WITHDRAWN

THE LIFE OF THE BUDDHA

The Life of the

BUDDHA

ACCORDING TO THE ANCIENT TEXTS
AND MONUMENTS OF INDIA

BY

A. FOUCHER

Abridged Translation by Simone Brangier Boas

Wesleyan University Press

MIDDLETOWN, CONNECTICUT

Library of Congress Catalog Card Number: 63–17795
Manufactured in the United States of America
FIRST EDITION

CONTENTS

ILLUSTRATIONS

Guide to the Pronunciation of Sanskrit Words

a   short, as in *amount*

ā   long, as in *father*

ai   as in *aisle*

c   midway between English j and ch as in *chart*

ḍ   like English d, but with the tip of the tongue turned up and drawn back into the dome of the palate

e, ē   as in *they*

ḥ   like English h

i   short, as in *pin*

ī   long, as in *police*

ñ   as in *singe*

ṅ   as in *sing*

ṇ   like English n, but with the tip of the tongue turned up and drawn back into the dome of the palate

o   as in *stone*

ph   two separate sounds, as in *uphill*

ṛ   like second r in *merrily*

ṣ, ś   as in *sure*

ṭ   like English t, but with the tip of the tongue turned up and drawn back into the dome of the palate

th   two separate sounds, as in *hothouse*

ū   as in *rule*

v   after a vowel, as in *ivy;* after a consonant, like English w

TRANSLATOR'S NOTE

WITH THE advice of scholars in the field, the decision was taken to shorten or to omit certain passages of the French edition that seemed cumbersome in English or of no immediate interest to the general reader. In other respects the translator has been faithful to the original text and has made every effort to preserve the quality of Monsieur Foucher's style and to allow his humanistic turn of mind to come through the translation.

When standard English versions of the original Sanskrit and Pāli works cited by Monsieur Foucher were available, they have been used instead of retranslations of the French translations made by the author. In such instances their spelling has been preserved even when it differs from that adopted throughout the book. The sources of these passages are given in the Notes. Some quotations in the original text have no references, consequently they have none in the translation. Volume II of the *Lalitavistara* was not available in English; hence Monsieur Foucher's translation was put into English and used in the text. Most of the illustrations are of monuments cited by the author, but they do not appear in the French edition.

The translator wishes to express her sincere gratitude to Messrs. A. B. Griswold of the Breezewood Foundation and John Spellman, formerly of Wesleyan University, for their help and encouragement. Mr. Spellman read the entire manuscript and made valuable suggestions, but he is not, of course, responsible for any errors that may remain in it. Dr. James W. Poultney, Professor of Classics, Johns Hopkins University, has most generously supervised the Sanskrit transliterations and spelling. Professor Benjamin Rowland, of the Fogg Museum, kindly allowed the translator to go through the files of slides, negatives, and photographs in the museum's Oriental Library. Several of the illustrations are a result of this generous privilege. Particular thanks are due Mr. John Rosenfield, Research Fellow at the Fogg Museum, for his kindness and for the use of his own photographs. Professor William Weedon, Wesleyan University, made available his Oriental library which was most helpful. Thanks are also due Mrs. Tania Senff and Mrs. Mildred Howard for their secretarial assistance, and to the staff of the Olin Library at Wesleyan University for their untiring cooperation in helping to secure the necessary books.

                                                          S. B. B.

Ruxton, Maryland
June 1963

PREFACE

Iᴛ ɪs said that when the Buddha reached perfect Enlightenment he hesitated a long time before preaching his doctrine, fearing that it would be a waste of time and energy. But he observed that, as there are three kinds of flowers in a pond of lotus, so in the world there are three kinds of souls. Some are too deeply sunk in the original mud to come up to the daylight, either in a season or in a lifetime; some are already near the light and have only a last effort to make; and some, rising above the level of the waters or of mankind—have come into blossom. Out of love for those in the second category he consented to preach the Doctrine.

In my humble sphere—a professor is not a prophet—I hesitated a long time before publishing this book, in view of the demands of three kinds of readers. First there is the general public, willing to be informed but unwilling to be stopped at each line by footnotes or to be burdened by technical terms and foreign words. Then there are the specialists (*genus irritabile*), who are only satisfied by an abundant *apparatus criticus*. Finally between these two extremes there are those who, desirous to know more about Buddhism, need to be both encouraged and guided into further research by a book that is easy to read. It is for these readers that I have written this book.

The most ancient Buddhist texts have naturally been my principal source of information and as such have forced me to repeat things often said. But they have not been my only source. No religion can express itself and be understood through its literature alone. A critique of a religion, such as Buddhism, in the abstract, can in no way give a full understanding of it to those who have not known it from childhood. To interpret it requires some knowledge of the milieu in which it developed and of the phenomena that grew out of it. These include social patterns, public and private ritual, missionary activities, architectural forms and their purpose, iconography, the sites and aims of pilgrimages, and so forth. In this study I have taken full advantage of the work of scholars who preceded me and of the progress they have made as a result of archaeological findings in India. They have presented known events in a new light, organizing them in a more vital and rational fashion around the remains of newly discovered religious centers. The localization of eight sacred places, today well established as the sites of the principal episodes in the life of the Buddha, not only clarifies the distorted accounts we have of these events, but also often reveals the cause of distortion. Thus the true facts underlying the legends emerge in sharp relief.

My task has been to sketch as close a likeness of the Buddha as possible, but I have been careful not to neglect reflections from the doctrine that have highlighted the face of its founder. This bit of novelty is my excuse for placing this book among those that have been and still will be written on the same subject.

THE LIFE OF THE BUDDHA

identified nor word of criticism has defined. That is the secret of these exceptional beings, and as this has been felt rather than perceived by their contemporaries, it becomes at once shrouded in mythical accretions, which by now make it almost impossible for us ever to recapture certain of their features.

The historical fact that no critic can ignore is that half of Asia, the mother of our religions, has elevated the Buddha to the rank of a god. This determines what our method will have to be as we study him. Not only are we confronted with an extraordinary personality, but indeed with one that has two faces, depending on whether we look at the man of daily life or at the figure that has grown within the imagination of the faithful. No part of the Buddha's life is so simple that the question of biographical truth versus legendary fiction does not arise. Because of his apotheosis, it could hardly have been otherwise. As he became divine, all his acts were transposed once and for all into the realm of supernatural miracles and myths. Our method of study may afford a Westerner, free from religious scruples and hereditary veneration, a unique opportunity to witness the mechanism of this inevitable transposition.

We can state briefly the facts at hand. At a time which practically corresponded to that of Zoroaster and Confucius, one hundred years before the time of Socrates and five hundred before the birth of Christ, a son was born in the family of a feudal lord in a far corner of the Nepalese Terai. From then on we have his biographical data: the death of his mother, his education, his marriage, and the birth of his son. At this time a revulsion against the world came over him and at twenty-nine he left everything—home, riches, family, and so on—to become a begging monk. From then on his quest was the solution to the problem of human destiny. Six years later, after his painful search, as he was sitting under a tree, he felt the truth come to him at sunrise and then he discovered the cure for the world's sufferings. After preaching the new doctrine to five companions, he found that the number of his disciples quickly multiplied, and his word spread. Forty-five years of teaching and traveling throughout the Ganges Valley as a mendicant brought the Master to his death in a small, obscure town in the same general region as that of his birth. This happened in 543 B.C. according to the Singhalese tradition; about 477 according to European calculations.

This is all that we know, or think we know, about the one who had become the Buddha, the "Awakened," or, as the term is usually trans-

INTRODUCTION

THE BUDDHA ŚĀKYAMUNI, "The Sage of the Śākyas," without doubt belongs to that extremely small human elite which rises above the general mass of humanity as a lighthouse which throws its beams over the surrounding darkness. Travelers to the Orient can bear witness to this fact. But this man who wrote nothing has had ascribed to him great tomes that are said to be his own words and that are constantly learned by heart, recited, incised in stone, and printed in ten living languages—Singhalese, Burmese, Siamese, Manchu, Japanese, and so on —to say nothing of European translations. This man who never reigned continues as head of a spiritual kingdom of millions of souls. This man who was seen daily begging in the Indian market places is now represented in golden images on the altars of pagodas throughout the Far East. There he sits enveloped in clouds of incense amid a buzz of prayers. All this in spite of his having forbidden it before his death. His disciples, believing him to have supernatural intelligence and moral power, have turned him into a god. Even those who are not Buddhists admit that this great figure is the one most human and most worthy of universal admiration ever produced by India. These are signs by which the world recognizes its saviors. It knows them and sees them, but when called upon to explain how a child born of woman can create so profound an impression on his own generation that, far from fading out with time, it is on the contrary amplified, human understanding is dazed. Believers hail such an event as a miracle, while the hypercritical prefer to doubt the actual existence of such a supernatural being. Those of us who treat the subject from a purely historical point of view, without preconceived intent, remain overwhelmed.

However far the search for truth has gone, there has always remained a mysterious deposit left at the bottom of the crucible that no test has lated, the "Enlightened One." Nothing can be more historical, in the usual sense, but also nothing can be less sensational. Yet hardly two centuries had gone by before the reputation of the Prophet and his doctrine had swept across the whole of India. For myriads of disciples and believers he had become the Predestined One, the Blessed One, the Teacher of men and gods. With more or less clarity and fidelity, his thinking lived on in their consciousness, but his image became less and less clearly seen as it was highlighted by too many refracted rays. His very existence became a tissue of miracles; nothing remained accidental or natural. Thus, popular imagination took over the biography of the man and, by virtue of its magic, transformed it into the legend of a god.

Two main approaches to the study of the life of the Buddha are found. First there is the work of Hermann Oldenberg, *Buddha, sein Leben, seine Lehre, seine Gemeinde,* a splendid book that has been translated into French and English, a book that is the champion of the historiographers. The second is Emile Senart's *Essai sur la Légende du Bouddha,* which treats the subject as a mass of mythical tales. Although Senart later recognized that he had gone too far in his system of interpretation, still he had launched one mode of approach. We should like to venture the statement that both Oldenberg and Senart are right and also wrong, right in what they admit and wrong in what they omit. In Senart's image of the Buddha it is the man that is missing; in Oldenberg's it is the god.

Thus, however great is our admiration for the erudition and the intellectual power behind these two European theories concerning the Buddha, we must admit that neither satisfies us completely. Therefore, we have no choice but to pursue our own path, set between the lofty heights of comparative mythology and the pedestrian way of factual history. For this we humbly cite a precedent. It is said that after Śākyamuni's death his great disciples felt the need to settle definitely the one legacy left them by the Master—namely, his doctrine. Consequently, they met in Rājagṛha and, drawing upon their memories, recited together the text *ne varietur* of the Good Law. They had barely finished when another monk arrived. It was Purāṇa ("the Ancient"), who had not been reached in time. He was told, "The Law has been well recited by the Elders: accept the Law as recited." To this he answered, "There is no doubt that the Law has been well recited by the Elders; but what

I have myself heard from the Buddha's lips, what I have directly received from his mouth, that I shall abide by."

In turn, let us say with due respect, "Truly, the life of the Buddha has been well studied by our predecessors and our masters; however, since they have taught us the rigorous methods of critical thought and constant reliance on the texts, their spirits will not blame us for going back to the sources. The rereading of the Scriptures, which hold all we can learn and know of Śākyamuni and his life, is our only recourse. The European scholars have spoken well, but let us above all return to the Indian tradition."

Whatever your choice of authority is to be, you are told, you will of necessity fall into the ways already established. It is well known by all Indologists that Oldenberg founded his theory upon the writings in Pāli, while Senart used the Sanskrit and Prākrit documents. The latter adhered to what is called Buddhism of the North, the former to Buddhism of the South; for there is not one great Buddhist tradition, but two. You must make a choice: either you adopt the orthodox version, based on the Singhalese canon, that was made popular in Germany by Oldenberg and for a time in England by Rhys Davids, or you remain loyal to the texts from Nepal, which, along with the French School, are somewhat suspect of heresy.

This argument might have seemed unanswerable in the past but it no longer is. Just as Christianity has both a Greek and a Roman Church, East Asia recognizes a Northern and a Southern Buddhism. As a matter of fact, there is a greater difference between a Chinese or a Tibetan lama on the one hand, and a Singhalese or a Cambodian priest on the other, in the domain of rites as well as of doctrine, than is found between a Greek pope and a Roman Catholic priest.

For one who deliberately remains within the frontiers of India proper, the antiquated classification of "Southern" and "Northern" texts must once and for all be abandoned, although the terms are sometimes convenient for reference. When Eugène Burnouf was the direct recipient of newly discovered manuscripts from opposite ends of the peninsula—some from Ceylon, others from Nepal—the two designations seemed logical. But with the advances made in the research he so brilliantly started, and also because of possible comparisons between original Indian Scriptures and Chinese or Tibetan translations of canons of various Buddhist sects, it has become steadily more apparent that, no

matter where the most ancient texts were found, they and Buddhism
itself originated in the Ganges Basin. Only those writings on palm
leaves and beech bark which in the course of their wanderings and
vicissitudes had found a safe haven either in the Nepalese mountains or
the Singhalese libraries have come down to us.

The fact remains that we have three series of documents in Indian
languages about the legendary life of the Buddha Śākyamuni. These
documents originated in three of the four broad sects into which Buddhism broke up early. Some are written in Pāli, such as the *Mahāvagga*
(the "Great Section" of the treatise on discipline) or the *Mahāparinibbāna Sutta*. They are part of the canonical writings of the *Sthavira-
vādins* or *Thēras* (Elders), the sect that has kept its identity in Ceylon,
whence it has spread into Indochina. Others are found in Sanskrit, such
as the *Lalitavistara* ("The Pleasurable Biography") and the *Divyāvadāna* ("The Divine Adventure"), which comes from the canon of the
Sarvāstivādin, "those who profess realism." The third group, written in
an irregular Prākrit, a kind of macaronic Sanskrit represented by the
Mahāvastu, "The Great Subject," also constitutes a fragment rescued
from the lost canon of the *Mahāsamghikas,* the "Great Community."

These, then, are our primary sources, and a priori we have no right
to adopt one to the exclusion of the others. The fact that we are faced
with several different versions of the same incidents can only favor research. What finally transpires is that the differences we find among the
various accounts are not as fundamental as the partisans of Singhalese
orthodoxy would have us believe for the sake of polemical expediency.
That all their sources were the same is revealed by the numerous iden-
tical expressions and similar parallel passages. Our task consists, if our
method is to be reasonable, of extracting the greatest degree of historical verisimilitude from a point-by-point comparison of the multiple
traditional offshoots. In so doing we shall contribute, within the limits
of our fragmentary sources, to the establishment of the Buddhist "Syn-
optic Gospels." At the same time we may be contributing to the understanding of the formation of a legend which remains the ultimate aim
of scholarly critical research. As archaeologists should not stop their
search before reaching virgin soil, so philologists should burrow through
the wordy accumulations until they have come, if possible, to historical
data.

Our study has been greatly helped by Indian archaeology, the con-

stant progress of which has not only revealed the sites of the eight holy
cities of ancient Buddhism but identified much sculpture unearthed
around the old sanctuaries. These monuments are as authentic as the
written texts. In a sense they offer surer testimony, for even when they,
too, have suffered from mutilations, they at least have not been altered
in later times and amplified for propagandist purposes. Their immediate
effect is to bring back to earth a legend which tends only too easily to
lose itself in mythical clouds. This is the important role of the scenes
represented in the bas-reliefs—practically the only remaining vestiges of
the art of representation of which painting would have been the most
beautiful example. When chronologically arranged, they give us a kind
of figured version that parallels the written version of the Buddha's life.
Sculptors are necessarily more restrained in their interpretations than
writers or even painters. It is characteristic of their craft to create gods
in the image of man and to keep miracles within the stone.

Buddhist art began in the third century B.C. with Emperor Aśoka
and was destroyed, in India, only by the Moslem invasion. It still survives in Tibet and the Far East. The two oldest schools happen to be of
primary interest to us. The older one flourished in Central India from
the second century B.C. under the dynasty of the Śungas, which left
us part of the sculptures which decorated the walls of the old sanctuaries of Bhārhut, Bodh Gayā, and Sānchī. Its most characteristic
trait is the retention of the principle of representing episodes of the
Buddha's last existence without ever showing him other than as a symbol. The Gandhāra school, which became active in the first century
A.D., several decades after the last Indo-Greek dynast had been sup-
planted by other invaders, on the contrary represented the Buddha in
the form of a semi-Hellenic, semi-Hindu figure. This caused a complete revolution in Buddhist iconography, and the success of this new
method was immediately made secure with its adoption by the school
of Mathurā, in Hindustan and the Deccan, and its final adoption by
all Buddhist Asia.

These later imitations have nothing to teach us. Nor should we retain
here those representations that assume a strictly conscious biographical
character, such as the long series on the temple at Pagan in Burma and
on the *stūpa* at Borobodūr in Java, for their nature is purely that of
book illustrations. The only useful evidence for our purposes is the ancient and original sculpture of artists from either Northern or Central

India who were still working according to specifications given them orally by donors and not from written descriptions. Thus these sculptures alone are able at times to give us an unknown form of the popular tradition; and they become an excellent counterweight to the flighty texts.

That is not the only purpose they serve. A careful study of the bas-reliefs carved on the lintels and the doorjambs of Sānchī's gates, since they are the only completed works extant, reveals the few exact facts about Śākyamuni that we have. The reason for their survival is probably that some of the scenes represented took place at that very spot, and, as is known, the Indians have a strong feeling about establishing and preserving what might be called the topography of their legends. Every Buddhist writer felt that he had to locate the site of the episode or the sermon that he was relating. A multitude of guides for pilgrimages, still in use, are imbued with that same spirit. The considerable role that the Eight Pilgrimages have played in preserving the legend is revealed to us in accounts written by the pilgrims themselves. By great good luck, for which Indologists are unfailingly grateful, the diaries and reports of several Chinese travelers who were attracted into India by their Buddhist faith have been preserved. These date from the fifth to the eighth centuries A.D. Particularly valuable are the reports of Hsuan Tsang, who repeated verbatim the lessons recited to him before the "sacred remains" concerning the miraculous manifestations of the "Honored One of the World."

A final word seems necessary. We shall on occasion compare Christian and Buddhist traditions. This can only increase the clarity of our study. Buddhism and Christianity have much in common, especially in their moral teachings. These two historical phenomena not only belong to the same planet but originated on the same continent at approximately the same period. In addition, they both show the same yearning for peace on earth promised to men of good will. We shall, however, reject all vain polemics, pro and con, as to which influenced which.

First of all, we must give up the idea that because of Buddhism's earlier date any analogy between the two doctrines means that the Christian borrowed from the Buddhist. Not only must we keep in mind the fundamental identity of the human spirit, but we must also deal with chronology. Chronology reveals that Buddhism remained obscurely in Central India for many years; for various historical reasons, it was only at the end of the first century A.D. or the beginning of the second that it began to make some claim to universality. Then, for propagandist purposes, the first "lives" of the Master were written. Furthermore, the supposed analogy fades as we continue our reading, and what at first sight seemed similar ends by disappearing. After several such repeated experiences, we are forced to conclude that the two traditions are absolutely independent of each other. Finally, it is a fact that neither of these religions has had any marked effect on the other. Their being too far apart in dogma and too close in ethics eliminates any possibility of confusion and any reason for dispute.

PART ONE

The Kapilavastu Cycle

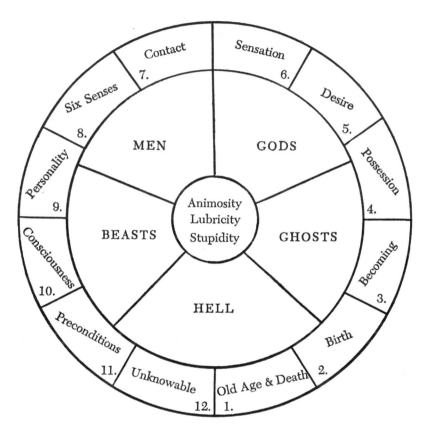

The Wheel of Life

CHAPTER I

THE NATIVITY (I)

Before Birth

THE BIOGRAPHY of the Buddha has to be taken for what it is, a mixture of history and legend, of truth and fiction. Instead of following Oldenberg's [1] attempts to explain it in rationalistic terms, or Senart's,[2] by the method of comparative mythology, we shall try, with the help of written texts and sculptured monuments, to determine how the Indians conceived and represented it two thousand years ago. The important thing is to ask neither more nor less of our sources than they can give us.

While we shall certainly not attempt to hide the tremendous appeal of the Buddha's admirable aspects, we shall not be blind defenders of his doctrine. Though the Christian and the Buddhist ethics really have much in common, they cannot be identified with each other, because their fundamental doctrines and the spiritual atmospheres that surround them are too unlike. This is strongly felt by the traveler leaving shipboard in Ceylon, the first Buddhist port of call on the long sea route through the Far East. Transported abruptly from the tumult and bright lights of the port to the dimness and calm of the nearest pagoda, he cannot help but wonder if the smile on the great Buddha's face is not caused by the vain bustle of our Western life and the useless noise of the age of steel. The contrast is so overwhelming that he feels as if he were entering another world. What follows will show that he is not far wrong.

The universe we are about to enter is by no means closed to our intelligence and sympathies; but it is based on a chain of ideas totally different from those we have accepted since childhood. We can understand Buddhism, like all products of the Indian genius, without accepting it. It is both close and distant, similar and different. This is the usual experience, and history easily explains it. The last people to colonize ancient India were of the same race and mentality as ours, which explains the similarity of both our moral concepts and our logical deductions. On the other hand, in the heart of that immense hothouse the Indo-Europeans were forced to mix and live with quantities of other peoples practically in geographical isolation, which explains the differences. What is true of the Doctrine is not less so of the Buddha's biography. No matter how human it is and, in many respects, how close to the lives of the saints in the *Golden Legend,* we shall only be able to understand it after making a certain kind of mental or optical adjustment.

Transmigration and Works

THE first surprise and difficulty we face is not knowing where to begin tracing the Buddha's existence, for there is no "beginning." The Blessed One proclaimed it himself:

> The transmigration of beings [*saṃsāra*], O my disciples, has its origin in the remote past. It is impossible to discover a beginning for the beings caught in ignorance, enmeshed by the desire for life, wandering from rebirth to rebirth, moaning and weeping and shedding more tears than there are drops of water in the great ocean . . .

Whoever the living being is whose biography is to be recorded, he can only be seized upon at a transitory moment of his multiple existences. Each of these lives is to be explained as the result of good and bad actions committed by him in a preceding life, or, in a word, because of *karma.* Therefore, in order to find his origin, it would be necessary to keep going further and further back into the past, in the darkness of time, obviously a futile endeavor.

The words and even the concepts of *karma* and *saṃsāra* [3] are already familiar to us. Regarding the first, we have read the Western formula of Victor Hugo: "Man has his own acts as judges; that is sufficient." As for the transmigration of souls, Pythagoras believed he had kept his memory of past experiences, and Caesar found the same belief among our Gallic ancestors. Although we find nothing very strange there and think we understand the two concepts, we must take care not to go completely astray. It is easy to admit that a being can change his body as he does his clothes, because—without worrying over the materialistic nature of this apparent spiritualism—we and the Brāhmans believe in the reality and permanence of the soul (*ātman*). Neither they nor we would feel able to speak of true moral sanctions if it were not that the same soul passes through successive destinies. Nothing could be more contrary to the Buddhist doctrine. According to it, the self, or ego, is only a perishable composite, as is the body, and both are dissolved at death. Our sense of logic is shocked by such a theory and the contradictions that it imposes, but we are not the first to rebel. Long before our era the Indo-Greek King Menander refused to admit that it was possible to speak of moral retribution if the being who inherited accumulated merit or demerit throughout an existence was not the same one who was rewarded or punished at the time of a new birth. In the Pāli dialogue which bears Menander's name, *The Questions of Milinda* (*Milindapañha*), the philosopher-monk Nāgasena attempts to show the king, through the use of many comparisons and parables, that the being who is reborn is both the same and another. To use a metaphor, although the oil that burns in a well-filled lamp which is kept burning at intervals throughout the night is the same oil, the flame is a different one each time the lamp is relit. It is thus with transmigration from life to life. It is not the same individual but the same *karma* that continues.[4]

We must be keenly aware of this distinction at the outset, for the contrast between Buddhist and Christian ideas will continue to remain important. According to Christian theologians, the human soul comes to life with the body or soon thereafter, and yet it is immortal. Though immortal, it has a beginning but no end. This the Indian thinkers find absurd, for they hold it as axiomatic that everything that has a beginning has an end. To them, this unknown quantity, which transmigrates from rebirth to rebirth, is eternal, not immortal. Having always existed, it has no beginning. And the only end it may have is the extremely rare one known as Nirvāna,[5] gained through unusual merits.

Based on premises so completely opposed, the two religions understandably have differing views regarding human destiny. For the Christian it is a tragic one, since eternal felicity or eternal sorrow for him depends on one existence alone. For the Indian his present life is only a passing moment in the course of an endless journey, during which he reaps the fruit of his past existences and sows the seed of those to come. Death for him will never be the moment heralding happiness without end or the irrevocable fall. It is only very slowly, through thousands and thousands of successive lives, that he can claim (or *did* claim, for

later Buddhism, the Mahāyāna, has accelerated matters) to come nearer
perfection and obtain that supreme reward, salvation, which Christian impatience demands at once. The Occidental, born yesterday,
wishes only to live. Because of this thirst for immortality, he does not
hesitate, in the event of missing Heaven, to accept a long or even endless period of suffering in Purgatory or in Hell. The Oriental, with an
eternity already behind him, is dreadfully tired of these lives or rather,
as he says, of these deaths indefinitely repeated. In short, the hope of
the Occidental is never to die, and that of the Oriental, never to be reborn.

Previous Births

WE have spent much time on general considerations in order to be able
to apply them to the particular case of the Buddha. His destiny will be
presented to us not as a brief tragedy in five acts but as a dramatic
legend in a thousand scenes. His past existences were innumerable, and
he climbed one by one all the rungs of the ladder of all living beings,
animal as well as human and superhuman, "from ant to god." He also
knew and exhausted all the joys and all the sufferings of life. If it is
true that to understand all things one must have experienced them
personally, then he felt for everything in the world. Nothing could any
longer tempt him, for he had tasted the vanity of every variety of regal
and voluptuous gratification, and the joys of heavenly felicity as well.
His wisdom and charity came from the conscious treasures of his prodigious experience, for, unlike common mortals, he remembered all his
past existences. His personal store of memories went back, we are told,
to ninety-one *kalpas* or aeons [6] that is, ninety-one times 432 million
years. He related these recollections to his disciples for their edification,
and they in turn kept records, several of which have come down to us.
Whoever goes through them finds numerous fairy tales, fables, verses,
adventure stories, and edifying statements, all attributed to the Buddha,
though many recall the folk tales of Europe. Because of their fanciful
nature we are often puzzled as to what we should retain from these
texts.

In the minds of Buddhists, these accounts of previous births are an
integral part of the personal history of the Master, and he never would
have attained the supreme rank of Buddha, the "Enlightened One," if
he had not in the course of his past lives practiced to the full the ten

ethical virtues: morality, renunciation, heroism, patience, truthfulness, resolution, good will, equanimity, and, above all, wisdom and charity. That opinion has always been held by and has grown in the bosom of the Order (*Saṃgha*). A poem of the seventh century A.D. by Śāntideva,[7] which is sometimes compared to the *Imitation of Christ,* attempts to show how everyone can eventually become a Buddha. These ten perfections (or at least six of them) stake out the long, arduous path to the shining goal which the Mahāyāna, the Greater Vehicle, would make accessible to all. Though in early Buddhism these virtues, faithfully carried out, were only the steps, they were the indispensable steps that had to be strictly followed by each of the exceptional beings predestined to achieve Enlightenment (*Bodhi*) and who were therefore called *Bodhisattvas.*

Thus Śākyamuni's past, which was the beginning of his journey towards the light, was necessarily a series of marvelous exploits and sublime sacrifices. These are all well exemplified,[8] and in the case of his charity they are admirable. Once, as a fugitive and refugee monarch, he had nothing to offer as alms, and hence let himself be turned over to his enemy by a beggar in exchange for the ransom placed on his head. There are other instances equally extravagant, such as his giving his own eyes to a blind man or his throwing himself to a starving tigress. Some seem cruel to us, as when, born a prince, he was unable to refuse anything to a beggar: neither his own nor the state's possessions, nor his children nor even his faithful wife.

Such superhuman actions and mad generosities are listed by the hundreds as mere incidents in the evolution of one being, constituting a continuous chain in his development. They eventually led the future Buddha to the fourth level of the heavens, from which he descended to earth for the last time. This final existence, crowned by complete Enlightenment (*Sambodhi*) and ending in definitive death (*Parinirvāna*), was itself the expected outcome of his fabulous destiny. We shall omit his innumerable previous existences and begin Śākyamuni's biography at a point just prior to his last terrestrial life, the only one that is at least partially historical.

Sojourn in the Tuśitas' Heaven

DURING the phase of his penultimate rebirth, the future Buddha of our epoch (for each aeon has its Buddha, and our Śākyamuni is only one of the series) was still dwelling in the Heaven of the Tuśita gods under the name of Śvetaketu, "the one who bears the white banner." From there he descended to be incarnated for the last time on earth in the womb of his mother, Māyā, for the future salvation of all. At least this is the way Buddhists speak and write, and when Europeans read these texts, they mistakenly think they recognize a doctrine already known to them. True, we are told that Christ came down to be incarnated in the womb of the Virgin Mary to save humanity, and the descent of the Son of God is the essential dogma and the greatest miracle of Christianity. What seems to us a unique and supernatural fact is to Buddhists a commonly accepted occurrence, as for them all beings are reincarnated. The two religions do not function on the same plane; and the same words, depending on the environment in which they are spoken, may have quite different implications.

Anyone not Indian born has much to learn and unlearn before he can penetrate deeply into Indian ideas. To start with, what is the Heaven of the Tuśita gods, "the Satisfied"? It is known as the Fourth Heaven, for in Indian mythology the heavens go up on different levels towards the zenith and the hells descend towards the nadir. The Bodhisattva was installed in the Fourth Heaven because it was inhabited only by gods who were so completely satisfied that they were free from all desire, and thus it provided a proper atmosphere of chastity suitable to a future Buddha. Actually, the accumulated merits of Śvetaketu, acquired from the practice of the ten perfections, would have made possible his rebirth at a still higher level in the celestial hierarchy; but he had already decided upon the role of world savior, which it had often been predicted would be his. Had he thought only of his own salvation, he would have either faded away long before or else been reborn in one of the heavens that were higher still. Those were the "Pure Spheres" where the beings who "never come back" went after having said a last good-by to humanity. There they directly attained sainthood and through it Nirvāna. But in Buddhist dogma only a man born of woman can become that "First of Beings," higher than the gods, a perfectly fulfilled Buddha. For that reason the Bodhisattva did not

wish to go too far from this earth to which he knew he must descend one last time.

For us, when a soul goes to Heaven it is forever. Not so for the Buddhist. For him, it may be for a prodigiously long time if counted in human years, but not forever. Neither Heaven nor Hell is eternal. They are only two of the five "Conditions" of impermanent rebirth: in Hell, as ghosts, as beasts, as men, and as gods. In each of these transformations a being can only expiate the sins committed, or live out the merits acquired, in the preceding life. Once the accumulation of his *karma*, good or bad, has been "consumed," he is forced to re-enter the cycle of transmigration. The great wheel of *saṃsāra* will then keep him within its perpetual rotation, unless one day he can escape by means of virtues and sacrifices—on a tangent, so to speak—and take refuge at last in the absolute peace of Nirvāna. The Buddha came to earth to enlighten both men and gods concerning this unique chance to escape.

The Buddhist texts tell us how one reaches a heaven and how one is dashed down again to earth. Not even a god can escape the law of nature. The sum of his accumulated merits constantly dwindles as he enjoys the celestial felicity they have brought him, and its end inexorably approaches. Sooner or later the five signs that portend his imminent downfall appear: garlands of flowers which have always kept fresh begin to fade; his clothes, which have always remained clean, begin to show soil; his breath becomes rank; sweat appears in his armpits; and the god begins to feel unsteady on his throne. Thus warned, he knows that the hour of change is near and that he may be reborn as a beggar or even as an animal. Though the inhabitants of the lower heavens, and even the companions of the Bodhisattva in the Heaven of the Tuśitas, live in danger of such a future, he himself is spared it.

The Four Investigations (Mahāvilokitāni) [9]

POSSIBLY at no other point in Śākyamuni's biography can we grasp more easily the play of the two opposing forces that fashioned it. The first, which grew with the fervor of each generation, tended to free the Bodhisattva from any limitation or impurity. The second, in contrast, compelled even the most exalted believers to admit certain facts concerning the Master, his family, his country, which were so well authenticated by tradition that it would have been sacrilegious, and consequently im-

possible, to deny them. Because of this, the legendary account has been
able to bring down to us some historical nuggets wrapped up in mystery. Coming upon the various versions of the Nativity, we find some
giving more credence to these recollections, and others to prodigious
inventions. In whichever direction they are slanted, they are all a compromise between the two contradictory tendencies. But even the most
extravagant accounts always contain a trace of the reality and of the
humanity so characteristic of Śākyamuni.

If this healthy balance had not existed, we should have been thrown
completely into the realm of the miraculous. Had a state of total mystery surrounded the origins of the Buddha, the legend would have
been much freer, and his divinity far simpler to claim. No doubt the
final rebirth of the Bodhisattva would have been like his heavenly one.
He would most probably have been born on a "lotus with a thousand
petals the size of a cartwheel," having emerged on a distant Himālayan
lake unknown to anyone.[10] That is easily imaginable, for in the accounts that follow, the lotus is constantly appearing—to distill Śākyamuni's food during the gestation period, to steady his faltering steps at
birth, and later to serve as pulpit for his sermons. How much simpler
to have had him born within the petals of this magic flower. But
whether we regret it or not, this sleight of hand was not possible, for
exact recollections and precise locations render these pious fantasies un-
sound. Willy-nilly, popular imagination has had to come to terms with
the facts, and the result of this compromise is the lopsided version that
we shall read.

Held in check by traditional data, the legend ingeniously circum-
vented the obstacle it could not remove. The Bodhisattva did reside in
the Heaven of the Tuśitas in conformity with universal laws; but when
he was about to leave, a supernatural element took over. As a unique
exception, justified only by the Bodhisattva's supremacy over all other
beings, the automatic power of *karma* became suspended in favor of
the god Śvēta-kētu. Never would he perceive on himself the five signs
of the coming fall. It was of his own accord and in full happiness, after
due reflection and twelve years ahead of schedule,[11] that he chose
the circumstances of his last existence. In order to do this, with the help
of his divine companions, he proceeded to the four great Investigations
or Observations, and in turn examined at what time and in which continent, country, and family it would be fitting for him to be reborn.

Some say that he even considered what woman he would elect to be his mother. In short, he alone among all living beings was able to determine what concerned his last rebirth. At least this is the tale that it pleases the believers to tell. It becomes a moral satisfaction in which they indulge, that of causing inflexible destiny to yield before their Master. There is no other way for them to make him sublime—and it is not too difficult to free him from the laws that they themselves have invented.

Let us now examine the results of the four Investigations. We shall see at once that, although a taste for pious fiction dominated the narrators, it could not lead them too far astray, for the boundaries were already set. Their Bodhisattva's choices had been settled long before, in spite of his searchings and prospecting with his heavenly companions, elaborating many hypotheses and investigating new worlds. In order that his teachings be accepted and be efficacious, he had to be born at a time when human life had a normal duration, neither too long nor too short, about one hundred years. As if by chance, that description fits ours. Among the four continents dominated by the central peak of Mount Meru, the Jambudvīpa (Continent, *dvīpa,* of the Rose Apple, *jambu*) had absolute priority, for it was in fact India. In India itself, all outlying regions being by definition eliminated, it was the "Middle Land" (*Madhyamadeśa*), which, as one guesses, was the only possible one.

Another choice to make was that of a suitable family, for a Bodhisattva could belong only to one of the superior classes, that of the nobles (*kṣatriya*) or that of the Brāhmans. Naturally the Buddhists turned towards the former, but as a concession to Brāhmanic pride they conceded that the future Buddha, Maitrēya, would be born in the priestly caste. After the Tuṣita gods had been warned of their companion's resolution, they discussed among themselves and reviewed the reigning dynasties of the capitals in the sixteen great kingdoms of central India. Each was found to have a prohibitive taint. It was Śvetaketu himself who came to their rescue by enumerating the sixty-four qualities that the family had to possess and the thirty-two necessary for the mother of a Bodhisattva who had reached "his last existence." All the required items were found only in the oligarchic clan of the Śākyas and in Māyā, the first wife of their chief, King Śuddhodhana.[12] The saintly historians could not do better than to dramatize with countless scenes a tale that held surprises for no one, and this part of the legend found its plot outlined by history.

By attributing to their Master a more than divine omnipotence, the worshipers of the Buddha found themselves in the paradoxical situation of having confirmed in our eyes the human condition of the man. The relatively recent date of his birth and the name of his country, of his native city, of his family, of his father and mother are all detailed information, the authenticity of which grows out of the fact that it has resisted to the end the corrosion of later devotion. Let us keep this small historical core and leave the entire field to the imagination of the hagiographers, for their wings are clipped. As could be expected, their imagination was not restrained in elaborating universal rules concerning all Buddhas, in their luxurious descriptions of the Bodhisattva's family, and their miraculous prophecies. In spite of these elaborations, they were unable to erase from the Buddha's biography the indelible marks of his human personality and history.

Conception

HAVING gathered some information from the hagiographers, we shall leave them to follow their own exaggerations and fantastic play on numbers as we try using those fictions which throw a psychological light on the inventors and their environment. For instance, the mobilization of hundreds of millions of divinities to serve as a retinue for the descent of Śvētakētu from the Fourth Heaven to earth may seem an extravagant fantasy to us, but it is merely the dressing up of what to the Indians was a common occurrence in order to give it a supernatural aura. The texts state the facts as follows:

> A widespread idea is that girls or boys come because of prayer. That is an error, for if it were true, each couple would have a hundred sons just as an emperor. It is because of the meeting of three conditions that boys and girls are born. What are these three? That the father and mother be united in love; that the mother be in a fertile period; and that a *spirit* be free at that time. It is thus from the concurrence of these three conditions that boys and girls are born.

Thus, for an Indian child to be conceived it did not suffice that a father and mother be ready. It was also necessary to have a being at the end of one existence and disposed (or more likely condemned) to begin

another life. That, as we have seen, was exactly the case of the Bodhisattva. But he distinguished himself from the commonplace by not
waiting for the end of his term in the Tuśita Heaven in order to be
reincarnated and also by choosing his father and mother as well as the
time of his rebirth.

We can skip rapidly through the good-byes of the Bodhisattva to his
colleagues in the Tuśitas' Heaven. Of course, he had to "indoctrinate,
enlighten, cheer, and comfort" them with a sermon before leaving, and
that is why the *Lalitavistara* gives over a whole chapter to his expound-
ing of the "one hundred and eight ways of the Law." [13] His friends
were so moved by his words that they wept, and this is what follows:

> And so the sons of gods reborn in the heaven of the Tuśitas fell
> at the feet of the Bodhisattva weeping and said, "In truth, Wise
> Man, how will the sphere of the Tuśitas retain its brilliance once de-
> prived of you?" And the Bodhisattva said to this great and divine
> gathering, "The Bodhisattva Maitrēya here will teach you the Law."
> And the Bodhisattva *having removed his crown, placed it on the*
> *head of Maitrēya,* saying, "You, Wise Man, will be the first after me
> to obtain supreme and perfect Enlightenment." [14]

It is excusable if what interests us most in this passage, and which we
have italicized, is not the spoken words but the gesture that accompanied them. This action has nothing Indian in character; quite the
contrary. The anticipated crowning of the Buddha-to-be has too familiar
a ring to Europeans not to awaken the thought of possible Occidental
influence. The fact that the passage is absent from the old Chinese
translations confirms its late origin.

The following lines, however, take us right back into local folklore:
"And the Bodhisattva, having thus enthroned the Bodhisattva Maitrēya in the Tuśita Heaven, turned again to his large divine assembly
and asked, 'Under what guise, O my friends, shall I enter my mother's
womb?'"

The gods, thus called into consultation, suggested all the divine
forms imaginable. But one of them, who because of his more recent
birth knew the writings of the Brāhmans better, closed the discussion
by peremptorily stating, "In the form of a white elephant having six
tusks." [15] It is easily understood that we may at first be surprised by
this choice. However, our astonishment may diminish if we stop to re-

flect that our symbols probably seem just as surprising to Buddhists. They would not more easily see why we should represent the Holy Ghost in the form of a dove. Furthermore, if Christians attach to the image of the lamb notions of purity and divine compassion, why should they not attach to the symbol of the white elephant notions of perfect wisdom and royal power? That is exactly what they did, and we might recall that the white elephant is for them one of the seven treasures of the Universal Monarch. The religious care that is lavished in Bangkok on the albino elephants of the king of Thailand is a direct heritage of these old Indian beliefs. As for the detail of the six tusks, it probably is a reference to a previous rebirth of the Buddha when he so generously forgave the hunter who had mortally wounded him and even presented him with his six ivory teeth.

We progress from miracle to miracle with ease, though we find them contradictory. For instance we are told that the Bodhisattva lived in his mother's womb and left it, when the time came, in the shape of a six-month-old child, but we are not informed at what moment he exchanged his animal form for a human one. The Chinese thought they solved this problem by imagining that the Bodhisattva entered his mother's womb "mounted on an elephant." We shall not quarrel with them as to the more or less incredible nature of the miracles. If we take refuge in the texts, we still find contradictions—often from one page to the next without any apparent uneasiness on the part of the writers. Thus, in the part of the *Lalitavistara,* in verse, the oldest version, we read that the Bodhisattva's descent in elephantine form was nothing more than a dream on Māyā's part. This statement would appease our scruples if we were not told in the very same chapter that it was an actual occurrence.[16] In despair we turn to the sculptured monuments for the key to these inconsistencies.

Fortunately, there are fragments of ancient sculpture still extant, even though early Indian painting has for the most part perished. The sculptor of the medallion decorating the balustrade from the *stupā* of Bhārhut, now in the Calcutta Museum, took on the task of illustrating the above-mentioned passage of the legend, and this he did in a naïve and clumsy manner. Māyā is shown reclining, her head to the left of the spectator, on a four-legged bed of webbing similar to the kind still in use today. A water pitcher and a lighted lamp (indicating that the scene took place at night) complete the furnishings. Maidservants, one holding a fly whisk, watch over their mistress' sleep, and above their heads floats the materialized vision of the divine young elephant. One difficulty is that he is much larger than his future mother; another is that the queen is lying on her right side, when it was written that it was this side the Bodhisattva entered and emerged from. The right side was also said to be the area the male progeny was privileged to occupy. The Amarāvatī artists, more careful of verisimilitude, gave the elephant tiny dimensions, and those of Gandhāra placed the queen on her left side. Still, each treated the same subject and the sculptor of Bhārhut, in his most beautiful calligraphy, inscribed above his medallion the words *Bhagavato Ūkramti,* "the descent of the Blessed." [17] This concrete representation of the Conception of the future Buddha was to be repeated and generally accepted throughout India. That the sculptor himself believed it is confirmed by the gesture of surprise of one of the queen's attendants, which is so well rendered by the artist's chisel that it proves that the vision of the elephant was not just part of the sleeper's dream as far as the sculptor was concerned.

The inevitable image was already in the minds of the people as early as the second century B.C., and from them it passed into the texts. What originally was and has remained in the Pāli tradition, and also in the verses of the *Lalitavistara,* a premonitory dream and a symbol of the Conception—in short, a kind of Annunciation in the Indian manner— became a genuine episode of Śākyamuni's life in the prose version of the *Lalitavistara* as well as in the *Mahāvastu.* Soon it was to become an absolute principle that a Buddha, either of the past or of the future, must enter his mother's body in the form of an elephant.

The sculptures not only clarify the story but indicate a fact of psychological importance. It should be noted that at the decisive moment of conception Māyā is always shown alone on her couch. In Bhārhut she has only her women about her; in Gandhāra amazons are guarding the approaches, leaning upon spears; at Amarāvatī the four gods, Guardians of the Four Cardinal Points, do likewise, sword in hand, at each corner of the bas-relief. Always and everywhere the husband is absent. This restraint cannot be attributed to prudery but to a far deeper reason. It was the religious conscience of the time that was reflected in the images and in the texts. It demanded that everything that had to do with the birth of the Buddha be physically and morally pure, and an increasing delicacy in handling the subject is apparent. It can be followed from one version to the other in the preserved writings: From the moment the Bodhisattva entered his mother's womb she became exempt from any impure act, word, or thought and became immune to all illness and suffering. Not only did she feel no carnal desire; she could no longer inspire it in anyone, including her husband.

Soon this absolute chastity following conception did not seem sufficient to the disciples, and even before conception Queen Māyā asked and obtained permission from the king to enter a sort of religious retreat. She then retired with her women to a secluded room situated on the highest palace terrace.[18] Not to be outdone, Śuddhodhana took and observed the same vows of religious continence. Thus, even if one may not speak of Māyā as a virgin, as one speaks of Mary, it is, however, strictly true to say that the Conception of the infant Buddha became for the Buddhists an immaculate conception. At the same time, even for India, it became a supernatural or at least a supraterrestrial event. Of the three elements necessary for the birth of a man—the father, the mother, and the being ready for reincarnation—the first has been purely and simply eliminated. Hence we are still completely within the realm of the miraculous.

Gestation

THE details given in later versions concerning Māyā's pregnancy are, if possible, more miraculous than the earlier ones. The oldest texts, however, tell us only that it is with full consciousness and complete understanding that the infant Buddha entered his mother's body. On her part, through a particular gift from heaven she saw him distinctly "as one sees the colored thread through a precious stone bead." This comparison apparently did not please everyone because it gave Māyā too important a role at the expense of her son; so it was thought better to say, "as one sees a cat's eye inside a crystal casket," or again, "as one sees one's face in a perfectly clear mirror." What must be remembered is that the Bodhisattva was already an infant with a complete set of limbs and organs. We are given to understand that he entered his mother's womb fully formed, and remained completely separate and independent while in his mother's body.

These rather complicated suggestions did not seem sufficiently precise to the author of one version of the *Lalitavistara,* and he attributed

1. Māyā's Dream: Descent of the White Elephant into her Womb.
Bhārhut Stūpa, ca. 2nd–1st century B.C.

2. The Birth of the Bodhisattva.
Gandhāra school, 2nd–5th century A.D.

to one of the gods the following statement: "How, upon leaving the Tuśita Heaven, could the Bodhisattva, this pearl among all beings, absolutely pure and with a suave odor, have remained ten lunar months in that stinking human receptacle which was the womb of his mother?" [19] One must pardon the crudity of these expressions, for they have the merit of rudely posing the problem as it was finally presented for the judgment of future generations. Its solution was not denied them. Without worrying in the slightest over what we have just found in the texts concerning the descent of the Bodhisattva in the shape of an elephant, the same writers then portrayed him leaving the Heaven of the Tuśitas in the midst of his retinue, but this time in human form sheltered by a tabernacle of precious stones.[20] This is how the conscientious artists of Borobodūr in Java depict him. Thus enclosed in that protective case, he is supposed to have entered his mother's right side and settled down inside her body. For ten months he had to sit cross-legged in Indian style inside this incorruptible tabernacle.[21] We must not lose track of the fact that he was already the size of a six-month-old child and had the thirty-two marks characteristic of a "great man." From there, due to magical transparency, he illuminated the whole universe. During this period of forced seclusion he used the time to preach his doctrine and convert to his Law, as a beginning, thirty-six times a thousand million souls.

The objection that was bound to be made, even at this early date, that an embryo could not subsist thus isolated and unable to participate in his mother's life, had been foreseen. On the very night of Conception a gigantic lotus broke through the earth and rose straight up to Brahmā's heaven. In the chalice of the flower all the essence and sap of the universe were distilled and concentrated into a unique drop of honey. This the god Brahmā brought to the Bodhisattva, who accepted the magic drop, knowing that he alone could assimilate it.[22] From this miraculous elixir he drew his strength until the end of his gestation period. And thus he was the only child born of woman preserved from any soiling blemish during his stay in his mother's womb. "It is well to speak of such blemish for others, as he alone was exempt," says the text.

As for the tabernacle of great artistic merit and splendor under which he was sitting, it was taken by the god Brahmā to his heaven at the time of birth and was made into a shrine. Should any doubt about this be entertained, it must be remembered that, at the request of the

Blessed One, Brahmā once brought the precious relic from heaven to show it to the Community (Saṃgha).[23]

Such were the supreme efforts made to ensure absolute purity for the Bodhisattva's final rebirth, and truly it would have been hard to do more. We have seen that the would-be father had nothing to do with the Conception; now we can ask what part his mother played in the gestation. When the Bodhisattva entered her body, his own was already complete and he was fully conscious of his intellectual and moral supremacy. Furthermore, there was never the slightest physical link between the two, and one wonders why he felt the need to be born of woman. Nothing would have been easier for him than to dispense with those ten months of imprisonment in the fetid atmosphere of a human womb. He, the supreme being, could have done without a mother as well as a father and been reborn by a spontaneous birth, which is the privilege of the gods. Without further ado he could have been born in the marvelous lotus that produced the precious drop of nectar which fed him during his mother's pregnancy. Why didn't the legend simply take this way out instead of becoming involved with a hybrid kind of generation that was neither entirely human nor entirely divine?

The texts are ready with an answer, and a most edifying one. If the Bodhisattva came into the world in the womb of a woman, it was purely because of his commiseration with the human race. Had he manifested himself as a god, we should all have despaired of being able to imitate him, much less of being his equal. It was to encourage us by his example in the practice of all virtues that he wished to be only a man. This is the sublime reason that is given; and, as the Christian dogma has not hesitated to do likewise, it must be admitted that the words have a familiar ring. Although this reason may be sufficient for the faithful, it does not impose silence on the historian. For he knows that in the course of transformation of a man into a god it is always easy to discard the father, sooner or later, but it is far less simple to do away with the mother. While the Buddhist legend did not hesitate to pile miracle upon miracle concerning the last reincarnation of the future Buddha, it never dared to have him born in any way other than from Māyā.

Birth

AFTER a Conception and gestation, so close to the supernatural, the birth, in this sequence of prodigious events, had to be equally sublime. There remains for us the indubitable *fact* that the future Śākyamuni was born, and we even believe that we know where. All the texts agree in setting the place of birth in the neighborhood of Kapilavastu, in the park of Lumbinī, today known as Rummindēi, in the heart of the Nepalese Tērai.[24]

Knowledge of the site has been ascertained due to the fact that the Emperor Aśoka, having become an ardent zealot of the Good Law (*Dharma*), when there on a pilgrimage about 244 B.C. and had one of his famous monolithic columns erected on the spot. When 880 years later the Chinese pilgrim Hsuan Tsang visited this holy place, which by then was practically deserted, his guides led him to the column. He found it already broken and split by lightning. The capital with a horse's head had been knocked down, and since then has been lost in the jungle which has spread over the area. Today the park and the ruined city are buried, and people can reach the sacred spot only on elephants. The truncated column, however, is still above ground, and a superficial search, directed in December, 1896, by Dr. Fuhrer, brought to light the inscription that Aśoka had had carved on its shaft for the benefit of a most distant posterity.

One can read in the clearest lettering, "By his Gracious Majesty, the Beloved-of-the-gods, who came in person twenty years after his coronation [this spot] was consecrated by saying, 'Here was born the Buddha, Śākyamuni.'" We must believe these royal words, recognizing how strong are memories attached to material remains in India, as elsewhere. Only a few generations separated Aśoka from the event he earnestly wished to commemorate on the very spot where it took place. This pious gesture proved most fortunate for the historians who came more than two thousand years later.

One of the details of the Nativity that would seem confirmed by the above is that it did not take place in the palace of Kapilavastu, but that it was during one of Māyā's usual outings to the pleasure gardens that she was overtaken by what in other women would be known as labor pains. At this point legend again assumed its task, if not its rights. First of all, the texts are unanimous in stating that Māyā gave birth standing up—a position that is as uncomfortable as it is unusual. They are equally unanimous in having her grasp the branch of a tree with her right hand at the final moment. It is only the species of the tree that becomes debatable.

For instance, Aśoka was said to have been taken before a tree bearing his own name (*aśoka*), known in India by its magnificent red flower, and there, due to the prestige that the sage Upagupta exercised over the gods, the emperor was able to converse with the dryad who lived under its bark. Consequently she had had the rare privilege of seeing the infant Buddha born. More than six hundred years later it was again an *aśoka tree* that was shown to the Chinese pilgrim Fa-hsien, and perhaps the same one, this time dead and withered, that was seen by Hsuan Tsang two and a half centuries later. Other texts state that it was a fig tree, *plakṣa,* which spontaneously bent down one of its branches towards Māyā's right hand.[25] Still others opt for a *śāla,* the most common species in the sub-Himālayan zone and the very same kind of tree that, eighty years later, shaded the death of the Blessed One. The important point to be remembered is that tradition attributed to Māyā, at the time, the sculptural pose *par excellence,* according to Indian aesthetics even of today.

All this is a prelude to the miraculous coming of the Predestined One, for let us not forget that the Nativity is one of the Great Miracles. The ten lunar months having come to an exact end, the time was set for the birth and, according to the more ancient texts, nothing more was needed. The later ones, however, were much more demanding in stating *how* the infant Buddha must be born. They called upon the precedent established in the Rig Veda, where it is told that the god Indra refused to be born in the normal way but insisted upon coming forth through his mother's flank. It is thus that the infant Buddha owed it to himself to follow Indra's example.

And, after all, it is not more surprising for the Blessed One to come forth from his mother's body from the same side he entered at the time of Conception.[26] The only precaution that must be taken in order to banish any scruples on the part of worshipers was to announce that in so doing the divine child never so much as hurt her. In truth, it was said that this kind of spontaneous Caesarean operation left not even the slightest scar. It was absolutely necessary that the Buddha's birth be superhuman, but it must not become inhuman.

CHAPTER II

THE NATIVITY (II)

After Birth

A T LAST the infant Buddha has been born. Our hope to be free of the risky mixture of mythology and obstetrics was not shared by the Buddhist Order. Lengthy explanations were written which tended to become an apologia for the mythical nature of the event. As time went on, the Greeks, the Romans, and the early Christians were called upon to sustain the truth of the legend by a long list of miraculous births.

Buddhist Legend and Christian Tradition

SAINT JEROME's words, "It is tradition among the Gymnosophists of India that the Buddha, founder of their doctrine, was born of a virgin and emerged from her side," [1] inspire us to bring the legend of the Buddha and that of Christ closer together. Though we have already been careful about setting up a detailed comparison and drawing conclusions that are only guesswork, it still remains that a number of analogies can be noted in passing. These are quite obvious to the Christian reader: the apparition of omens, the fulfillment of prophecies, the annunciations, the vows of chastity of the wedded couples, the immaculate conceptions, the heavens which open and from which descend legions of angels or *dēvaputras* (sons of god), all have a familiar ring.

And when we read that the trees of the Lumbinī park burst into blossom to celebrate the birth of the future Buddha, we recall that according to a certain apocryphal gospel the vineyards on the hills of Bethlehem came out of their winter torpor and bloomed with joy on Christmas night. If even closer likenesses are desired, one has only to read the following passage concerning the happiness brought to the whole universe by the coming of the Predestined One:

> All passion, all hate, all excess, all pride, all sorrow, all depression, all fear, all lust, all jealousy, all selfishness disappeared. All evil acts ceased. Illnesses were cured, the hunger and thirst of the hungry and thirsty were appeased, the intoxication of those drunk on strong liquor was dissipated, the deranged recovered their reason, the blind their sight, and the deaf their hearing.[2]

How can one fail to hear an echo of the words in the Gospel according to Saint Matthew: "The blind recover their sight, the lame walk, the lepers are cured, the deaf hear . . ."?[3] A whole volume of similar parallels could be gathered, but what would this prove? Nothing more than the same tendency to exalt and transfigure the personality of the Master and to glorify the coming of the Kingdom of God to earth.

These superficial similarities do not hide from those well acquainted with the texts the fundamental differences that separate the two traditions, nor the worlds in which they have grown. No fugitive analogy can bridge the gap between the rustic and touching poverty of the manger and the humble carpenter's shop on the one hand and the luxuriant display of the gardens and palaces of King Śuddhodhana on the other. The atmosphere is aristocratic in India and democratic in Galilee; and though the same supernatural aura attends the conception of each of the predestined beings, the miracle ends much earlier in the Christian than in the Indian legend. Before birth the infant Jesus was not given a protective tabernacle in his mother's womb and his birth was like that of other children. Furthermore, the Gospels have practically nothing to tell us of Christ's first thirty years and deal only with His short public life. As against this, the *sūtras* of a biographical nature overflow with verbose details about the childhood and youth of the Bodhisattva and become abruptly arid at the start of his long teaching career. Though we are told of numerous episodes preceding the First Sermon of the Buddha and may be tempted at times to make a comparison between them and some of the apocrypha, we must remember that the idea of reciprocal borrowing is philologically undemonstrable.

The Reception of the Infant Buddha

UNLESS the analogies mentioned above are to be used for polemic reasons or as a means of propaganda, there is little in them except amusement for the dilettante. But, as we have said, the Buddhist Order (*Saṃgha*) was avid for any information about circumstances following the Nativity of the Blessed One. Many questions were raised by the zealots but too late to have an historical answer, that is, one based on contemporary testimony worthy of belief. In the absence of precise evidence, imagination had a free play and Buddhist writers did not hesitate to improvise in the most extravagant manner. Even if certain episodes seem to contain some basic truth, the variations in the texts themselves point to their fictitious character. It would not be worth reporting them if it were not for the considerable role they have played in the later imagery, thus showing the importance they had assumed in popular devotions.

First of all, it was accepted as absolute fact that only divine hands could be worthy of receiving the Bodhisattva when he came from his mother's body. India did not worry about introducing male gods beside the half-naked woman and, according to the northwestern version, Indra and Brahmā officiated as midwives. Later the Sino-Tibetan account had the infant come forth through a wide sleeve and insisted that the gods be transformed into matrons before coming close to Māyā. On the early monuments with figures, Indra is closer at hand while Brahmā is pushed further back because of the perspective, or even to the other side of the panel. The sculptures of Amarāvatī, as in the Pāli tradition, show the Guardians of the Four Cardinal Points holding between them four long receiving blankets upon which the future Buddha is represented only by his sacred footprints. We need not make a choice between which of the two versions we will accept, for when Hsuan Tsang visited the park of Lumbinī, he was shown the two places side by side: one where Indra had received and swaddled the miraculous infant and the other where the "Four Celestial Kings" had done the same with the same divine cloths. Such duplications of sacred sites are frequent enough for us not to be worried by them.

The Bath

THE Bodhisattva rapidly left the hands that received him and we soon find him with a parasol and fly whisk over his head, both emblems of royalty, standing on a lotus that miraculously emerged from the earth to protect him from a coarser contact.[4] We are puzzled to find that our sources give two immediate activities. One is the usual bath and the other "the seven steps" which the infant Buddha is said to have taken "right after birth." We must not forget that he knew both how to walk and how to talk spontaneously. The Gandhāra school showed the latter to be first, while later steles from the Ganges Valley combined, as best they could, the two episodes in the same framework. We shall follow the Pāli texts in telling of the ritualistic bath.

Concerning the bath, tradition is most shaky and there are many variants in the accounts, even though the perfect purity of the Bodhisattva should have made it a simple formality. On one point the texts are curiously in accord: both cold and hot water were used. Sometimes it was from the earth that two springs emerged and filled two tubs in which the child was bathed "like a golden statue." At other times the water seemed to fall from heaven like rain. Someone invented something even better. In accordance with an old belief, widely found in India and still prevalent in Kashmir, water spirits, called *nāgas,* which haunt springs and ponds, came forth on this auspicious occasion. Two of the most famous ones, Nanda and his younger brother Upananda, are shown as half human and half serpent, naked to the waist, and directing a double jet of water upon the Bodhisattva. Both ideas were found so good that in the garden at Lumbinī two places were shown: one where the "dragons" had showered the divine infant, and one where the twin springs had miraculously arisen to furnish water for his bath.

All of this must have seemed too simple and unimpressive. Therefore, the great divinities had to be brought into the pious act and hundreds of thousands of gods, preceded by Indra, Brahmā, and the Four Guardians of the World, sluiced the infant Buddha with perfumed waters over and over again.[5] No one could have been more copiously cleansed of an impurity already declared inexistent.

Naturally the sculptured monuments reflect the variations of the texts. At Mathurā the two *nāgas* come halfway out of the earth, while

on the Benares stele they pour the contents of two round jars on the
head of the Bodhisattva, which is the Indian way of anointing kings as
well as of bathing children. In Gandhāra the two usual assistants, Indra
and Brahmā, are responsible for this function as well as for that of
carrying the white parasol and fly whisk that accompany the walk of
the Predestined One.

The Seven Steps [6]

THE episode of the seven steps, whether it preceded or followed that
of the bath, was far more original and was presented with fewer variants. This is how it is given in the oldest tradition:

> Just born, the Bodhisattva stands firmly on his feet and takes seven
> steps, his face towards the north. Shaded by the white parasol, he
> looks to each cardinal point and speaks the following words in
> stentorian tones [some say like the roar of a lion], "I am the first;
> I am the best of all beings."

This behavior, unusual for a newborn child, could only have been believed after knowledge of the supernatural nature which was eventually attributed to him. The commentators consequently felt the need
to show that there were precedents, and recalled that at the time of his
two prior births, immediately preceding this last one, the Bodhisattva
had spontaneously begun to talk. The first time he happened to be
holding a bit of sandalwood in his closed hand and when his mother
asked him what it was, he answered, "It is a cure, Mother." The second
time, when he was reborn as Prince Viśvantāra and a paragon of charity, this is what happened: "As he came forth from the maternal womb
he held out his right hand, saying, 'Is there nothing in the house,
Mother? I should like to make a donation.' His mother answered, 'My
darling, you are born into a rich family.' Taking her son's hand in hers,
she put into it a purse." [7] Such tales go on and on and remind us of the
no less miraculous stories in the *Golden Legend*.

The various texts concerning this early episode are fairly uniform,
with only slight embellishments. There was the addition, for instance,
of lotus flowers blooming under the infant's footsteps and that of an
editor of the *Lalitavistara* who felt that the early account was too simple.
Walking towards the north was not enough. So he had the Bodhi-

sattva take seven steps towards each of the cardinal points, plus heaven and hell, but each time he also had to speak with an allusion to the specific direction taken. As Indians orient themselves by facing east, the Orient is the cardinal point that comes *first,* and the Bodhisattva started out by taking seven steps towards the east, declaring that he was the one who walked "first" among people of good will. Thus, walking towards each point, he made a statement making use of an insipid pun in referring to his direction. Then, with his head bent down to earth, he predicted not only the defeat of Māra, the Buddhist Satan, but also the good that would come to hell from the "beneficent rain of his Law." Finally, since during his last seven steps he had his face raised to the sky, it meant that all beings must forever look up to him. Even this curtailed account will give the reader an idea of the long-winded character of the Buddhist books.

The Simultaneous Births

WE must now turn to the miraculous phenomena that accompanied the Bodhisattva's birth. We have already mentioned some of them earlier. Since the newborn baby's horoscope had not yet been read at the time of his birth, his future destiny is supposed to have been uncertain. That it was to be exceptional was recognized, but he was to have the privilege of choosing between the role of monarch of the world by right of conquest or the still more exalted, but completely peaceful, role of religious savior. No one in India was unaware that the Universal Monarch possessed by right of birth seven great treasures, namely the most perfect of wheels, elephants, horses, precious stones, women, ministers, and generals. It was then obligatory that these seven treasures should manifest themselves at the same time as the heir to the throne of the Śākyas.

None of our texts disputes this, but even the conscientious efforts made by all to agree could not be expected to meet with complete success. The discus or "wheel" easily became symbolic of the Wheel of the Doctrine, and its being set in motion for the first time was synonymous with the First Sermon. The precious stones and the ministers often were left out because they were of no use. It was also difficult to have a large ceremonial elephant born at the same time as the prince, for the growth of such an animal is notoriously slow. This objection did not hold true for his favorite horse or his future wife. Finally, with a little good will, the word *parinayaka*, leader, could be understood not as a commander of armies but simply as a groom. Thus at least four of the treasures remained useful for the future. To be on the safe side, at the time of the Nativity, there also were born 5000 boys of noble birth, 10,000 girls of good family with Yaśodharā, the future bride, among them, as well as 800 women servants and 800 males slaves, including Chandaka, the future "leader" of the horse. Ten thousand mares foaled and among the foals was Kanthaka, the Bodhisattva's future steed. A long list of gifts and happy events followed this enumeration to indicate the universe's gratitude for the coming of the Predestined One.

The Singhalese commentator not only included in his list of the seven "born together" Udāyin, who became the playmate of the young prince,[8] but also named the *ficus religiosa* as the tree under which the Bodhisattva was to attain Enlightenment. Not to be outdone, the Tibetan texts found it important to name in advance the kings contemporary with the Master and with whom he would later come in contact: namely, Bimbisāra of Magadha and Prasenajit of Kośala. Finally, they did not refuse the same kindness to the familiar jinni who, thunderbolt in hand—whence his name, Vajrapāṇi—was to constitute himself the bodyguard of the Blessed One and follow him as his shadow—in our terms, his guardian angel.

The custom in India is that a child is given a name only a few days after his birth and, as far as possible, in memory of a circumstance attending it. So one pious recorder tells us that as all desires (*sarva*) and material needs (*artha*) of Śuddhodhana were fulfilled (*siddha*) by the qualities of his supposed offspring, the king decided to call him Sarvaarthasiddha or, for short, Siddhārtha.

The Presentation at the Temple

AFTER the birth, the bath, and the seven steps, it seems in agreement with historical facts that the Bodhisattva and his mother be brought back from the Lumbinī park to the palace in Kapilavastu. Even this simple act became complicated by the myths surrounding the whole question of the Buddha's birth. The *Lalitavistara* organized on the spot the pomp of a triumphal procession, composed of two hundred thousand men, women, horses, and elephants, with an air-borne retinue of several thousand divinities who accompanied the procession, all the while dropping clouds of paradisiac flowers, while the Bodhisattva sat in a chariot drawn by twenty thousand celestial nymphs, all magnificently adorned. Who could do more? [9]

It is understood that we drop this phantasmagoria inspired by excessive devotion. But we are told of one episode on the way that causes us some astonishment, being unexpected by an Indian or a scholar of Indian lore, and we quote directly the *Lalitavistara:* "Śākyas with their elders, both male and female, came to Śuddhodhana and said to him, 'May it please your Majesty, the Prince must be taken to the house of the Dēvas.'" [10] (There follows the usual account of the decoration of the streets and the organization of the procession.)

> Thus did King Śuddhodhana, amidst a mighty host of kings, with royal magnificence and kingly majesty, take the Prince to the temple, and enter it. Now, when the Bodhisattva set his right foot on the floor of that temple, all the inert images of the Dēvas, such as Śiva, Skanda, Nārāyana, Kuvēra, Chandra, Śurya, Vaiśravana, Śakra, Brahmā, and the Guardians of the four quarters, rose from their respective places, and fell at the feet of the Bodhisattva. . . . And the gods whose images were in the temple made manifest their respective shapes and recited these Gāthās [in his honor]. . . . On the entrance of the Bodhisattva into the temple thirty-two hundreds of thousands of Dēvaputras had their mind directed to the sequence-less perfect Sambodhi. This . . . is the reason, this the result of the indifferent Bodhisattva entering the temple.[11]

If we compare the above with the following passage from the apocryphal Gospel of Matthew on the infancy of Jesus, we find a great similarity:

> They came into a city called Sotinen; and because they knew no one from whom to seek hospitality, they entered a temple called by the Egyptians *Capitol*. In this temple there were three hundred and sixty-five idols before which in turn each day of the year were performed sacrificial honors. When the Blessed Mary entered the temple with the little child all the idols fell to the ground. . . . And so were accomplished the words of the prophet Isaiah (19:1), "Behold the Lord rideth upon a swift cloud and all the idols of Egypt shall be moved at his presence."

No one will deny that the bare elements of the two accounts are the same. In one as in the other, the images of the ancient gods had to bow before the superiority of a little child who was to be the founder of a new religion. These accounts, however, indicate that the surrounding factors are dissimilar, but what is more important and decisive is that the intentions of the narrators are shown to be diametrically opposed. The Egyptian idols, flung from their pedestals by a force hostile as well as supernatural, struck the earth, never to rise again. They were false gods and Christ had come to abolish their worship. The Indian divinities, on the contrary, received a courtesy call from the infant Buddha, and it was with complete spontaneity that they hastened to forestall his homage by offering their own. If they thus prostrated themselves before him, it was to rise again and resume their places on their own altars, for the Predestined One had "come as he has come" for the salvation of the gods as well as for that of humans. Thus we see that the two passages quoted could not be more different in spirit.

The contrast between the two legends becomes even more accentuated if one follows their portrayal in religious art. In Christian representations the idols are shown again and again not only falling down but breaking up; while the Chinese pilgrim Hsuan Tsang found in the temple outside the gates of Kapilavastu a statue of someone in the act of rising to bow in salute. The old image-makers of India, like those of our medieval cathedrals, understood perfectly and translated into visible form the intimate sense of their own religion.

The Horoscope

KING ŚUDDHODHANA had no sooner reached his palace than his first concern was to have the horoscope of the newborn baby read. Again it would seem that the texts reported an actual fact, and this time we detect in none of them the slightest dissonance due to foreign influence— that is, nothing that sounds in discord with what we believe is true of the old Indian folklore. Not that the practice in question, which was still current in Europe in the sixteenth century in all noble houses, was peculiar to India. Only every account given us describes what took place in accordance with the rites that belong to its great antiquity.

To begin with, we must understand by the word "horoscope" not an astrological operation but, in its broadest meaning, a prediction about the future of a child, made without reference to the position of the stars at the time of his birth. Of course, tradition ended by fixing the Buddha's birth in the month of Vaiśākha (April–May) and by taking account of the asterisms in view at that time of the year. But the old Brāhman diviners who were called in for this horoscope were not yet true astrologers. They were content with being fortunetellers. As is indicated by their name, their role was to observe the corporeal aspects of the subject brought to them and to prognosticate, according to these, the destiny that awaited him. That is the first point to retain.

The second question is: How did they proceed? In a completely methodical fashion. According to the systematic genius of the old Indian theorists, these signs, which were purely physical, had been classified, numbered, and divided into two lists. One list consisted of thirty-two principal characteristics; the other contained eighty secondary indications, which were really only more detailed listings of the first. Consequently, all that had to be done was to go through the items of a catalogue, which contained both these lists and look for them in the subject—much the same way that tourists spend their time verifying on monuments the items listed in their guidebook.

It was noted, in turn, that the newborn baby had a large skull, evenly rounded, glistening black hair that curled to the right, a broad and even forehead, a small circle of hair between the eyebrows, black eyes, forty-two even white teeth, a long and flexible tongue, a lion's jaw, fine golden skin, well-set-up shoulders, and so forth. The width of the chest, the length of the arms, which must reach down to his knees, and legs, which must have the elegance of a deer's, were all noted, ending with a look at his toes. This first examination being finished, another was started in reverse order, following the eighty secondary characteristics, beginning with the toenails and ending with the top of the head. We shall spare the reader the tiresome enumeration; all he needs to know is that the child who fulfilled all the requirements, and of course Siddhārtha did, had to become a "great man." [12]

Thirdly (we, too, must be methodical), it emerges, from what has been said, as Emile Senart well knew, that the catalogue of principal signs and minor signs is neither the invention nor the composition of the Buddhists and that it existed long before they used it. Far from denying this, their texts insist upon its being among the old technical

Brāhman manuals. Nevertheless, it remains that they are the ones who, by applying it point by point to the body of their Master at birth, have brought it to our knowledge—and to that of the innumerable converts of Central Asia and the Far East. Thus it was inevitable that in time it became considered as an integral part of the Buddhist Scriptures. When the time finally came, four or five centuries after the Master's death, to conceive, draw, or model his image the worshipers were only too happy, in the absence of all documents and actual memories, to turn to this enumeration of all the marks of beauty and grandeur. It was then and for that reason that it became a description of the Buddha, not at birth but fully grown, and thus the divinatory manual became a sort of iconographic memento. It is as such that both the Tibetan and the Chinese presented it to the first European exegetes.

When, reassured by this information, we come back to the accounts of the horoscope, we are not too surprised to find that the exaggerations and uncertainties have denatured the actual event. Its usual nature seemed to guarantee its authenticity. None of the commentaries has been willing to simply accept the result of the consultation that King Śuddhodhana held with the astrologers who were part of his court and who had previously given him the interpretation of Māyā's dream at the time of Conception. The written explanation of the doubt is that, though the horoscope forecasted the greatness of the newborn baby, it did not specify what form it was to take. Our Middle Ages would have stated it as possibly becoming one or the other of "the two halves of God, the Pope or the Emperor," and the Indian idiom was "Universal Monarch or Savior." Because the Brāhmans were unable to decide between the two conjectures, the gods were called upon. But even they were hesitant, and it was left to an old *rishi* to come down from his mountain hermitage and settle the question. This version became so popular that it was the subject of numerous pictorial representations, which still remain. For Hsuan Tsang, our Chinese traveler, there is no doubt that it was Asita, the *rishi,* who alone was clairvoyant enough to forecast clearly the Bodhisattva's destiny.

Asita's Prediction

THE word *"rishi"* evokes, in the Indian mind, the image of someone similar to what a Westerner might call a patriarch—but an ascetic patriarch without descendants and living the life of a hermit. The *Lalita-vistara* gives us the following account of the *ṛishi's* prediction:

At that time there lived on the side of the noble Himavat mountains a great sage named Asita. He was versed in all the five sciences, and lived with his nephew Nāradatta. At the moment of Bodhisattva's birth he beheld many extraordinary, wonderful, magical occurrences. He saw Dēvaputras moving about in great joy under the sky, and, high in the void above, resounding the name of Buddha. The wish arose in his mind, "I must inquire into this mystery." With his intellectual eyes he surveyed the whole of the Jambudvipa. He beheld in the great city called Kapila, in the house of king Śuddhodhana, a prince was born, who was refulgent with the light of a hundred virtues, who was the adored of all regions, who bore on his person the thirty-two signs of greatness. Having beheld this he addressed his pupil Nāradatta: "Know ye, my pupil, that a precious jewel has been produced in the Jambudvipa. In the great city of Kapilavastu, in the house of king Śuddhodhana has been born a prince who is refulgent with the light of a hundred virtues, who is the adored of all regions, who bears on his body the thirty-two signs of greatness. Should he remain at home he will become a great sovereign, owner of a fourfold army, an emperor, victorious, virtuous, master of religion, ruler of countries, possessed of great might, and endowed with the seven jewels, and these will be the seven jewels, *viz.,* the jewel wheel, the jewel elephant, the jewel horse, the jewel ruby, the jewel wife, the jewel lord chamberlain, the jewel commander-in-chief. Unto him will be born a thousand sons, valorous, heroic, handsome, and oppressors of enemy armies. He will conquer the whole circle of the earth to the brink of the ocean through his impartial discipline, his arms, his religion, and his might, and reign over all with supremacy and power. Should he, however, retire from urban life to a hermitage, he will become a Tathagita, an Arhat, a knower of the perfect knowledge, a leader of unfailing policy, a lawgiver, and a perfect Buddha in this region. I should therefore, proceed to see him."

Now, the great sage Asita, along with his nephew Nāradatta, rose up like a goose in mid-air, and passed on to where the great city of Kapilavastu stood. Arrived there, he suppressed his miraculous power, entered on foot the city, and, arriving at the house of king Śuddhodhana, stood at the gate. There the divine sage Asita saw hundreds of thousands of persons collected near the gate. Then, approaching the warder, he addressed him, saying, "Do you go and inform king Śuddhodhana, that a sage awaits at his door."

"Be it so," replied the warder and, then proceeding to where king Śuddhodhana was, joined his hands and said, "Be it known to your majesty that an old, emaciated octogenarian sage awaits at the gate, and says, 'I am anxious to visit the king.' "

The king, having ordered an appropriate seat to be got ready for the sage, said to the warder, "Let the sage enter."

Now the great sage Asita repaired to where king Śuddhodhana was, and, standing before him, said, "Victory, victory to the great king! May you rule all life through! May you conduct your royal duties according to law!"

Then king Śuddhodhana, having welcomed him with the offering of Argha and water for washing his feet, and enquired of his welfare, invited him to take a seat. Knowing then that the sage was comfortably placed, the king respectfully and with due regard addressed him thus: "I cannot say, O sage, that I have desired your visit. What may, please, be your object in coming here and what do you require?"

Thus addressed, the sage replied, "Mahārājā, a son has been born unto thee, and I am come with a desire to see him."

The king said, "The Prince is sleeping now, great sage; wait for awhile till he is awake."

The sage said, "Mahārājā, great personages like him do not sleep long; such great personages are usually very wakeful."

Then through the blessing of Asita the Bodhisattva became awake. King Śuddhodhana, with his two hands taking up the Prince Sarvarthasiddha, carefully and gently brought him before the great sage Asita.

The great sage, beholding the Bodhisattva with his person adorned with the thirty-two signs of great personages and eighty subsidiary signs, with his body superior in excellence to that of Śakra, or of Brahmā, or of the guardians of regions, endowed with greater might than that of hundreds of thousands, with every member developed to perfect beauty, burst forth in this exclamation: "A wonderful soul has appeared in this region!" Then rising from his seat, and joining his hands, he fell at the feet of the Bodhisattva, circumambulated his person, and, then taking him in his hands, sat in contemplation . . . Beholding him thus, the sage cried much, shed profuse tears, and sighed deeply.

King Śuddhodhana, seeing that the sage was greatly agitated, horripilated, crying, shedding tears, and heaving sighs, humbly asked him, "Why do you cry? Why do you shed tears? Why do you heave deep sighs? May no evil befall the Prince!"

Asita replied, "I cry not, O Mahārājā, for the sake of the Prince, nor is any evil to befall him. I cry on my own account."

"And what is the reason of it?"

"I am, Mahārājā, an old, emaciated octogenarian. The prince Sarvarthasiddha is sure to acquire the sequenceless perfect knowledge, and, acquiring it, he will turn the wheel of the never-to-be-equalled religion, which cannot be turned by any Śramana, or Brāhmana, or Dēva, or Māra, or any other of the same religion. He will impart religion for the good and gratification of all beings, including gods. He will expound the religion which is auspicious at the beginning, auspicious at the middle, and auspicious at the end, of good purport, well arranged, unequalled, complete, perfectly pure, well-environed, . . . and ends in virtue. Those, who follow religion by hearing it from us, will throw aside all trammels of caste, and be free from disease, death, grief, lamentation, pain, melancholy, injury, and labor. By raining the water of true religion the Prince will gladden the hearts of those who are oppressed by the fire of passion, envy, and delusion. He will bring to the straight path of Nirvāna those wicked persons of vicious motives who are traveling in wicked ways. He will untie the bonds of those persons who lie fettered in the cage of worldliness and pain. He will create the eye of knowledge for those whose eyes are enveloped by the dense darkness of utter ignorance. He will pluck out the dart of affliction from the sides of those who have been pierced by it. For example, Mahārājā, even as the fig blossoms rarely and at some places, so on rare occasions, and at certain places, in course of millions of years, adorable Buddhas are produced on this earth. This Prince is one of them. He will for certain understand the sequenceless, perfect Bodhi knowledge. Having understood it, he will rescue hundreds of thousands of millions of persons from the ocean of worldliness and establish them in immortality. But I cannot behold that Buddhist jewel, and hence it is, Mahārājā, that I am crying, and am deeply grieved, and heaving deep sighs."

[There follow the enumerations of the thirty-two principal characteristics and the eighty secondary ones represented in the child and the inevitable conclusion repeats itself: "Undoubtedly he will go into religion."]

Pleased, exhilarated, glowing in affection and delight, by hearing

this account of the Prince from the great sage Asita, king Śuddhodhana, rising from his seat, fell at the feet of the Bodhisattva and recited this verse:

> "Thou art to be praised by the Suras including
> Indra, and worshipped by R̥ishis; thou art the
> physician of the universe. I perform obeisance
> to thee, O Lord."

Then . . . king Śuddhodhana, offered refreshment to the great
sage Asita and his nephew Nāradatta, and, having refreshed them,
bade them adieu after offering them suitable presents of cloth, etc.

Through his miraculous power the great sage Asita passed away
through the sky, and reached his hermitage.[13]

We have no difficulty in recognizing a pattern already familiar to us,
beginning with the celestial activities of the "sons of the gods," which
only slightly recall the choirs of angels that alerted the shepherds of
Bethlehem the first Christmas night. The gestures of Asita, however,
are surprisingly like those of Saint Simeon, according to the Gospel of
Saint Luke. In order to settle our suspicion of imitation in the two accounts, we shall now turn to the much less verbose Saint Luke
(2:25-34):

> And behold, there was a man in Jerusalem, whose name was
> Simeon; and the same man was just and devout, waiting for the
> consolation of Israel: and the Holy Ghost was upon him.
> And it was revealed unto him by the Holy Ghost, that he should
> not see death, before he had seen the Lord's Christ.
> And he came by the Spirit into the temple: and when the parents
> brought in the child Jesus to do for him after the custom of the
> Law,
> Then took he him up in his arms, and blessed God and said,
> Lord, now lettest thou thy servant depart in peace, according to
> thy word:
> For mine eyes have seen thy salvation, . . .
> A light to lighten the Gentiles, and the glory of thy people Israel.
> And Joseph and his Mother marvelled at those things which were
> spoken of him. And Simeon blessed them . . .

The analogies that at first seem to appear tend to disappear upon
reading the two accounts, and are replaced by a number of differences.

First of all, the settings as well as the circumstances of the two inter-
views are completely different and in either case equally likely. What
seems of greater importance is that, in spite of the similarity in gesture
on the part of the two old men, their mental attitudes are diametrically opposed. Asita weeps, while Simeon rejoices. The former is distressed because he has to die too soon and the latter sings a hymn of
joy because he has lived long enough; each is justified within the context of his statement. In all, the likeness between the two episodes may
be reduced to the fact that in each case an inspired old man holding a
predestined child in his arms predicts before his admiring parents the
coming of a savior of the world.

Surely no one will deny the interest of the analogy, but we must
also recognize that in both cases the incident is pretty much demanded
by the legend. The destiny of the founders of these two great religions
was necessarily visible as early as the cradle to those who knew how to
see, and the logical visionary in each case was a saintly old man. The
fundamental accord between the two predictions remains, then, purely
theoretical: they are so different in context that no reciprocal influence
seems possible.

Māyā's Death

As much as Buddhism and Christianity are similar in the use they
made of earlier beliefs for the sake of spreading the doctrine, as much
do they differ in the role they assigned to the Savior's mother. Each
made the mother divine after death; but, whereas the humble Virgin
Mary was transformed into a Queen of Heaven sitting beside her son,
Queen Māyā was assigned to the Second or the Fourth story of Heaven.
The Assumption of the Virgin is a miracle, a just one as an exceptional
reward for all she suffered; while the rebirth of Māyā in heaven and
her promotion to the masculine sex were simply the necessary results
of her being the Bodhisattva's chosen mother. Thus, in spite of the
homage paid by Buddhists to the personification of the feminine ideal,
Māyā never became the object of any particular cult such as the Catholic
world has devoted to the Virgin Mary. The images that remind West-
erners of their "Madonna and Child" are of a completely different
deity.[14] It is all the more amazing to discover, beneath the differences
and similarities, the interplay of the same scruples and aspirations.

The Virgin Mary not only lived many years after the birth of her son, she survived his death as well; Queen Māyā died seven days after the birth of the Bodhisattva, according to all Buddhists. The texts agree upon this fact and nothing makes it unlikely, certainly not the improvised delivery of Māyā while on a walk in the country. Again, of course, the legend could not leave a simple fact untouched, and her death became the cause of endless speculations. The basic reason for this was the necessity of absolutely exculpating the infant Buddha from the possible accusation of causing his mother's death.

The first thesis, expounded by an old hardhearted monk, stated that things took place like this because they could not be otherwise: it is an absolute rule that the mother of a Buddha must die seven days after his birth, and he is in no way responsible for it. In fact, at the time of the Investigations preceding his last rebirth, the Bodhisattva in his omniscience chose as his mother a woman who had just ten months and eight nights to live.

The second argument, coming from a more delicate and subtle theologian, stated that, since the Blessed One forbade the pleasures of love in his sermon, it would have been improper for Queen Māyā to resume her married life. So she died. Another added that the womb which had once held the Bodhisattva was "as a sanctuary" and should never have another occupant.

The second argument seemed too absolute to the writer of the *Lalitavistara* and he chose a kinder reason of his own: "The mothers of past Bodhisattvas had also died seven days after giving birth. And why is that? It is because once the Bodhisattva, grown and in full attainment of his powers, when the moment came for him to leave home to take up the religious life, his mother's heart would have been broken." [15]

Thus we can choose between the premature death of Māyā as the result of an inexorable fate, of theological protocol, or of a merciful destiny. Of course none of these reasons has the slightest historical value or authenticity, and the original fact, which seemed at first so clear, remains forever dim. If the first and last reasons given do not trouble us, the second is deeply troubling. What guarantee have we, after what we have just read, that the Buddhist teachers did not promptly do away with Māyā in order to eliminate the same kind of thorny question that has troubled Christian Fathers, namely: What of the earthly brothers and sisters of Jesus Christ? Since Saint Jerome, Christian orthodoxy has continued to deny their existence, so shocking would it seem. For us as for the Indians, the mother of a savior must nevermore conceive or give birth.

The Buddhist legend, as we have seen, attempts to soften whatever cruelty is in Māyā's fate. Not only did she escape the sorrows of life, but her apotheosis in masculine form delivered her from all care, terrestrial or maternal. Her relations with the child of her previous incarnation were practically nonexistent. Only once, during a rainy season, did the Buddha, moved by filial piety, ascend to heaven just to teach her the Good Law. So thought and spoke the severe scholars, but even they had to give in to popular imagination. Not only did the worshipers keep a place for Māyā beside the Buddha, when he was grown up and even old; they continued to evoke her in her original feminine and maternal aspect and not in the form of the god into which her *karma* had transformed her. When the Blessed One endured terrible austerities before his achievement of Enlightenment, at one point he was believed dead by the gods, and then "Queen Māyā" hurriedly appeared, disheveled and in tears.

A later legend, told by Hsuan Tsang, even brought her to the scene of the Ultimate Death. When the Predestined One was put in his coffin, the monk Anuruddha, due to his magic powers, ascended to heaven to inform Queen Māyā of her son's death. She came down to earth immediately, accompanied by a number of deities, and wept before the traditional relics: the coffin, the monastic robe, the alms bowl, the beggar's staff—all that was left of her child. Then, due to the Buddha's divine power, the lid of the coffin lifted and the Blessed One, brilliantly lighted, sat up and, bowing before his mother, spoke a few words of consolation to her. This was a new lesson in filial piety left for future generations, and probably that is the reason why this episode has become so well known in China. It is only through Chinese texts and superb Sino-Japanese paintings that we know it now, but that it is of Indian origin is proved to us by the fact that Hsuan Tsang saw a monument representing it in Kuśinagara at the place where Māyā wept over her dead son. Both the Buddhist and the Christian traditions insist that the Savior's mother be present at the scene of his death.

We may conclude from the above that it can be useful, and it is also moving to note that even in completely different times, environments, and circumstances there are such similar desires and expressions.

In both cases, religious conscience demands that the Savior's mother remain forever chaste and, to satisfy popular devotion, that she be associated with the scene of her son's death, whether she be dead or alive. Both of these demands and emotions are found independently and unknown to each other. While such unconscious and similar efforts seem to lessen the differences between Buddhist and Christian traditions, neither detracts in the least from the originality of the other. They only attest, through time and space, to the deep unity of the human spirit.

CHAPTER III

CHILDHOOD AND YOUTH (I)

Social Life

T HE HOROSCOPE of the child and the death of the mother bring to a
close the fifteen episodes of the second cycle of the Nativity. The
greater cycle of Kapilavastu, however, continues and furnishes us the
framework for the ensemble of traditions concerning the childhood of
Siddhārtha. There is no doubt that the writers of the texts filled in this
traditional outline with whatever their imagination could provide as
well as what they thought they knew. We have no hope of finding in
these writings the elements of a true biography, and we read them as a
completely romanticized life of the "Sage of the Śākyas." Though tiresome because of their ridiculous exaggerations, they at times are fasci-
nating.

A novel is not history, but it often possesses more psychological truth
and even more objective reality than a methodically compiled treatise.
Never shall we know the exact details of the Buddha's life as a child, an
adolescent, or an adult. But at least we shall learn what the Indians of
two thousands years ago thought was a fitting education, marriage, and
private life for a prince. Furthermore, since this prince decided one day
to enter the religious life, we shall find out what the obstacles were he
had to overcome in doing so. Such knowledge is certainly not to be
scorned by an Indian scholar nor by historians, nor even by anyone interested in religious questions. If we remember that what we like to call
historical truth is often only the conjecture upon which some sincere
scholars agree, then we shall not turn a purist's mind to these writings.
The unanimous agreement of the biographers in this case will at least
give us what one might call traditional truth. Although the admission
that there might be several kinds of truth is repugnant to the logical

mind, even this truth is at least worth having, and we remain free to accept it with the necessary grain of salt.

To its documentary interest, there will also be added the pleasure derived from the voluptuous and melancholy charm of the literary and dramatic descriptions of customs of the times. Turning to the Bodhisattva's youth, we find mystical and sensual yearnings translated into sudden surges of asceticism and of passionate languor, thus giving us two aspects of the eternal Indian soul. Let us not forget what we have already read: the Bodhisattva was to be outstandingly superior in all things. But on this fundamental theme our authors have embroidered two series of clearly contradictory variations both in tone and in inspiration. On one hand Siddhārtha is not only the heir to his father's throne, but he is at the same time emperor designate of the world, if he consents. Thus it becomes necessary to endow him and his environment with all the splendors, the riches, and the enjoyment that normally go with a more than regal life. But on the other hand, everyone knows that this excess of luxury, this overabundance of pleasures, were unable to retain our hero in his century. It then becomes necessary to indicate, through the descriptions of this none-too-edifying, worldly life, the early signs of the later amazing reaction that transformed the prince, surfeited with voluptuous satisfactions, into the begging monk. The edification is the greater because of the sharp contrast between the life he left and the one that his religious vocation made him follow. The task of outlining the dual chronicle of an existence that appears to be a double one was accomplished by the biographers as best they could. We shall not be greatly surprised to find that only one among them, Aśvaghoṣa,[1] has succeeded to a certain degree in tracing step by step, in the *Buddhacarita,* the gradual moral evolution that finally determined the Bodhisattva's preference for the poverty of a wandering monk rather than all the gifts brought by fortune. The lack of transition between erotic scenes and those showing piety, often varying in their order from text to text, led to the decision to treat first the secular and then the religious life of the Buddha. We could not pretend to succeed where Indian authors had failed, and it is now too late to attempt an agreement in the order of the various episodes.

The Coefficient of Reduction

The above decision greatly simplifies the order of the next two chapters, but it does not suppress or alter certain difficulties that arise, the most important of which can easily be guessed. The historian who believes that Śākyamuni actually lived has to admit that, in part, he shares the beliefs of the faithful Buddhists. The problem is to stake out the boundaries of his credulity. Even if the line of demarcation is at the limit of the miraculous, after common facts are accounted for, even there the exaggerations of the *sūtras* are of such a nature that one is at a loss to know by what measure they should be reduced. Not only do the figures noted differ from one text to another, but the lack of proportion makes it impossible to establish a coefficient of reduction. When the *Lalitavistara* [2] gives the infant Buddha 32 nurses, it is easy to divide the number by 4 or even 8, but when the same text later speaks of 84,000 wives (others say 60 or 40,000), how many zeroes should be dropped, out of sheer respect for the prince as well as likelihood? A common divisor is obviously impossible.

Perhaps we will do better if we start by asking a few simple questions. What was the social status of the Bodhisattva's family? What kind of kingdom did his father rule? How much land and how many subjects did he have and what was his income? We shall have to subtract much from the evaluations in the Buddhist writings, for the greater the sacrifice, the more sublime did the renunciation of the Predestined One become. Seeing through the multiple Buddhist boastings, European historians in general agree that the "great king of the Śākyas" was really a modest little monarch,[3] the ruler of a small oligarchic vassal state more or less subject to the great monarchy of Kosala, the capital of which, Śrāvastī, was only about a hundred miles from Kapilavastu. This state, barely as large as one of the old provinces of France, stretched into what is now called the Nepalese Tērai and spread out at the foot of the high snow-covered Himālayas, its rich rice fields abundantly irrigated by mountain streams. These fertile areas, once able to feed a large population at the cost of much labor to keep them cultivated and irrigated, became fever-infested marshy jungles by the time the first Chinese pilgrims arrived.

Siddhārtha's father was himself a large landowner and did not scorn presiding over the plowing festivals. That he owned riches could not be doubted, nor that through him the Bodhisattva belonged to the noble class of the *kṣatriya*, or, as we would say, to the nobility of the sword. The entire Indian tradition, even the Brāhman, recognized in him a prince. That he received the education then considered proper for a young nobleman, that he had horses, carriages, elephants, numerous servants, and that his father was in a position to provide him with a life of luxury after his marriage, seem all most likely. Let us not ask for more.

Education

THE legend manifests no feeling that fate, which took his mother so rapidly, in any way wronged the child. Upon the advice of the Śākya elders of both sexes, the care of the child was given to his maternal aunt, Mahāprajāpatī Gautamī, who was also his father's second wife. She carried out the task with as much success as love, and we shall see later what her reward was to be. We are told that she was assisted in her care by no less than thirty-two nurses—an exaggerated figure but not so much as one might believe, due to the division of labor among Indian servants.[4] Current custom never assigned less than four nurses to the son of a wealthy *bourgeois:* one to nurse him, one to bathe him and wash his clothes, one to carry him, and one to amuse him. King Śuddhodhana could hardly do less than multiply this number by 8, and we must praise the writer of the *Lalitavistara* for his restraint. This same traditional account, incidentally, tells us how infants were fed at the time. The Orient, in general, separates foods into two kinds—hot and cold. So let us trust the Bodhisattva's nurses to have fed him, as is written, with "sweet milk, sour milk, melted butter, and other particularly caloric foods."[5] Let us also believe that due to this rich diet, full of vitamins, he grew as rapidly as "the lotus in pond water" or the "new moon in the sky of the clear half month."

This, however, is all we are told of the period during which the Bodhisattva was in the care of women—namely, until he was seven. Information concerning the period of his education is far more abundant, and we are not spared one of the sixty-four subjects listed on the educational program.[6] Indians would not have been true to themselves had they not listed letters, sciences, arts, and technical knowledge as subjects with which the son of a "good family" had to be familiar. In order to reach the honorable number of sixty-four, they left nothing out and enumerated one by one the most diverse of subjects: grammar, sports, arithmetic, music, chess, massage, cleanliness, fortunetelling, the art of combining perfumes, strategy, and so forth. In this welter of knowledge each could choose according to the professional necessities of his class. Thus the son of an important merchant could limit himself to eight types of studies most useful in his business, starting with writing and arithmetic and going on to various kinds of appraisals. The young nobles were expected to follow a broader program, including the studies suited to all men of noble birth as well as the practice of sports suited to future warriors.

In the case of the Bodhisattva, this dual obligation was well in accord with the double eventuality concerning his near future (which must always be kept in mind). Thus, at the time of the pilgrimage of the Emperor Aśoka to Kapilavastu, he was shown by the guide the two places known as the "schoolroom" and the "gymnasium" of Siddhārtha: "It is here, O great king, that the Buddha learnt to write, and here that he became an expert, as suited his noble birth, in the art of handling elephants, horses, chariots and the use of arms, etc."[7] One of the paintings at Ajantā represents the young prince sitting and writing in class, and right next to it he is shown standing shooting arrows. All this is normal and in conformity with such reasonable precedents that we shall not separate the Bodhisattva's intellectual training from his physical instruction.

Not being moved by religious zeal, we have no cause to follow the biased order that the writer of the *Lalitavistara* adopted. He did not fail to speak of the dual "manifestation" or "demonstration" concerning both the scholarly and the physical development of the Bodhisattva; but he brought up the question of sports only much later, at the time of the tournament just before the marriage of his hero. As a writer he drew from this the advantage of doing away with inevitable repetitions, but as an apologist his fervor was aiming much higher. Since nothing had been said earlier of Siddhārtha's athletic training, his crushing victory over his rivals in all sports seemed even more marvelous. His eulogist only forgot that to win without effort means to triumph without glory. And, besides, the element of surprise was too obviously obtained at the cost of the most likely probability.

Scholarly Manifestation

HOWEVER, with our usual care let us see what the tenth chapter of the *Lalitavistara,* entitled "The Manifestation in the Writing Room," has to tell us. In passing, it is well to note the name given by all ancient texts to the school, although today in India it would be called the "reading room." We should be the first to be disappointed if on the occasion of the Bodhisattva's entering school our authors did not organize a magnificent procession in well-known style, with pomp and showers of heavenly flowers. The whole clan of the Śākyas, with Śuddhodhana leading, was mobilized to accompany the Bodhisattva, along with ten thousand other young boys his own age, to their teacher, who bore the illustrious name of Viśvāmitra, in the best Brāhman tradition. At once a miracle took place. Veneration for a teacher is well known in India, and we have seen the pupils of great scholars in Benares prostrate themselves, with their heads at their master's feet. Here, in an inconceivable reversal of the code of youthful respect and courtesy, it was the professor who, "incapable of bearing the blinding splendor of the Bodhisattva, falls before him, his nose on the ground." This eloquent gesture tells us at once the superhuman nature of the pupil with whom we both have to deal.

What followed does not conflict with this amazing introduction. While the group of nurses and attendants waited outside and the family returned to their occupations, the large class settled down somehow, possibly in the shade of some great trees, ready to listen to the first lesson. Second surprise! It was not Viśvāmitra who spoke but Siddhārtha, who asked at once, "What writing are you going to teach me, O my master?" And without waiting for a reply he enumerated at least sixty-four to choose from. Viśvāmitra, completely overcome, admitted with good grace that it was the first time he had heard the names of most of them. With this we agree, for the first two are known to us from inscriptions, while others are geographic or ethnic names, some real, some imaginary and others pure fantasy.

The author omits to say which was the final choice, but it goes without saying that it could only have been the first named. We do learn that the class continued and that a third surprising event took place: "Thus these 10,000 little boys in the company of the Bodhisattva learnt writing and, while under his direction, as they spelt out the alphabet, each letter became the first in a moral statement." So for forty-five of the forty-nine letters of the Brāhminic alphabet the Bodhisattva was able to show his supernatural influence, and a lesson in grammar became one in morals as well. But it was in order to bring maturity to the minds of all these children and to turn them towards Enlightenment that the future Buddha was willing to go to school. And though we are told at the beginning of the chapter that the Bodhisattva's companions numbered 10,000, by the end the force of exaggeration made it possible for him to convert 32,000 boys as well as 32,000 girls who had never been mentioned before.

If slightly amused, we can in no way doubt the popularity of this scene. Numerous bas-reliefs from Gandhāra represent it, and some say that the artists, duly indoctrinated by the donors, conceived it as it has just been described. Each time the Bodhisattva, seated in the center of the composition, holds in his right hand his reed used for writing and on his knees the little tablet he used as a slate, similar to the ones used by most Indian pupils today. On at least two of the known reliefs the sculptor was careful to carve on the tablet a few letters in Aramaic, a script used by the scribes of the Achaemenids and still in use in northwest India.[8] Whatever interpretation we give these graffiti, there is contained an evident allusion to the moral maxims always present in a class reciting the alphabet under the magic power of the Predestined One.

Physical Training

THE scene of the Bodhisattva's athletic exploits changes completely, but the monotony of his constant triumphs remains. This matters little, for what we are seeking is what India at that time considered to be an integral part of a young nobleman's education. The short passage from the *Divyāvadāna* that we have noted reveals that at least four sports were essential: equitation, the art of riding elephants, driving chariots, and handling arms—naturally steel arms. Of these the text mentions three: the sword, the lance, and the *aṅkuśa,* a sort of gaff the metal point of which ends in a hook. Furthermore, from the long and confused Chapter XII of the *Lalitavistara,* we can reconstruct a kind of Indian pentathlon.[9] As in Greece there was running, jumping (both broad and high), wrestling with various kinds of holds—of body, hands, feet, and even hair—the use of bows and arrows, but no mention is made of discus throwing. Still, India knew well this favorite weapon of her great god Vishnu in the form of a large flat ring with a sharp outer edge. Today the old Sikh warriors, guardians of Amritsar's temple, are said to hide in their turbans this object, probably archaic but which, if thrown by a strong and sure hand after having been swirled around the fingers, could at a certain distance cut off a head. The throwing of a lariat was also mentioned in passing.

Whenever it is a question of noting concrete realities long in disuse, their names alone would be of little assistance if the figured monuments did not help us to visualize them. For instance, the numerous representations of Māra's army put before our eyes the shape and the way of carrying the short, wide Indian sword, such as is described by Arian from the diaries of Alexander's companions. At the western door of the balustrade of the great stūpa at Sānchī a jinn stands guard with a heavy pike in hand. But where the ancient sculptures are most useful is in showing us in every detail the trappings of horses and elephants and the construction of chariots. Thus we learn that in India two thousands years ago horses were ridden without stirrups, with only a saddle cloth and a simple snaffle. The elephant's rider, holding the special hook, straddled the animal's neck with his legs tucked behind the large ears. That, as a fact, is the only comfortable place on the enormous beast, whose shoulders are too steep for comfort. The servant was perched as best he could behind the master, holding onto a rope that acted also as a girth. It was only with the invention of the fixed howdah, placed on top of the elephant's back, that the groom took over the master's place and instrument.

The lintels of Sānchī leave nothing to guess about the construction and the harnessing of the chariots used in that distant land and ancient epoch. The scenes represent the too generous gifts of Prince Viśvan-tāra, and we are shown side by side the horses and the chariot which, as a punishment for his having given the kingdom's wealth to a beggar, was taking him, his wife, and their two children into exile. First there is the equipage going forth with the entire family standing in a chariot, quite similar to a Roman one. The prince himself is holding the reins, but the horses are not held to the chariot by any traces. Their tails are carefully rolled up and brought forward, as their hindquarters practically touch the chariot and these improvised fly whisks could easily sweep the faces of the occupants. In the next scene, when the horses have been unharnessed, we can see that the shaft ends in a sort of yoke, to which they are tied by a halter. This means that the horses can pull only with their necks which explains why there are four to a cart.

The evidence of the sculptors, in complete accord with that of the writers, would indicate that fencing, running, and jumping were of no great moment, for they are never represented or described, while wrestling and archery are favorite subjects. Wrestling has remained so to our day, and the announcement of a wrestling match in Lahore, as we saw, brought out the entire population. The Gandhāra bas-reliefs show us the young Śākyas wrestling, wearing nothing more than shorts, as do the modern athletes, for no sport needs fewer accessories. Archery, on the other hand, is far more complicated. We are told at length how the field had to be paced, the distances set, targets put in place. These, we read and see, were usually drums or metal kettles or even palm tree trunks and images of boars. The classic pose of the archer who lunged forward on his left leg, contrary to the swordsman, had a special Sanskrit name. Let us not forget that Herodotus claimed that the Indian archers, contemporaries of the Buddha, showed up well in Xerxes' army. Mardonius is said to have kept a contingent of them which perished with him at Plataea (479 B.C.).

The Engagement

WHILE we were busy gathering specific information here and there, the young Siddhārtha grew up. He was now nearly sixteen and, in a country of early marriages which India has always been, it was high time to find him a wife. No doubt his father had thought about it but the *Lalitavistara* wished Śuddhodhana to wait upon the advice of his councilors, and this he did with much good will. Chapter XII opens with the customary interview between councilors and ruler, and it was agreed that the time had come to settle the prince with a household if he was to be retained in the world as Universal Monarch, an honor to the whole clan. Each in turn offered a daughter, but the king's response was as follows: "The prince is difficult: we must begin by asking him which girl he likes." [10]

Obedient to the royal command, the councilors went in a body to find the Bodhisattva and to advise him of what was being done. "You will have my answer in seven days," said the Bodhisattva. On the part

Victoria & Albert Museum. Crown copyright

3. The Bodhisattva Going to School.
Gandhāra school, 2nd–5th century A.D.

Eliot Elisofon

4. Ancient Indian Trappings of Horses and Elephants.
Sânchī Stūpa, 1st century A.D.

of one of such fine presence (one is a "young man" in India when with us one is a mere adolescent) a certain indifference is felt towards his approaching marriage. We must not forget, however, that this story was written by a monk and that he could only write it from his point of view. The essential feature of the Buddha's doctrine is complete condemnation of all desires, carnal and others, and at this point he is preparing himself for the pleasures of love in contradiction to all his future precepts. The biographer thus finds himself caught between the desire for grandiose exaggeration of both the voluptuous pleasures and the austerities that in turn wcrc in storc for the Predestined One, and he seeks comfort in the following oratorical warning:

> And this came to the Bodhisattva's mind: Well known to me are the evils without number caused by desires, sources of pain with their endless conflicts, animosities and sorrows, similar to a fatal cup of poison, similar to the flame and to the cutting edge of the sword;—as to me I am exempt of all passion and am not happy in the company of women;—why can I not live in silence in the forest, my soul appeased by the peace of meditation and ecstasy.

Much against its will, the Buddhist Order admitted that the Master was married, and wanted it to be also against his. This is an important point. All this involvement is to us the best proof of Siddhārtha's marriage, for had it been possible for the Buddhist monks to remove from the Master's biography this embarrassing concession to human weakness, it would have been done. Since in the conflict between ideals and tradition the latter proves to be the stronger, we are led to believe that it is based on genuine memories.

However, the delay of seven days came to an end and the prince remembered that the Bodhisattvas of the past had all been married and that their saintliness had been no more affected than is the purity of the lotus flowers by the mud of the pond. Resigned to this inevitable destiny, he wrote in his own hand and in verse a description of the ideal woman he would eventually consent to marry, albeit without enthusiasm. As was fitting, he made her moral qualities of primary importance. She must be of maternal or sisterly gentleness, charitable, sincere, without cunning or jealousy, without excessive taste for strong drink, parties, and public performances. She also had to be the perfect daughter-in-law and mistress of her slaves—the first in the house to rise and the last to retire and so forth. But he did not omit that she must be in the flower of youth and beauty and yet show no vanity for this. It was a great deal to ask for, but less than others had done before him. As soon as Śuddhodhana received this descriptive statement, he sent for the officiating priest attached to the family and, handing him the prince's request, said:

> Go, O great Brāhman, from one end of Kapilavastu to the other and, entering each house, scrutinize each young woman. The one who possesses these qualities, whether she be the daughter of a noble, a Brāhman, a merchant, or a peasant, make her known to me. "And what is the reason for this?" Because the Prince cares nothing for race or family; he cares only for qualities.

This Buddhist disdain for distinctions of class was held only within the Order, and our author forgot that on the preceding page of his account of the versified statement Siddhārtha had stipulated "a perfect purity of birth, of family and lineage."

However, the seeker did not have to go far in his quest, for he found in Gopā, daughter of the noble Śākya, Daṇḍapāṇi, the living embodiment of the prince's feminine ideal. That, at least, is what Gopā herself told him with a smile when she saw the written description—a proof that she could read. The Brāhman believed her on the spot and reported to the king that he had discovered a young woman answering in every way the requirements of his son.

Less credulous than his chaplain, Śuddhodhana was not certain that the perfect fiancée had been found, "for women are quick to attribute to themselves qualities which they do not possess." Consequently he devised another scheme by which he could ascertain in advance his son's consent. The same version appears in the *Mahāvastu,* but in that one the fiancée was called Yaśodharā, the daughter of the noble Śākya, Mahānāman. In spite of the Indian tradition that epic heroines chose their husbands from among crowds of pretenders, the Bodhisattva's biographers did not hesitate to reverse the roles. The king, having had handsome ornaments made, sent word, with drums resounding throughout his capital, that in seven days the royal prince would receive at court, and on this occasion would present jewels to the young girls of the Śākyas. Nothing more was needed to make them all appear. As each came before him, Siddhārtha handed her a jewel, but his heart yearned for none, and they, "incapable of sustaining the brilliance of the Bodhisattva," withdrew rapidly, taking their presents with them. At last Gopā arrived with her suite, and she alone was able to look at the prince without blinking. But by then the stock of jewels was exhausted.

> When Gopā came nearer the prince she said with a smile: "Prince, what have I done that you disdain me?" He answered, "It is not that I disdain you but that you came last." And, removing from his finger a most valuable ring, he handed it to her. She then said, "May I really accept this present from you, Prince?" To which he replied, "This jewel is mine, accept it." "No," said she, "Our aim is not to despoil the prince of his adornments, but rather to become an adornment to him." And having thus spoken she withdrew.

Well may we appreciate this gracious interplay, which comes as a charming oasis in an arid desert. The behavior of the young people did not escape the attention of the secret agents on the watch for the outcome of the reception. After hearing their report the king believed the affair settled; but, against all expectation, it bounced back. Only a short while before, every Śākya was offering his daughter to become the king's daughter-in-law; now, when Śuddhodhana sent his chaplain to Daṇḍapāṇi with the mission to seek Gopā's hand for the royal prince, he met with an insolent refusal. The excuse was the well-known incapacity on Siddhārtha's part for all athletic sports, and truthfully no one had ever seen him participate in any—at least in the course of the preceding chapters of the *Lalitavistara*.

The Athletic Competition

ŚUDDHODHANA was deeply mortified, as was to be expected, by Daṇḍapāṇi's humiliating refusal, but instead of imposing his will upon a subject, he bore the affront in silence. Apparently he was not a supreme ruler and within his clan his power was limited. The son was finally able to pry from the father the secret cause of his depression and, giving him an absolute guarantee of success, persuaded the king to challenge in his name all the young Śākyas of his age to a tournament. The city's drum and crier again went forth through the streets of the capital proclaiming that in seven days there would be an athletic competition at which the prince would demonstrate his talents. Five hundred well-trained young athletes responded, and Gopā, by common accord, was named the "Prize of Victory," to be awarded to the victor of three contests: fencing, archery, and wrestling.[11] This was an excellent chance for a grand program, and the population of Kapilavastu turned out *en masse* on the athletic field.

Let us keep to the description of the three sports specifically noted, or even to the last two, for fencing with swords, jumping, and running are hardly mentioned. Nothing is more boring than the account of the wrestling, for whether the thirty-two contestants assailed the Bodhisattva one by one or in a group, he stretched them out flat with a flip of the hand as if they were straw men.

The archery contest was the *pièce de résistance,* and the various competitors followed each other in an ascending series, reaching more and more distant targets. When the Bodhisattva's turn came, all the bows brought to him broke as twigs in his hand. He then turned to his father and asked him if there was not in the city a bow strong enough to withstand the power of his arm. His father answered that in fact there was: the one used by his grandfather, Simhahanu (Lion's Jaw), but added that since his death it had remained in a consecrated temple because no one had been capable of lifting it, much less of stringing it. The prince ordered his ancestor's bow to be brought forth, and it was mere child's play for him to use it and surpass all his rivals. Not only did his arrows pierce each target one after the other, even the most distant; they still had enough strength to bury themselves into the ground right up to the feather. The Śākyas acclaimed all these exploits on the spot, and even today Buddhists marvel at them.

The writers did not fail to use the athletic competition to introduce some of the personalities who were to be of importance later on in the Bodhisattva's life. First, there was Nanda, called the Handsome, his half-brother, whose forced conversion we shall read about later; then came his cousin Ánanda, who became in time his devoted disciple and remained at his side until the very end; and last of all came his cousin Devadatta, for whom the role of villain was reserved. The affection of the first two for the Bodhisattva needs no explanation, but that is not true of the jealous hatred of the third, which goes far back. Both were barely twelve years old, we are told, when one day Devadatta wounded the wing of one of the fine royal geese with an arrow. The bird fell at

Siddhārtha's feet. He picked it up to bind its wing to heal it, refusing to give it to his cruel cousin, who wanted to kill it.[12] Such was the cause of the latter's animosity—at least in this life, for it goes without saying that this hostility had been constantly reborn from one existence to the other and loses itself in the darkness of the past.

At the time of the tournament, Devadatta gave full proof of his antagonism. At the gate of the city, he came upon the large white elephant that was going to fetch the young prince to take him to the athletic field and he fell into a fit of rage as gratuitous as it was sudden. Catching the elephant's trunk in his left hand, he killed the beast with a blow of his right fist (for after the Bodhisattva, he was the strongest of their generation) and walked off, leaving the animal halfway through the city gate. Thereupon came the handsome Nanda who, finding the entrance blocked, pulled the enormous beast out of the way by his tail, a task that no one had been able to perform. Finally the Bodhisattva arrived in a chariot and learned of the wicked act of his cousin and the kind help of his half-brother. He blamed one and praised the other; then, reflecting that the odor from the rotting corpse would pervade the whole city, he put out one foot and, with his big toe under the tail of the elephant, tossed him over the seven ramparts and the seven moats surrounding the city. Of course this exploit only increased Deva-datta's antagonism, which was not decreased by the consideration that the Bodhisattva, always forgiving, showed him during the wrestling match, when three times he threw him down without hurting him.

Marriage

NOTHING and no one stood in the way of Siddhārtha's marriage, and we might be expected to rejoice at the thought of reading a description of princely nuptials held in India twenty centuries ago. This anticipation is shattered, as, evidently, a Buddhist monk could not bring himself to elaborate on such a profane subject. Fortunately, the two essential rites of the ceremony are known to us: the joining of hands and the triple circling of the fire by the bride and groom.[13] This last scene is represented on the bas-reliefs of Gandhāra but in the most restrained of settings. The same is true of the timid representations of the traditional procession led by musicians, with the groom on horseback followed by the wife on a litter as they are escorted to the husband's house.

When we are told that Śuddhodhana gave his son no less than three personal residences, it might seem like gross exaggeration until the Indian seasons are considered. There are three in number: the relatively cold one, the extremely hot one, and the rainy one (most important because of its food-giving character). Indian architects, not hampered by the cost of land or labor, have solved the difficulties imposed by these varied seasons by designing three different types of houses suitable for the cold, the hot, and the wet periods. Even a minor *rājā* could well afford such comforts for himself and his heir. Another such apparent extravagance was the possession of private parks, located on the outskirts of crowded, walled towns and dotted with lotus ponds, where rich merchants and their families went to refresh themselves in the shade of the trees and cool waters. Later we shall see how early converted wealthy bankers transformed these charming areas into hermitages for the Order of Buddhist monks.

To learn more of Siddhārtha's way of living we need only to turn to the texts. In one curious passage the Buddha felt called upon to explain to his disciples how completely his father had indulged him: "I was, O monks, a fine royal prince, the paragon of beautiful crown princes, and to the handsome prince that I was my father, the Śākya, gave [such and such gifts] for my enjoyment, my pleasure and my use." There followed a long enumeration of these presents, beginning with three palaces, for winter, summer, and the rainy season, and ending with four pleasure parks, each situated at one of the cardinal points of the city. With each the quoted sentence is repeated like the refrain of a ballad. The litany goes on to enumerate: precious couches, each covered with rugs and surmounted by a canopy of equal richness; ointments and perfumes; garlands of sweet-smelling flowers; garments of fine silk or wool cloth; foods as varied as they were refined; elephants, horses, chariots, barges, and litters for transportation; a parasol, practical as well as honorific; a well-outfitted corps of guards; and so forth, including the many things known to be part of the external princely existence. But what follows next makes it possible for us to penetrate more deeply into this princely life. To his handsome heir the king furnished five sensual gratifications: first, dancing, consisting, in the Indian manner, of a sequence of more or less stylized poses combined so as to represent certain legendary dramas; second, singing, probably already of the high-pitched tonality that delights Orientals; third, music solos, which made string or wind instruments such as flutes or harps "speak"; fourth, orchestral music with the sustained rhythm of drums that accompanied the dancing; fifth—for one must finally admit it—women.[14]

Such is the list, authentic and complete, of what might be called the five capital pleasures of that time. It gives us direct insight into the private life of the prince, regardless of the writer's puritanical notions. It is the life of the Arab's harem, the Persian's *anderoun* and also the Indian's *antahpura,* and at once we realize what the bas-reliefs confirm—namely, the importance of dance and music. Torn between the demands of their propaganda and their scrupulous consciences, the writers completely lost their common sense. The *Lalitavistara,* for instance, admits (Chapter XIII) that the Bodhisattva lived in the "private apartments" amid all the luxurious refinements and voluptuous pleasures in the company of eighty-four thousand women, all as beautiful as goddesses. On the other hand, it is maintained that even in this period the Bodhisattva never ceased to lead a life filled with devotion, for the chords of musical instruments only reached his ears transformed into highly moral stanzas, and this edifying flood of sound finally overcame the multitude of women and "many hundreds of thousands of divinities."

These obvious contradictions again indicate that we have to keep to the middle of the road in order to be just. Not being monks, we have no reason to contest the statement that Siddhārtha humanly enjoyed for a few years the pleasures of life made available to him by his fortune. However, the fact that he broke away proves clearly enough that he was not blinded, as so many Oriental princes are, by the perpetual search for new pleasures. In all fairness it must be noted that no one has ever thought of accusing him of having a thousand offspring, as became a Universal Monarch (or even seventy, as was the case of an emir of Afghanistan still reigning early in this century). He had but one son, and Gopā-Yaśodharā was the mother; so that it was as if she had not only been his "first queen" but also his sole legitimate spouse.

The other female inhabitants of the inner apartments, once their number is reduced to a reasonable figure, were mostly the numerous ballerinas and musicians whose duty was to entertain the prince, whose main amusement was to enjoy opera at home. Even in our time Indian *rājās* all had their ballet corps and a feminine orchestra, until British prudery became alarmed and the English governor insisted that they be replaced by a band of musicians in the European fashion. If modern ideas or questions of budget should bring about the disappearance of the dancers at the Cambodian court, those of us who have appreciated the charm of their pantomime will feel that art has lost more than morality has gained. In short, though we are unwilling to be shocked by the worldly life led by the Bodhisattva, we refuse to seek in it a subject for edification, and we firmly believe that we shall no less understand clearly, when the time comes, the intimate reasons for his religious vocation.

CHAPTER IV

CHILDHOOD AND YOUTH (II)

Religious Vocation

O UR task grows in difficulty as we reach the point where we must attempt to look into the soul of the Bodhisattva in order to trace with some degree of exactitude the psychological evolution that, starting with a usual heir apparent, brought him to the condition of an ascetic, and, from one ascetic among many others, to that of one of the saviors of humanity. Fortunately for us, Siddhārtha was not the first Indian to give up the pleasures and worries of the world, nor has he been the last, so that we are not restricted solely to Buddhist writings for our study. What is more, even great spirits in spite of their originality never quite free themselves from the ideas of their epoch. With all his compatriots at this time the Buddha had faith in the transmigration of souls. With them also he believed "that there was salvation only away from the home." The oldest texts, supposedly from his own lips, repeat this again and again: "The layman's life is a constraint; it is full of impurity. It is under the open sky that the religious life is led." Because he believed it he renounced the world.[1] This is the dominant idea that we must always keep in mind.

It would be important to learn whether in the course of his childhood and youth, any incident occurred to unveil or even stimulate the secret aspirations that were finally to win the day and force him to break the ties, however strong or tender, that bound him to his world. Pious generations have thought the same and have found no less than three of these preparatory episodes, namely the First Meditation, the Four Signs, and the Instigation to the Great Departure.

The First Meditation [2]

It was on the occasion of a country outing to the "plowmen's village" that the first sign foretelling the Bodhisattva's religious vocation manifested itself. All the texts agree on this, but one of them wished it to be at the "feast of sowing," in which the king and his court participated. The prince was a baby; nevertheless, his father had him brought along and settled in his cradle in the shade of a tree. Then Śuddhodhana with a golden plow and each of his one hundred and seven ministers with silver plows walked back and forth making furrow after furrow, thus setting an example to the peasants of the neighborhood, possibly a thousand plowmen. The nurses, unable to resist the attraction of such a fine show, left the infant alone.

Taking advantage of his solitude, he pulled himself up and sat cross-legged like a yogī and likewise controlled his breathing, and at once reached the first of the four degrees of meditation. Certain biographers, probably doubtful that so young a child could be capable of such a mental effort, delayed this event until the eve of the Great Departure. For once, the *Lalitavistara* professed a conservative opinion and placed the event between the scholarly manifestation and the sports competition. The desire for exaggeration, however, took its revenge by having the adolescent master not only the first but successively the four degrees of meditation. These range from the one which holds attention, reason, and intimate joy to the one where the soul, casting off all logical process, all sense of pleasure and pain or indifference, is only pure lucidity.

We must admit that even reduced to the first statement this psychic demonstration has a touch of the miraculous about it, although it is an inner miracle known only to the individual himself and unperceivable to those around him. Have we then any proof of the miracle? Two have been given, but one is only for those who fly in the sky. Due to the magic powers that we know the *rishis* were able to fly over the plains of the Ganges when traveling between their summer habitat near the Himālayan lakes and their winter retreats in the passes of the Vindhya Mountains. During one of these flights five of them, flying just above the spot where the young prince was meditating, were stopped by an invincible force. Looking below them and seeing the Bodhisattva shining brightly with mystic fervor, they wondered what powerful god they had encountered and were soon told by a passing deity. The five *ṛishis* at once came down near the young Śākya and each recited a prophetic stanza, greeting him in turn as the lake, the lamp, the ship, the liberator, and the doctor, who was to refresh, illuminate, traverse, liberate, and heal the world. Only then could they resume their course.

The other surprise in store for the common laymen was the fact that when the attendants returned to the infant (or when the ministers looked for the adolescent) they found him beneath his pink apple tree, the shade of which had remained piously immobile for the protection of the future Buddha. A miracle was at once noted, and for the second time Śuddhodhana worshiped his son.

These are the often-repeated features of the first manifestation of Siddhārtha's religious vocation, and yet little was made of them in the writings. What seemed more important in the scene was the brutal aspect of the plowing, which was destroying growing and living things, scarring the earth, tiring men and oxen which must have "upset the spirit" of the Bodhisattva. Aśvaghoṣa actually forgot to mention the immobility of the shade, and the *Lalitavistara* coldly called the chapter "The Plowmen's Village."³ In the past we have accused the figured monuments of being responsible for this emphasis, because the only way that sculptors could represent the psychological miracle of the First Meditation was to let real objects symbolize the event. The oxen and plough were the chosen symbols. The frequent use of this representation on monuments may have influenced the shift of interest, but it might possibly be explained by the contempt that Indian intellectuals had for agriculture. The first sight of such a fundamental human activity may have startled Siddhārtha's conscience and caused him to turn later to the contemplative life, and there his biographers have rightly seen the awakening of his religious vocation. Their brief indications contained the seed of the prolonged growth of popular ballads still in existence which take up point by point the absence of worry on the part of the ascetic as compared to the anxious life led by the landowner. There is no doubt that monks are as free "as the birds of the skies which neither sow nor reap."⁴ Fortunately, others do it for them!

The Four Signs

THE scenario of the second experience that was responsible for encouraging the Bodhisattva in his dislike of the world is composed of four scenes based upon one of the most often-repeated precepts of the Buddhist texts. What makes it necessary for Buddhas to appear on earth is the need for someone to cure the three great evils common to all humanity: old age, illness, and death. We readily admit that the sight of these painful miseries was the principal determining factor in the Predestined One's religious vocation. According to the earliest texts he himself told his disciples that it was his reflecting upon these three evils that had made it impossible for him to share man's inconceivable indifference to them. This reflection also stifled the joys of youth and of health and even the joy of living. It is perhaps difficult to understand why the Bodhisattva reacted so violently to the sight of these three miseries, because we know that most people become accustomed to seeing them from childhood on. His reaction can be understood only by learning that Śuddhodhana, always haunted by the fear that his son might enter the religious life, had succeeded in keeping such sights from him until his manhood. The stage is now set and, if the sequences follow in the right order, all will be well.

Siddhārtha, alone in his chariot with his groom, left Kapilavastu by the east gate to go to his pleasure park. Of course his father gave orders —as is still done for official visits—that nothing unpleasant be allowed to offend the prince's eyes. But the gods "of the Pure Sojourn," who from their sublime sphere were watching over the Predestined One's vocation, frustrated the precautions of the king and his ministers. As a result, Siddhārtha suddenly found himself facing a man white-haired with age, wrinkled, toothless, and bent over his stick. Before this sight, new to him, he turned to his groom to ask the cause of it and if the man's condition was particular to him or his family. Upon learning that this is the fate of all men and that he himself would not be spared, the prince gave up the outing to the park in search of the "five kinds of voluptuous pleasures" and, in spite of the groom's objections, turned back. The second time the same scene was enacted outside the south gate of the city before "a diseased man, dried up, overcome with fever, weak, with his body immersed in his own filth, helpless and protectorless, and breathing with difficulty." [5] The third time, leaving by the western gate, the prince encountered a funeral procession, such as one still sees today, with the corpse simply wrapped in a shroud and carried on a stretcher followed by his parents, crying and moaning, their hair disheveled, and beating their breasts. At once all life's pleasures lost their appeal for the young prince, and to complete the conversion the watchful gods needed to produce only one more episode. In the course of a fourth outing there appeared a begging monk, bowl in hand, serene, his eyes lowered, decently robed, and showing by his whole exterior the complete peace of his soul. This sight consoled the prince by indicating to him the way of life, and from then on he was ready for religion.

The early ignorance of the Bodhisattva once admitted, the development of this scenario does not lack for either dramatic gradations or philosophical meaning. Its weakness in the eyes of the old sculptors must have been its monotony, for the only figured representation we have found is on the façade of the first chamber at Ajantā. On the other hand, Javanese decorators welcomed these repetitive scenes as decorations for their long galleries at Borobodūr, as did the reciters of Buddhist legends and their audiences.

The popularity of the episodes spread beyond the Indian frontiers, for we find the painter of the frescoes of the Campo Santo in Pisa using the same idea in a scene showing cavaliers in the prime of their youth coming upon open coffins revealing the corpses they contained.

Consequently, we could grant the story of the Four Signs a complete success if the writer of the *Lalitavistara* had not spoilt it all by his desire to outdo everyone. In the fourteenth chapter, entitled "The Dreams," he began by describing the horrible nightmares that warned Śuddhodhana of the imminent catastrophe threatening the future of his dynasty. Thereupon the king decided to keep his son virtually a prisoner, as within a hothouse, amid the delights of his harem. This, however, did not mean that he did not permit the Four Outings and do so without conditions—only one more inconsistency. A far more serious one is that, forgetting the convention upon which rested the dramatic element of the experience, the scribe could not tolerate the idea that the Bodhisattva, omniscient from birth, should receive any information from a simple servant. So before each of the prince's questions, he slipped in two small words—"Although knowing"—without realizing the damage he had done to the pious drama.

The Instigation

Now we have the Predestined One aware of both the unavoidable calamities of secular life and the serenity of monastic existence. This did not mean that his decision had been taken but only that time was growing short if the world was to be saved. Śuddhodhana had already begun preparations for the crowning of his heir, and in seven days (the great god Brahmā had announced it) the "Seven Treasures" were to appear at the prince's palace—and, once Siddhārtha awakened as Universal Monarch, he would forfeit any chance of becoming the Buddha. Tired of waiting, for he was now nearly thirty, destiny would have chosen for him between the two possibilities. At this same moment, according to some, his son Rāhula came down from the Tuśita Heaven into his mother's womb; according to others, he had just been born. "It is a link which has come to me," said Siddhārtha when he heard of his first-born and only child, meaning that it was another tie added to those already holding him back. But truly this was not a valid claim and legend knew well what to do. Rāhula could not have chosen a better time at which to be born in spite of his father's pessimistic welcome. His coming is not one more bond but a liberation according to Indian ideas, for it was a custom that a man could not enter the religious life before having seen his son's or grandson's face. This was the only way to ensure the continuity of a family and of the funeral sacrifices to the ancestors' spirits and thus settle one's debt to them. The road to salvation was now open to others as well as to the Predestined One. The only thing needed for the final decision was a psychological shock or a word from above.

Tradition had those ready. The first is found in a Pāli text, the *Mahāvastu,* which linked it to the Fourth Outing. When the Bodhisattva cut short his country ride he had to come through the streets of Kapilavastu, and it was natural that the women of the city leaned out of their windows to watch him drive by. One of them, filled with admiration, sang the following stanza:

> Blessed indeed is the mother, blessed indeed the father,
> Blessed indeed is the wife, whose is a lord so glorious! [6]

The prince heard this admiring song but fastened only on the epithet used by the singer that brought to his mind supreme beatitude and absolute peace—in short, the idea of Nirvāna. Marvelous power of a word, which, as a crystal dropped in a saturated solution produces crystallization, gave form to all his aspirations still vague and scattered. At that moment he spontaneously discovered the goal towards which his life had turned. The various texts are in disagreement as to the singer's recompense. The Singhalese tradition had the prince send her a string of pearls from around his own neck, a gesture she took to be a sign of love; while the *Mahāvastu's* writer, fearing all women, did not even grant her a glance from Siddhārtha.

It should be noted that the above version in its fidelity to the spirit of the original Order is free of any divine intervention. However, the later *Sutras*—so-called "advanced"—having so often called upon hundreds of millions of gods to escort the Bodhisattva, could hardly refuse them a hearing in a circumstance so full of importance for humanity. Still the *Mahāvastu* spares them only a few lines, to the effect that the "Gods of the Pure Spheres" simply reminded the Bodhisattva that until then he had performed everything on time and that he must not fail them when a whole people, yearning for salvation, had its eyes fixed on him as peasants fix theirs on a cloud bringing them rain. The *Lalita-vistara,* as usual, mixed things up. In that version, "The Instigation" (Chapter XIII) is placed immediately after Siddārtha's marriage and is a long exhortation to put an end to a life of pleasure. In Chapter XV, when we come to the "Great Renunciation," the divinities had nothing more to do than make the news known among themselves and help Siddhārtha in his departure. The figured monuments are simpler in their representations and the Gandhāra bas-reliefs show that the two motifs—the Instigation and the Great Departure—are equally popular.

The Women's Sleep

It must be recognized that the episode of the women's sleep is seldom represented among the series of biographical bas-reliefs preserved from Gandhāra. It seems to have found more favor when taste turned from biographical to iconographical representation. It then gave the artist an easy excuse to group around the Buddha sitting on his throne numerous mythological figures and to even bring the donors into this flattering company. The representation of Siddhārtha's religious crisis seems originally to have been done in three sections. Marriage was followed by the life of pleasure in the harem. This caused distaste, and it brought about the Great Renunciation. Such a sequence was most logical and possible but seemed far too simple to the biographers, who felt the need for complicated amplification. On one point, however, both writers and sculptors are agreed: The final point that sealed the prince's decision to renounce the worldly life was the sight of his women asleep.

The *Lalitavistara's* author, though a mediocre novelist, was an austere moralist, and he could not admit that the Bodhisattva, who was the model of all virtues, should have deliberately disobeyed paternal will. Let us read his account:

> Now . . . the Bodhisattva thus reflected, "It would be unbecoming and ungrateful on my part if I should go away without informing the great king Śuddhodhana and obtaining the permission of my father." Accordingly, in the depth of the night, descending from the palace in which he was dwelling, he went and stood before the palace of the great king Śuddhodhana. As he stood, the whole of the palace became ablaze by the light of his person. The king was thereby awakened, and seeing the light, he called the warder and asked, "Warder, has the sun arisen from which comes this light?" The warder replied, "Lord, the first half of the night has scarcely transpired."

And the account continues with a popular poem:

> This light . . . lord of men, is pleasant and gratifying; it . . . produces no burning sensations; of walls and trees there is no shadow: it is doubtless due to [our] attaining this day some merit.[7]

The king quickly realized that the light emanated from his son's body. Standing before him, the Bodhisattva begged him not to oppose his departure, for the time to leave had come. But the king with tears in his eyes promised him everything if he only would not leave him or the royal family and the kingdom. And again in a soft voice the Bodhisattva took up his renewed pledge to remain if his father would guarantee that he would forever be exempt from old age, sickness, and death.

Naturally Śuddhodhana answered that it was beyond his power to do so; therefore the son begged him to cease opposition to his vocation. Finally the king was supposed to have given in, for one must not torment good souls. "And then the Bodhisattva went back to his palace

5. (Upper panel) The Four Encounters. (Lower panel) The Buddha Preaching
to the Nobles of Kapilavastu.
Sānchī Stūpa, 1st century A.D.

6. Life in the Palace: (Upper panel) Prince Siddhārtha Lying on his Bed.
(Lower panel) The Prince Sitting Up, the Women Asleep.
Karachi.

and sat on his couch and no one had seen him go and come." This mysterious interview could thus remain the secret of the author who invented it, for it changed nothing in the course of events. At any rate, Śuddhodhana took every precaution to prevent his son's flight and mobilized all Śākyas capable of bearing arms to guard the palace exits.

The artists' sculptures take us into the prince's bedroom with two successive representations. In the first one, the prince is lying on his bed, and seated at his feet is his first wife. As great a number of women as the panel will hold surrounds them. With the exception of the amazons leaning on their lances guarding the vestibule, they are dancers or musicians. The latter are playing the harp, flute, or tambourine while the former are exhibiting their graceful dancing poses, and each is outdoing the other in carrying out the king's recommendation to Queen Mahāprajāpatī to have them rouse the prince from his melancholy. But all they succeed in doing is to put him to sleep.

In the second scene the positions of the principal characters are reversed: Gopā-Yaśodharā is lying down and even asleep while Siddhārtha, who has just wakened, is now sitting on the bed. The dancers and musicians, having seen the prince asleep, have followed his example and have fallen asleep here and there at the very places they occupied when dancing and playing. Tall candelabra still light up the scene. We can easily understand why the prince, tired of his existence, which is constantly idle and given over to sensual pleasure, is overcome with nausea at the sight of this sea of human flesh still moist with sweat.

For the monastic authors, this is too good an occasion to resist the temptation of gratifying their hatred of their most feared enemy—women. All the rage inspired by the fear of a temptation that is too tempting and by the exacerbation of desire unsuccessfully suppressed, all the bitterness squeezed forth from the depth of devout souls, is spread over the innocent group in the most abusive language. The descriptions become revolting in their crudeness and of such language, in Sanskrit, that translation would transgress the limits of decency. The *Lalitavistara* ends its statement by putting into the mouth of the Bodhisattva thirty-two moralizing considerations, most unkind to the feminine sex. Since sleep is not without resemblance to death, the prince ends by feeling that he is in a place of cremation surrounded by corpses. He has only one thought: to flee from his harem. He calls forth his groom and orders his horse.

At that moment, according to the Commentaries of the *Jātaka,* the Bodhisattva stopped and thought: "I must see my son"; and rising from his couch, he went to the residence of Rāhula's mother and opened the door to her room. A light was burning in the chamber. Rāhula's mother was asleep on a bed covered with sweet-smelling flowers, her hand on her son's head. The Bodhisattva, with one foot in the doorway, stopped and watched. "If I lift the Queen's hand to take my son in my arms she will awaken and thus my departure will be hampered. When I shall become Buddha I will come back and see him." [8] And with these words he left the palace terrace. We learn at the same time why he did not see fit to say farewell to his wife. Since his decision was irrevocable, he found it preferable to avoid the scene of cries and tears that usually takes place on leavetaking.

The Great Departure

In the palace courtyard the groom Chandaka and the horse Kanthaka were already waiting for their master. We have met both before, for we saw them born. Anticipating the future, we knew that the prince would need them for this last ride, but neither horse nor groom showed any eagerness to perform the task for which they were born. The horse neighed hoping to arouse everyone, and to this the groom added his verbal protest. "Chandaka's Protests" take up only a few lines in the *Mahāvastu,* but in the *Lalitavistara* seven pages are given over to them as the Bodhisattva refuted them point by point.[9] Thus the extent of the Bodhisattva's great sacrifice was recalled: pleasure, well-being, riches, social condition, rights to the throne, caste, family, and so forth, as well as the contrast between the ease and delights of the life he was leaving and the privations, miseries, and constant difficulties which would be his lot as a beggar. How would he endure the life of a wanderer, spent in the dust of the highways without even a thatched roof to protect his head, after enjoying a soft and harmonious existence in palaces and gardens? It was not as if he were old and incapable of enjoying these pleasures—and we must remember that it was not as a decrepit old man, worn by age and illness, but as a youth, in the prime of health and strength, that the Bodhisattva "left home for the absence of a home" and swore that he would discover the remedy to ills the effects of which he had not yet felt.

Realizing that their Master's resolution was as unshakable as Mount Meru, both groom and horse decided to help him. But how? All the doors and gates were well guarded with at least 500 men each and the gates themselves so heavily reinforced that each needed 500 or 1000 men to push them open; furthermore, the grating of their hinges could be heard for miles around. Fortunately, gods and jinn were there to assist. The Four Guardians of the World had already established their positions, with their armies at the four cardinal points; meanwhile, the "Thirty-three," with Śakra, Indra of the gods, leading them, were hovering over the zenith. Their first task was to put all of Kapilavastu's inhabitants, without exception, into such a profound sleep that no sound whatsoever would awaken them. And to be even safer, the jinn (some say the Four Guardians themselves) held Kanthaka's hoofs in their hands to soften their pounding on the ground. There still remained the problem of the heavy gate of the city. "That is of no moment," thought the good steed. "With my Master on my back and Chandaka hanging on my tail, I shall jump over the city wall with one leap." Even that was unnecessary, for the door opened as by enchantment. In short, due to this supernatural assistance, all went well and the nocturnal flight was accomplished. Spontaneously all the manifestations worthy of Great Miracles took place, such as divine acclamations, showers of heavenly flowers, airborne drums, and six kinds of joyous earthquakes. And, in fact, it *was* the fifth genuine miracle, worthy at times of being substituted for the Nativity on carved stele, for it meant the beginning of a new life for the Predestined One.

To learn whether popular tradition associated other characters with this decisive scene, we can do no better than to turn to the figured monuments. Whether represented in profile or full face, the departure through the city gates always shows the prince, the groom, and the horse. The groom carries the royal parasol by its long handle although it is the dead of night. Among the entourage of gods and jinn constantly present in these representations, three particular figures can be noticed, one of them female. She turns out to be the goddess of Kapilavastu, known by her crenelated crown, thus representing the distressed city. The *Lalitavistara* had her harangue her son but to no avail and we shall not see her again. The two other figures, however, will remain closely linked to the Predestined One's activities until the end, though with diametrically opposed intentions. The first has a mute role: he is

Vajrapāṇi, "the Carrier of the Thunderbolt," whose birth we noted at the time of the prince's and who now became his bodyguard. The other divinity, of a much higher rank and sometimes seen carrying Love's bow, is no less than Māra, who has been called the Satan of Buddhism. Without success he tries to hold the Bodhisattva back by promising him the empire of the universe within seven days; having failed, he dogs his footsteps "like his shadow," on the watch for a momentary weakness. This we should keep in mind for future reference.

Chandaka's Return

NEITHER the material obstacles put in his way nor Māra's temptations nor the wails of his native city stopped the prince. Kanthaka galloped wildly through the remainder of the night with Chandaka hanging onto the horse's tail. Daybreak found them some say eighteen miles away, others say thirty-six miles, and still others say ninety miles, southwest of Kapilavastu and there they stopped. The prince judged the distance sufficient to separate him from the emissaries sent out in pursuit by his father, and he did not wish to exhaust his horse and groom. All at once a rush of events took place. The Bodhisattva first dismissed the numerous gods who had escorted him to this point for, as we shall see, he no longer needed their services. Then without hesitation he proceeded to adjust his external appearance to his new condition. He ripped off his princely adornments, cut his hair with his sword, and exchanged his silk garments for the tattered clothes of a huntsman. Each gesture was another step in the transformation from layman to monk. We must remember that "all this was seen by Chandaka," for it was important for someone to be able to testify before Śuddhodhana that the sacrifice had been completely consummated and that there was no hope of seeing the prince again until he had attained his goal. The farewells were brief, and Chandaka, burdened by the prince's jewels as well as the ever present parasol, spent no time in demonstrations, as revealed in the texts and on the bas-reliefs. As for the horse, who can tell us whether he illustrates verse 53, Book VI, of the *Buddhacarita* or whether, on the contrary, he inspired it? Kneeling on his forelegs, "he licked [his master's] feet with his tongue and dropped hot tears." [10]

In Kapilavastu the cry of alarm was given by the prince's women who, having searched in vain the three palaces for their lord, "screeched like ospreys." This tumult aroused Śuddhodhana, who in turn called together the Śākyas to learn what he might have guessed. With all gates closed, the city was searched for the missing prince; then the king sent his agents coursing on horseback in all directions with the order to return only with his son. Those who left by the same gate that the Bodhisattva used saw his tracks still outlined by the heavenly flowers showered upon him by the gods. In short order they met the huntsman with whom Siddhārtha had exchanged garments and they arrested him, fearing that he had murdered the prince in order to rob him. Fortunately, Chandaka arrived in time to exculpate him. The groom also convinced the pursuers that it was useless to continue their search, and since nothing more could be done, they all returned to the palace, where the greatest of confusion reigned. Of course the sight of the princely adornments weighing down the groom's arms increased the lamentations and tears, but since on this earth no one—not even the Bodhisattva—is indispensable to others, no human heart was broken. Only Kanthaka would not survive his master's departure. However, do not pity him too deeply for he was an old horse and he was to be reborn among the gods.

The *Mahāvastu* admitted that Siddhārtha gave his groom a message for his father, his stepmother, and the rest of the family "except his wife alone." The author of the *Lalitavistara*, less of a ferocious woman-hater, consented to have Chandaka console the heartbroken wife in particular by telling her that one day she would again see the one who had just left her. As for the adornments, no young Śākya was of a stature to wear them and the queen, feeling that as long as they met her eyes sorrow would not leave her, wisely threw them into a pond. The king then set his dynastic hopes on his grandson and thus were the sorrows of the world appeased. The dust of time little by little settles over the emptiness left by absent ones.

Epilogue

WITH Chandaka's return the first and the most important part of the Kapilavastu cycle comes to an end. Seven or eight years later it comes to light briefly when the Bodhisattva, having become a perfect Buddha, returned to his native city to convert his people. Thus, Kapilavastu, chronologically the first of the four great Buddhist pilgrimages, was the richest in scenes connected with the Predestined One's last existence. Hsuan Tsang, in the long chapter given over to it, enumerated no less than twenty sites. His guides showed the pious traveler the location of each of the episodes that were successively mentioned in the course of the first four chapters of this book, and they provided a running commentary summing up quite exactly the accepted tradition concerning the first twenty-nine years of Śākyamuni's life. Although the Chinese account is frequently nothing more than a restatement of the same texts we have been using, it must be said that they in turn, barring their diffuse amplifications, are but an echo of the oral accounts that were recited before each of the stations of the Kapilavastu pilgrimage as well as at the other holy places.*

* From a comparison of both the Chinese account and the *Lalitavistara*, Foucher draws the conclusion that the Chinese traveler and the author of the *Lalitavistara* used the same "guidebook for pilgrims" as the source of a great deal of their information. The Moslem conquest of India has long since destroyed any vestige of oral commentaries concerning the once-sacred sites or any original interpretations of the figured monuments. For knowledge concerning both, we are now indebted to what modern archaeology can contribute to the actual location and identification of the eight saintly places—from Kapilavastu, city of the last Birth, to Kuśinagara, city of the Ultimate Death.—Tr.

PART TWO

The Magadha and Benares Cycles:
The Second and Third Great Pilgrimages

CHAPTER V

THE SEARCH FOR
ENLIGHTENMENT

T HAT the Predestined One's religious vocation was brought about by
the events described in the preceding chapter no one would swear.
But that it removed him from the world is a historical fact needing no
explanation. Christian annals are full of such psychological transformations and escapes. In Europe as in Asia, numerous seekers of salvation
have believed in the efficaciousness of virtue or, better, in the primary
necessity of renunciation, poverty, and chastity. We think immediately
of Saint Francis of Assisi and see a close resemblance between the
Franciscan and the Buddhist orders. Ignatius Loyola, also a young
noble, sent back home groom, horse, and arms when he yielded to the
irrevocable pull of his religious vocation. Though the times and the religions were far apart the gestures and aims were the same. Marco Polo
saw it clearly when living at an epoch of strict faith, but, made tolerant
by his travels, he revealed to us that he found the life of "Sagamoni-
Borcam" highly edifying. We cannot resist the pleasure of quoting from
his book the account of the legendary pagan as told him by "idolaters":

> Ceylon, as I told you earlier in this book is a large island. Now
> it is a fact that in this island there is a very high mountain, so ringed
> by sheer cliffs that no one can climb it except by one way, of which
> I will tell you. For many iron chains have been hung on the side of
> the mountain, so arranged that by their means a man can climb to
> the top. It is said that on the top of this mountain is the monument
> of Adam, our first parent. The Saracens say that it is Adam's grave,
> but the idolaters call it the monument of Śākyamuni Burkhan. This
> Śākyamuni was the first man in whose name idols were made. Ac-
> cording to their traditions he was the best man who ever lived
> among them, and the first whom they revered as a saint and in

whose name they made idols. He was the son of a rich and powerful king. He was a man of such virtuous life that he would pay no
heed to earthly things and had no wish to be king. When his father
saw that he had no wish to be king or to care for any of the things
of this world, he was deeply grieved. He made him a very generous
offer: he promised to crown him king of the realm, so that he should
rule it at his own pleasure—for he himself was willing to resign the
crown and all his authority, so that his son should be sole ruler. His
son replied that he would have none of it. When his father saw that
he would not accept the kingship for anything in the world, his
grief was so bitter that he came near to dying. And no wonder, because he had no other son and no one else to whom he might leave
his kingdom. Then the king had recourse to the following scheme.
For he resolved to find means of inducing his son to give his mind to
earthly things and accept the crown and the kingdom. So he housed
him in a very luxurious palace and provided 30,000 maidens of the
utmost beauty and charm to minister to him. For no male was admitted, but only these maidens; maidens waited on him at bed and
board and kept him company all day long. They sang and danced
before him and did all they could to delight him as the king had
bidden them. But I assure you that all these maidens could not
tempt the king's son to any wantonness, but he lived more strictly
and more chastely than before. So he continued to lead a life of great
virtue according to their usage. He was such a delicately nurtured
youth that he had never been out of the palace and had never seen
a dead man nor one who was not in full bodily health. For the king
let no old or disabled man enter his presence. Now it happened
that this youth was out riding one day along the road when he saw
a dead man. He paused aghast, as one who had never seen the like,
and immediately asked those who were with him what this was.
They told him that it was a dead man. "How then?" cried the
king's son, "Do all men die?" "Yes, truly," said they. Then the
youth said nothing but rode on his way deep in thought. He had
not ridden far when he found a very old man who could not walk
and had not a tooth in his head but had lost them all through old
age. When the king's son saw this greybeard, he asked what was
this and why he could not walk. And his companions told him that
it was through old age that he had lost the power to walk and his
teeth. When the king's son had learnt the truth about the dead man
and the old one, he returned to his palace and resolved that he
would stay no longer in this evil world but would set out in search

of him who never dies and who had created him. So he left the palace and his father and took his way into the high and desolate mountains; and there he spent the rest of his days most virtuously and chastely and in great austerity. For assuredly, had he been a Christian, he would have been a great saint with our Lord Jesus Christ.[1]

One could not say more, and, as a matter of fact, the great traveler was not aware of the truth of his statement. The Bodhisattva did become a saint of the Christian church two and a half centuries later under the name of Josaphat. On the authority of the Syrian John of Damascus, Pope Sixtus V inscribed his name in the Calendar of Saints on November 27.[2]

Transformation from Layman into Monk

IN such a spirit of broad understanding we continue the study of the Buddha's life. Our feeling of closeness towards him is particularly striking if we stop to realize that twenty-five centuries and a quarter of the earth's circumference separate him from us. However, the traits upon which we must insist as they appear in this universally human canvas are those which restore to him his particularly Indian character. To begin with, we must recognize that the Bodhisattva's flight represented an act of genuine courage and great moral strength, for civic obliteration awaited him at the end of his last gallop. We must try to understand the contradictions that are Indian and exemplified by the following. The sale of aphrodisiacs in India is greater than anywhere else; yet nowhere is there such veneration for chastity. All around there is talk of rupees and still in no other land is voluntary poverty more deeply respected. This great peninsula actually feeds freely at least six million wandering ascetics and beggars. These are referred to as "men of virtue" and yet their status is most ambiguous. They are shown profound deference, and merit is acquired by feeding them. One must ask their advice—much to the envy of the Brāhmans—and yet they have lost their caste and are not allowed to remain inside cities or villages. The texts reveal kings bowing before them and ferrymen refusing to take them on their ferries. They are invited to dine and it is a privilege to serve them because they are saintly, but it would not occur to their hosts to share their meal, for saintliness does not prevent these men from being impure. In modern terms one could not define them better than to say they are honored pariahs. It is, then, this mixture of regard and constant poverty for which the Bodhisattva gave up his luxurious and unique social status. He would no longer be an heir apparent, a prince, a noble, a head of a family, or a member of Indian society; nor would he be called Siddhārtha, for he had no civic status. Since he still had to have a name, he borrowed one from the Brāhman who, as the family's spiritual adviser, had previously guided him. Until he became the Buddha he was known only as "Gautama the Ascetic."

Such a total change in personality had to be accompanied by an equally radical transformation in physical appearance. As we have seen, the Bodhisattva so completely believed this that as soon as he was off his horse he performed three major operations to ensure this necessary change: he removed his adornments, he cut his hair, and he changed his clothes. None of these gestures need surprise us, for in our land the same sort of thing happens under similar circumstances. Again the Bodhisattva behaved in a way well known to us, and it is from the Indian point of view that his three gestures need some explanation.

The commentary on the first can be brief. In "divorcing himself from his adornments," which was in keeping with his new condition, Siddhārtha teaches us nothing new concerning the Indian taste for jewelry, which in other lands is left to the women. We knew this from Greek sources, and a glance at the Sānchī or the Gandhāra figures will confirm it. The head ornaments included not only those of the turban but also enormous earrings, which when removed left the lobes of the ears pierced and distended because of their weight. When the Indo-Greek artists represented the Buddha, they retained this particular trait, and later the Tibetans and Chinese, without understanding the reason for this deformity, saw in those unusually long ears a sign of wisdom. Necklaces, some rigid and others flexible, covered the torso, and the fingers and arms were encircled by rings and bracelets. Though decorative anklets were left to the women, sandals were highly ornamented, especially in the northwest, where the climate made wearing them necessary. The Gandhāra pedestals of broken statues reveal at once whether the figure was that of a Bodhisattva or the Buddha, depending on whether the remaining feet were in sandals or bare. Those were the adornments that Siddhārtha placed in the arms of his horseman to be returned to his home, and faithful to their tradition the Indo-Greek sculptors did not fail to include the turban, which their Central Indian colleagues show us as taken to Heaven. All these details are of antiquarian interest but the point most interesting to the social historian is that the prince evidently did not consider jewels as his personal property— any more than Loyola his armor—but as family possessions owned by the royal clan of Śākyas. The idea of distributing them as alms did not even occur to him.

Nor were we unaware that the ancient caste Indians wore their hair long. A remnant of this custom survives in the topknot that the orthodox Hindus still keep on their heads. In the Ganges region they used to wrap their hair in the numerous folds of a long band of cloth, which they then wound around their heads as a protection against the sun. Thus, when the Bodhisattva cut off his hair with his sword, he also severed the turban of white lawn, so that when he let it go it was "as the flight of a swan over a pond." Of course the gods immediately seized this precious relic, for—the legend holds—since it is nowhere on earth it means that it was taken to Heaven.

The bas-relief from Bhārhut, which is inscribed as such, shows us the "feast of the hair" being celebrated by the Thirty-three in honor of the Bodhisattva's shorn locks, and there the entire headdress is shown inside the sanctuary. Later worshipers were not satisfied to have the Master's hair cut so unceremoniously and with such an inappropriate instrument. The Order, wishing that their founder had at once assumed the true appearance of the future members of his Order, arranged for a god disguised as a barber to appear in the jungle at the right moment and shave the Bodhisattva's head in proper monklike fashion.[3]

At this point it is necessary to consider an archaeological question. The insistence and agreement in the texts concerning the hair-cutting make it more than surprising that the Indo-Greek artists should have refused to cooperate. For once they are in complete rebellion against tradition. On the bas-reliefs they represent the removal of the adornments and the exchange of garments but never the cutting of the hair. The statues of the Buddha do not have the princely headdress, but the head is not shaved.

Two reasons can be given for this break with tradition: one aesthetic—it would be ugly—and the other iconographic. How could the

Buddha be distinguished from his monks if he looked just like them? To better understand the sculptors' hard-headedness it must be known as we do, thanks to them, that in Northern India the turban was a ready-made headdress, usually of three folds of cloth draped around a conelike cap and affixed to it by jeweled ornaments. What is of particular interest here is that the turban was completely independent of the hair. When the Bodhisattva is shown to us bareheaded in his bedroom, his long hair is piled on top of his head. It was over this kind of knot that the turban was set, as a hat is put on. When Chandaka is shown bringing up his master's horse, in the figured representation of "The Sleeping Women," he also carries the ready-made headdress.

As to the treatment of the hair, it naturally conformed to the Greek technique and was waved. It was thus carried over from the Bodhisattva to the perfect Buddha. Fortunately, the famous list of the thirty-two traits of the great man was presented in time to settle by compromise the dispute between tradition and aesthetics. It may be recalled that one of the attributes of the wonder child was hair tightly curled to the right. In time that description became the accepted iconographic one for the adult Buddha, and his image was allowed, even by zealots, to retain the hair—as long as it all curled to the right. At this time sculptors, who were not less careless than docile, mechanically modeled curls on top of the usual knot of the idols representing the Master and thus created the apparently bony lump on top of the skull. For lack of a better name this bump was called *ushnisha,* which the North Asian Buddhists finally explained as "the bump of wisdom." What a thorny thing is a marriage between orthodoxy and art!

The last question to settle is that of costume. We could settle it more rapidly if Siddhārtha had decided to follow the example of those naked ascetics (or, as was said, ascetics "clothed with the surrounding air") who roamed through the countryside as well as the cities of India. The French traveler Bernier came upon them in the seventeenth century and noted that no one's prudery seemed offended. But it was not part of the Predestined One's character to be extreme in anything, including the vow of poverty, and he wished to have his followers decently dressed, even though the habit was supposed to be made of bits and pieces. The huntsman's rough garment for which Siddhārtha exchanged his silk clothing had nothing in common with the monk's habit except its reddish-brown color, which came from the cheap Kasāya dye prescribed for all outcasts. This color is still used by the monks of Northern Asia, while the Singhalese and Cambodians have adopted a beautiful yellow.

The monastic habit consisted of three separate pieces: an undergarment, over which the monk wore a kind of long tunic that hung to his knees and exposed the right shoulder, and, when he was on his begging journey, a cloak that completely covered him. This cloak was so ample that the Gandhāra sculptors often draped it in the Greek fashion. But the fine cotton of Central India could not rival the soft woolens of the north in drapery and in the religious images of India we find the folds becoming thinner and thinner until the *sanghāti* is plastered against the body.

The transformation of the prince into a monk was abrupt, and we can even say that it anticipated the actual events, for the Bodhisattva took on the aspect of the Buddha before becoming one. There would, therefore, be only two typical representations of the Predestined One in Buddhist art—the one as a young layman and the other as the Buddha—if the Indo-Greek artists had not created a third to depict the terrible austerities he temporarily inflicted upon himself. It is to this third image, which comes between that of the Bodhisattva Siddhārtha and the one of the Buddha, that the designation "Gautama the Ascetic" is most applicable.

To finish with these brief iconographic indications, shall we ask the question that the faithful thought of asking too late? There exists in the world innumerable images, painted or carved, of the Buddha as well as of Christ, but have we a *portrait* of either of them? The answer is completely negative. Surely in Asia as in Europe, miraculous or apocryphal images did not fail to appear in quantity, with the likeness guaranteed, but it is too evident that they were mere inventions and that the justifying captions were thought up later. Of the true face of Śākyamuni we can only repeat what Saint Augustine said of the face of Christ: "Our ignorance of it is profound." [4]

Our disappointed curiosity can only accept the lesson that the Master would himself have inflicted upon it. When his great friend, King Bimbisāra, ordered artists to paint a portrait of the Blessed One, they gave up trying to paint a likeness which so overwhelmed them. The Buddha then had a canvas brought forth, upon which he cast his own shadow, and after having had this silhouette colored, he ordered the principal articles of his doctrine to be inscribed below it. That was all posterity need know of him.[5]

The Dismissal of the Gods

PRINCE SIDDHĀRTHA was no more; he had been replaced by Gautama the Ascetic. And as such he found himself in an indifferent world, without guidance or support, confronted with both the noble task of seeking mankind's salvation and the lowly but pressing one of securing his daily food—for before philosophy comes living. Nowhere has it been written that his courage failed him, but it has been stipulated that he no longer counted upon help from above. We saw that he dismissed the many gods and jinn of every sort who were supposed to have helped him greatly and whose numerous troop felt it necessary to escort him on his departure. In truth, however, we shall not bid good-by to those millions of adoring divinities, who played such an active role in all the scenes of Siddhārtha's childhood and youth. Although they will make fewer appearances, they will still people the skies and from there send showers of flowers or sing hymns of praise. Probably Brahmā and Indra wished to serve the ascetic as they had the prince; but he never again accepted their kind offers, though he may sometimes have fulfilled their requests. As for Māra, whose rank placed him between the two great gods just named, he now entered into open struggle with the Bodhisattva. In short, during the quest for Enlightenment and after attaining it, Gautama the Ascetic systematically did without any supernataural help.

This point is important and worthy of emphasis. Nothing conforms more completely to the ancient Buddhist ideas than this putting aside of the gods. The original Order, without denying the existence of the traditional divinities, was convinced of their utter uselessness, as were the early Epicureans. For both, the salvation of mankind was entirely the task of man. We can be certain that the constant celestial interventions witnessed until now were neither liked nor invented by members of the Order. However, the faithful masses understood things differently. That the Predestined One should have attained his lofty goals solely through his own intelligence and without divine help was taken on faith by the scholars, especially since this made him greater in their eyes. On the other hand, that the gods should not have been interested

7. The Great Departure.

(Above) Sānchī Stūpa. 1st century A.D.

(Below) Amārāvatī, ca. 2nd century A.D.

8. From Prince to Monk.

(Above) Figure Showing Monk's Robes. Amāravatī, ca. 2nd century A.D.

(Left) Standing Figure of the Bodhisattva. Gandhāra school; from Foucher Mission to Shabaz Varhi.

9. (From Prince to Monk, continued)

(Left) Inscribed Image of the Buddha. Mathurā, ca. 5th century A.D.

(Below) Representation of the Buddha, Showing Early Indian Manner of Treating Hair. Gandhāra school, 2nd–4th century A.D.

10. Head of the Buddha.
Sārnāth, ca. 5th–6th century A.D.

and involved in all the phases of his life, including the Great Renunciation, was unthinkable, and the people made this clear. It was as a consequence of these popular beliefs that the biographical texts became so heavily laden with mythology, which could never be quite given up. While the Community was willing to give in to the fantasy of its zealots concerning the youth of the prince, it refused to do likewise for the biography of the Master. The sayings and doings of the Ascetic were of too great importance for the Order to let them go out of its hands, and from then on the theologians guided the pens.

Orientation of the Buddha and Buddhism

GAUTAMA the Ascetic was now on his way, barefooted in the dust of the dry season. Tradition has set the Great Renunciation, this second birth, on the same date as his Nativity. Thus, it was spring. The birds were singing and the trees were in bloom, but no song, no perfume, nor any spectacle evoking the past could have caused the Disenchanted One to turn back. The only question that confronted him, as it does us, was: "In what direction shall I turn my footsteps?" Without hesitation he continued on his way due southeast, as if he were letting the rivers from the Himālayas to the Ganges carry him along to the Indian Ocean. He had no thought that some fifty years later, heavy with glory and the weight of years, he would travel the same road in the opposite direction, only to die on the way in the small town of Kuśinagara.

It is thought that the names of the first two Brāhman women who invited him to their hermitage are known. There they gave him food and shelter. Thus from place to place he went until he reached the free, flourishing city of Vaiśālī, today known as Basārh in the Tirhut, where he remained for some time. As soon as he crossed the river he found himself in the beautiful land of Magadha, which was to become his chosen country and therefore one of the Holy Lands of the ancient world. It is now the province of Bihār, which name was given it by the Moslem invaders because of the large number of Buddhist sanctuaries which they found to destroy. Finally, after a brief sojourn in the neighborhood of Rājagṛha, the capital of Magadha, he made his way further south to the town of Gayā, which has remained sacred. It was near there that the intrepid seeker was able to overcome destiny and learn its secret.

On all these points there is agreement, and the Order apparently managed to retain a fairly exact memory of the Master's itinerary so that we are able to follow it on the map from Kapilavastu, the point of the Great Departure, to Bodh Gayā, the place of the attainment of complete Enlightenment. The most important factor, in our eyes, was the initial direction chosen. At that moment the die was cast. The Master's personal future, as well as that of half of Asia, and the nature of his thought, as well as the character of his religion, were really determined by that initial choice.

Although it is vain to speculate upon what might have been, imagine what might have happened if the Bodhisattva had taken the opposite direction and trudged toward the northwest, which direction would have brought him into "the land of the Brāhman wisemen." Had these men communicated their wisdom to him, he probably, because of his intelligence, would have become a brilliant champion of the Upanishads. But, although these mystical texts remain the source for all renovators of Brāhmanism, they never were and never could become the gospel of a new religion, and India would have known neither the Buddha nor Buddhism.

While in the mood for purely imaginary assumptions, let us use to the full the liberty allowed us by this confession and suppose that Gautama's wandering spirit had led him farther north. There is little chance, from what we know of the Master, that he would have become a member of the Śivaite sect of the Pāśupata, those half-naked ascetics who, covered with ashes and wearing great topknots as well as flowing beards, dominated the region at that time. However, a strange adventure would very likely have been in store for him. If the Buddha actually died around 477 B.C., at the beginning of the reign of Xerxes-Ahasuerus, he was alive at the time of the conquests of India by Cyrus the Great and Darius I. According to cuneiform inscriptions, these conquests extended over the whole Indus basin. Both the armies and the Achaemenid administration introduced in "White India," as it was called, not only the Aramaic alphabet but also the cult of the great Ahura Mazda as well as the Zervanite and the Zoroastrian doctrines. How the Bodhisattva would have reacted to Iranian dualism and the religious concepts of Zarathustra we cannot guess. All we wish to indicate is that by heading northwest he would have been caught and possibly destroyed by rigidly set forms of civilization far different from the social and ideological climate in which he was to move with such ease and lasting success.

When the Bodhisattva crossed the Sadānīra River to reach Vaiśālī he definitely turned his back on the land of meat and wheat eaters and drinkers of alcoholic beverages. Without doubt he knew them too well as a violent people, keen on satisfying their lust for pleasure and power, jealous and proud of the purity of their race, and ready to bow to the hierarchy of castes. They practiced bloody sacrifices which were an occasion for both revelry and an exchange of promised kindnesses between themselves and their gods, for their spirit was of the body and they were most unsure of the hereafter. Because of their faith in the divine origins of the Vedas, they submitted to the prescriptions, rites, and doctrines of their magician-priests and firmly believed in the supreme reality of the essence, the self, and consequently of their own ego. They also were deeply attached to the ancestral optimism brought from the highlands, and they were as well born believers in a pantheism based on an ecstatic use of principles of permanence and identity.

On the contrary, Siddhārtha's heart and soul responded to the vegetarian populations of the rice fields, drinkers of water, favorable to abstinence, mercy, and peace; of mixed races but untroubled by this fact; somewhat effeminate because of their cereals poor in vitamins and their debilitating climate. These people were horrified by the sight of any victim's blood and offered to their local jinn only innocent fruits and flowers. They remained perfectly incredulous of the pretended divine authority of a Veda of which they knew nothing; but, on the other hand, they all believed in the "transmigration of souls" (a concept that, as the old Upanishads bear witness, was still in the northwest only the esoteric belief of a few theosophists).[6] At the same time, finding both their psychic personality and the physical self perpetually disintegrating they were quite unsure of what was transmigrating. They were without illusion about the cruelty of destiny but also were without revolt. In the realm of metaphysics, they knew only pure doubt, having witnessed for generations on end the external world disappear as a mirage in the pale incandescence of a sun on fire.

It would be difficult to conceive of two more different worlds than existed on the two sides of the Sadānīra River. The choice between the two had already been made, and it was to the east that the Bodhisattva was to turn for the elements that would make up his system—half-

philosophical and half-religious—for no matter how great or how original a man is, he always starts by belonging to his milieu and his time.

We thus reach the conclusion that it was first of all the East Indian
voice, free from Aryan overtones, which is to be heard by the future
Buddha. He later transmitted it to us, distinctly phrased and transposed
into a way of salvation. In order not to mislead the unprepared reader,
we should warn him that, until recently, this was not the accepted
theory concerning the origins of Buddhism. The orthodox view was
that it came forth as a whole from Brāhmanism of the northwest,
slightly modified by tendencies which sporadically appear in the Upanishads. It could not be otherwise, for the early European scholars were
the docile students of the Calcutta Brāhmans. To them and their successors it appeared that all the societies and religions of India, however
diverse, emerged from the one and only Veda, just as an oak with all
its branches emerges from one acorn.

The excavations of the archaeologists at Mohenjo Daro have overthrown these seductive theories by revealing that the Indus Valley had a
well-developed urban civilization long before the invasion of the Indo-
European barbarians.[7] In all probability the same was true of the richer
and more heavily populated basin of the Ganges, though the climatic
and geological conditions there are such that there is little hope of finding any traces of this. It is now impossible to reject the primordial fact
that the great peninsula as created by successive invasions was originally
made up of several very different Indias. It was too easily forgotten that
the inhabitants themselves counted five of them long before the Moslem
conquest occurred and further complicated the situation.

King Bimbisāra's Visit

THE search for Enlightenment has a traditional itinerary, and tradition
has also fixed its time. The seven years that it took are divided into two
unequal periods: one of study, the other of mortifications, which, we
are told, were as useless as they were severe. The first period lasted only
one year and was divided between two areas, while the second had
neither interruptions nor change of scene for six years. We must recognize some historical truth in this except for the respective duration of
each.

Legend includes two episodes before the Bodhisattva becomes an ascetic, and in these we need put little historical faith. The first is hardly worth mentioning, since it only serves as an advanced compensation to the humiliating admission that the Buddha started by being the disciple of Brāhman teachers. The Brāhman Bhārgana having invited the Bodhisattva to share his hermitage, the latter refused and delivered himself of a denunciation of the life of hermits.

The next episode is the coming upon the scene of Bimbisāra, and that is more defensible. True, the oldest and most creditable tradition placed the meeting of the Predestined One and the king of Magadha after the Enlightenment. But in view of the fact that Gautama had been in Rājagṛha before this, how could it be admitted that his presence was not noticed by the population, the royal police, and the monarch himself? Moreover, the second meeting was more likely if it had a precedent, so our usual sources all agreed that Bimbisāra took the initiative and called on the unknown ascetic. We have a particular reason not to show ourselves more recalcitrant than our sources.

This visit came between the Bodhisattva's period of study with Arāda Kālāpa in Vaiśāli and the one undertaken with Rudrāka in Rājagṛha. Having come to the capital of Magadha in the course of his wanderings, Gautama settled himself for the night on the slope of one of the hills near the city. When morning came, he left his hard bed and taking his alms bowl went into the city, entering through the Gate of the Hot Waters. The nearby springs are still hot. Of course his beauty, the majesty of his walk, and his composure amazed the people, who took him for a god who had come down to earth. Soon the city was enthralled: a crowd followed him through the streets, women were at all the windows, and all business transactions stopped. The king, having been notified, watched and admired the charming monk (some say "from the towers of his palace," others "through a round window"). He had him followed when, the round of begging finished, the beautiful ascetic turned back to his rustic retreat. Then and there the king decided to go in person and pay him a visit. At dawn the next day he started out, traveling in a chariot as long as there was a road, and then continuing on foot over the stony hillside. When he reached the ascetic the king showed his profound respect by bowing to the ground and, under the spell of the noble aspect, at once offered him half his throne. Of course the Bodhisattva refused that which was even less than he had voluntarily given up. However, the king did not leave before extracting the promise—which was kept—that the monk would tell him the secret of salvation as soon as he had discovered it. Such was the origin of the long friendship that was to last until the monarch's tragic death.

What impression does this anecdote make upon us? First of all, it is a vivid illustration of what has already been said about the mixture of grandeur and poverty which was a part of the begging monk's life. Also, it is impossible not to be touched by the simplicity of the customs and not to admire the sovereign's sincere respect, shown by his bowing the royal turban before the monk seated peacefully on the grass. And are we not somewhat moved by this budding friendship, though we do not understand it?

What the scholars wished us to see here was that the king was tempting the ascetic by his enticing offers and trying to deter him from following the way to Enlightenment. Thus, even if he was not really one of Māra's aids, he at least assumed that role. The spontaneous, cordial offer therefore becomes a satanic ruse, and Gautama's refusal to be seduced the occasion for a long sermon by the theologians on the vanity of worldly pleasures. And so a charming encounter is destroyed by the moralizing mania of the scholars, which was certainly not shared by popular imagination when this tale was invented.

Period of Study

ANOTHER fault of our biographers was their incapacity to imagine the future Buddha in any way but as invested with shining glory. We can easily believe in the personal charm of the Bodhisattva, but it is quite likely that, as one among many other monks, he was not noticeable, and that kings waited until the voice of the people had consecrated his fame to venerate him. As a matter of fact, he himself realized his lack of preparation for the spiritual conquest he had set upon, and he felt the need to follow the teachings of those who had preceded him in the religious vocation. This fits in with our conception of his character, but we are surprised to find that legend has accepted this year of study, which probably proves its authenticity. Our authors have tried to reduce to a minimum the Bodhisattva's period of study as well as the need of it. If we are to believe them, he guessed all the answers before they were given him, and was quick to make his teachers feel their incapacity to teach him. He soon decided to leave Arāda Kālāpa, even though the latter offered to share with him the direction of the community of scholars. Thus our authors, blinded by fanaticism, failed to see that, according to Indian ethics, they were portraying the most unfaithful and insolent of pupils. The *Lalitavistara* even attempted to put this unworthy version in the mouth of the Buddha, but sometimes forgot to change the verbs from the third to the first person.[9]

Having left Arāda's community in Vaiśālī, the Bodhisattva came to Rajāgrha where, as we have seen, he at once met King Bimbisāra. The account goes on to say:

> At this time Rudrāka, son of Rāma, had settled in the outskirts of Rājagrha with a great crowd of disciples—seven hundred disciples; and he taught the attainment [of a psychic state] where there is no longer consciousness nor unconsciousness.[10]

The story goes on much as the above, attributing the same kindliness to the master and the same presumption to the so-called disciple. This time we are even told that the Bodhisattva only became Rudrāka's pupil in order to reveal the faults of his teacher's doctrine both to himself and to others. Because we feel that the foolish biographers, not the Bodhisattva, were responsible for these unfortunate statements, we need not spend more time on these particular readings.

The teaching of Arāda to his numerous disciples was summed up in the *Lalitavistara* as the "insubstantiality of all things" and would lead us to believe that it was an ancient and aberrant form of Sāṅkhya and that in the case of the Bodhisattva it did not fall on deaf ears.[11] We have formal confirmation of this from Aśvaghoṣa.

Let us go on to Rudrāka's teachings. The Bhagavad Gītā, that breviary of the noble warrior, constantly associates Sāṅkhya and Yoga. The latter is considered to be the practical side of the speculations of the former. And its final aim, through its well-known practices of special postures, breathing exercises, intellectual operations, and mortifications, is to enable the practitioner to become completely master of himself, thus making him able to control all his bodily functions, mental as well as corporeal, and even to separate his spirit from his body. Purified and systematized by generations of thinkers, Yoga is found at the birth of all Indian sects and, as Emile Senart has strongly brought out, it had considerable influence upon nascent Buddhism.[12] The Order not only attributed to its Master and saints the magic powers we have just listed, but it also borrowed from Yoga its main spiritual exercise, namely a concentration of mind reached by a meditation more and more ecstatic in character, with all the details and technical forms pertaining to its successive stages. It was exactly on such a practice that Rudrāka's teachings were based, so that ultimately the Buddhist tradition accused the Bodhisattva's second master of having been a mediocre and fallible yogī.

True, there was at the very beginning of Buddhism a flagrant disagreement with Yoga, but only after the Master had submitted with docility to the tyranny of ascetic practices. Of course legend would have the Bodhisattva follow the course of austerity with no illusions but only to better prove to the world its futility. No matter, but it still remains that after leaving Rudrāka and taking with him five of his disciples, we find him behaving like all yogīs of his time and ours; and it is difficult not to believe that he was simply following the example of his last teacher. At the same time we learn that the period of austerities should not be considered as a break in his studies but simply a natural continuation, as a practical assignment is the obvious complement of theoretical instruction.

The Practice of Mortification (Dushkara Caryā)

OUR biographers' ideas are by now so familiar to us that we know their plan. The first axiom is that the Bodhisattva is omniscient; consequently, he must, against all appearances, know beforehand that the austerities he is about to undertake are vain. Otherwise, he would be acting as a simple heretic, which no real believer can admit. The second axiom is that the Bodhisattva is superior to all creatures in every way. So now, even when knowingly engaged on a false path, he must carry out his vagaries further than any have done before or could do after him. Strengthened by his experience of austerity as well as of sensuality, he would thus be able to condemn the excesses of asceticism and its opposite and lay down the "middle way," which will be recommended to the world in the Good Law.

So now we find the Bodhisattva again on his way south with five companions, traveling towards the city of Gayā, which has remained sacred. The small group traveled on foot across a beautiful valley, from which here and there rose rocky hills, usually crowned by temples to

11. The Cult of the Turban.
Bhārhut, 1st century B.C.

12. Austerities: The Fasting Bodhisattva. Lahore, 2nd–3rd century A.D.

which pilgrims climbed through trails and steps. Several have become well known because of the sermons that the Buddha later delivered there.

After many stops they reached the village of Urubilvā, and there the Bodhisattva

> ... saw the river Nairānjanā with its pure water, its descending steps, the lovely wooded shores, the shepherd's hamlets which border it. There the Bodhisattva's spirit was truly charmed. Certainly this was a welcome corner of the earth, lovely, favorable to meditation, and perfectly suitable for the retreat of a young gentleman. And this is just my desire so I must settle here.

He did just that, and this bit of countryside, which holds the spot where the Bodhisattva reached Enlightenment became, along with Benares, Jerusalem, and Mecca, one of the great religious centers of the world. The village still exists under the name of Urel and the river, now called Lilâju, still flows into the Phalgu, with which it has sometimes been confused. The site has not lost its peace, calm, and silence made up only of rustic sounds, in spite of the daily visits of pilgrims who come in increasing numbers from all of East Asia. It is still favorable to an intense spiritual life: it is as if the very air were impregnated with the serene thought of the Blessed One.

So it was in this peaceful and charming setting that the Bodhisattva's frightful austerities, followed by equally terrible struggles against the forces of evil, were crowned by the final triumph of his keen intelligence sustained by an indomitable will. Our author begins by having him go over in his mind all the varieties of strange behavior, food, clothing, and cultural practices as well as the physical torments imposed on themselves by the ascetics of his time in the vain hope of escaping from the whirl of rebirths. The list is long, for human imagination, so restricted when it comes to describing happiness, shows an unending fecundity in inventing tortures. Many of these penances are still practised—for instance, forced postures which stiffen the limbs; complicated fasts that follow the moon, with the number of daily mouthfuls going from fifteen to one during the dark of the moon and increasing again from one to fifteen with the new moon. There is also the rite of the "five fires," in which the self-appointed victim sits in the center of a square formed by four burning fires, the fifth fire being the sun overhead. It is interesting to note with what independence and broad-mindedness the Buddhist monk rejects and scorns all these notions and superstitious practices.

If the Bodhisattva was certain of the absurd vanity of these mortifications, why did he set out to practise them to the most extreme degree? There is only one answer, and it has been given to us. Full of pity for the blindness of the human race, which is forever seeking ways of torturing and hampering itself by means that have no rhyme nor reason, the Bodhisattva felt that the only way he could force mankind to see clearly and to return to the right path was to strengthen his words with the authority of experience. Though the idea of loving humanity and of suffering for humanity might arouse the Christian concept of Redemption in our minds, nothing could be further from any Indian belief.

The texts show us how the Bodhisattva outdid the yogīs on their own ground, the fasting ascetics, and the *rishis* of legend by surpassing the physical strains of the first, the abstinence of the second, and the absolute immobility of the third. First, for six years Gautama sat upon the hard earth in the traditional pose: torso and head erect; legs tightly crossed with soles upturned on his thighs; and hands, with palms upturned, meeting in his lap. He began by making his thoughts master his body. As a strong man might hold a weaker one, shaking and tormenting him, so his will held his body, torturing it with such mastery that even during winter nights sweat poured from his brow and armpits onto the ground. Soon he ceased breathing, and, when respiration was thus suspended, there came from his ears a great noise such as issues from a blacksmith's bellows.[13] When in turn his ears were closed, a tempest blew against the top of his skull with such force that it seemed as if his head were cracked open with either a blunt or a sharp instrument. Did he at that point fall into a cataleptic state such as is artificially induced by the yogīs of today? However, the gods feared among themselves that he was dead, as he seemed to be. An officious divinity hurried up to the Heaven of the Thirty-three to alert his mother. Against all expectation, it was as a woman that Māyā came down, followed in genuine queenly fashion by a procession of nymphs. In this form she was able to weep maternal tears, and he could offer her filial consolation, and the devout, in turn, could be moved to sadness.

After this sentimental interlude the Bodhisattva began the second series of mortifications. This time he went on an extraordinary fast, eating only one grain of jujube, then only one grain of rice, and finally only one grain of millet a day. Then, with greater and greater self-control, he refused all food. We do not have to guess the effects that these privations had on his physical being, for artists and writers have shown and described them to us. It would be interesting to know whether such and such statues have been made from a written description or whether, on the contrary, the *Lalitavistara,* for instance, was inspired by them when its writer tells us that Gautama's limbs became like knotty sticks and that his spine—which could be grasped from the front through the flabby skin of his abdomen—was like the rough weave of a braid. His protruding thorax was like the ribbed shell of a crab, and his emaciated head was like a gourd that had been plucked too soon and had withered. His eyes were like the reflection of stars at the bottom of a nearly-dried-up well.[14] However, when Aśvaghoṣa tells us that even when the Bodhisattva was only "skin and bones" he still charmed the eye—the way a new October moon, however slight, delights the lotus—it is difficult not to feel that these words were written with one of the fine painted or sculptured images of Gautama the Ascetic in the mind, or actually before the eyes of the writer.

The third type of mortification again demanded that the Bodhisattva do as well and better than his predecessors. Committed to complete immobility, he did not move, either to seek shade or sunshine or to shelter himself from wind or rain. He did not move a finger to protect himself from horseflies, mosquitoes, and various reptiles. We are told that during these years no functional waste was emitted from his body. The Predestined One simply existed, his body tarnished by the elements, his senses dulled; he no longer perceived objects, neither did he see nor speak nor hear. He lost his human appearance and, still alive, he became of the earth. "And the village boys and girls, the cowherds, shepherds, and those who gathered grass, food, and dung, all took him for a dust demon and made fun of him, throwing dust over him." At last it could be said that he had reached the lowest depth of mortification and his apologist refused to invent new torments.

The Last Meal Before Bodhi

IT was high time for the Bodhisattva to abandon this disastrous pursuit, which he had chosen for the love of humanity. Of the thousand and one particles of life only one remained when he decided the experiment conclusive and that he was ready to proclaim once and for all that "this was not a road which led to Enlightenment in order to end birth, old age, and death." He had to choose another, but what would it be? Then he remembered his First Meditation, in his father's fields, and he saw clearly that it was in reflection guided by reason, and by the use of the mind alone, that he could discover the secret of salvation. But, the exhaustion brought to his body by mortification and his mind having been kept so long in disuse, how could he assiduously apply himself to the solution of destiny's problem? His whole organism, both physical and mental, needed to be restored; therefore the first step was to break his fast. Legend would have it that at that moment certain gods, guessing his desire, came to propose a secret vital insufflation through his pores. The Bodhisattva indignantly refused to lend himself to such a fraudulent trick. He was, in the eyes of the peasants, a total abstainer and he would fail them completely if he seemed to remain so and yet secretly received food by supernatural means. Since it seemed necessary to do so, he had to take food honestly, in sight of all.

> And so the Five of the fortunate group thought thus: In spite of such practices and attainments Gautama the Ascetic has not been capable of discovering a noble doctrine superior to the current ethics. How could he do so now that he is eating food and living normally? He is nothing but a fool, an imbecile. And with such thoughts they left the Bodhisattva and having gone to Benares settled in the Deer Park.

There he was soon to find them, much to their confusion, and for their own salvation as well.

The Bodhisattva was again alone and in the weak and destitute state just described. Hardly could he stand and his garments, which for six years he had not taken off, fell from him. So the son of a king was reduced, in order to cover his nakedness, to stealing a shroud from the corpse of a young servant girl which had been left for cremation. Having thus acquired a piece of linen, he then had to wash it, and in order to do so in the Indian fashion he had to have not only water but a stone. The water appeared when he struck the ground with the flat of his hand, and today there is still a pond known as "Struck-by-the Hand." Śakra, the gods' Indra, was on hand to bring the necessary stone and even offer to do the menial washing. The Bodhisattva refused and stepped into the pond, from which he would not have had the strength to emerge if a dryad who lived in one of the large trees on its edge had not at his request held out a helping branch. Having left the pond, he sat on the bank in the shade of the tree and set to work to a make a monastic cloak out of the coarse piece of cloth he had just cleaned. At the time of our author the place of this achievement was still shown to pilgrims. Hsuan Tsang himself saw the pond, the stone, and the place where the Bodhisattva had put on the "old garments." In the interval these had become the gift of a poor dying woman.

Sujātā (that is, Eugenia) a young woman who, since the arrival of the beautiful ascetic in the area, had maintained a tender interest in him, at once prepared some new rice cooked in the cream of a thousand cows. While this most tasty and nourishing dish was cooking over the fire in a new pot, all sorts of symbols of good omens were seen on its surface. It was this rice that the Bodhisattva received as the first gift when he came the next morning, decently dressed, begging for food in the village. Sujātā insisted that he accept the golden vessel into which she had poured it and he could do little else, since the gods had neglected to give him a begging bowl.

Taking this provision he went straight to the river Nairānjanā to bathe. This bath takes on a particular solemnity after six years, and the divinities of the waters and the earth and the heavens were all there.[15] They vied with each other in showering flowers and perfumes on the water that was to touch the body of the Predestined One. A number of them even collected some of it as holy water and it is thus that still today at Gayā the pilgrims solemnly drink the water which has become sanctified by running over the feet of the Brāhmans of the area.

At the same time the Bodhisattva found himself shorn of his hair and his beard, which Sujātā piously gathered in order to raise a shrine to them. At last he ate the rice pudding (which, it must be said, was to sustain him for fifty days), and no sooner had he done so than he instantaneously recovered his beauty in all its past splendor. As for the gold vessel he threw it in the river where Śakra fought the undines for it and carried it to the Thirty-three, who celebrate each year a religious feast in honor of the gold bowl and the Bodhisattva's turban.

So, empty-handed and freshly shorn, with new garments and bearing again all the characteristic signs of the great man, the Bodhisattva set out towards the fig tree which was to shade the accomplishment of his final Buddhahood or *Abhisambodhana*.

CHAPTER VI

ENLIGHTENMENT

A T LAST we have come to the decisive moment towards which, from time immemorial, through untold rebirths, and thanks to limitless sacrifices and perfections, the human being destined to become the Savior of this epoch of the world had been moving. Just as "Prince Siddhārtha" was transformed into "Gautama the Ascetic," the latter was about to become "Buddha Śākyamuni," and this ultimate metamorphosis would be the culminating point of his career. Having reached that height, he would remain there, for once a man (and it must be a man) has reached this supreme elevation, he can neither rise higher nor be demoted. It is easy to understand the interest that the Buddhists of India and Asia have had in that memorable moment in which they saw the fulfillment of ancient prophecies and the beginning of a new era for humanity.

Two Aspects of Abhisambodhana

THE exuberant Indian imagination could not refrain from adorning the Buddha's definitive triumph over the powers of evil with rich coloring and a grandiose setting. Among Indian and European scholars these elaborate accounts, mixed in with allegories, became subjects of controversies, which we shall leave aside and turn, as we have done before, to the old Indian texts themselves.

Turning to the *Lalitavistara,* we find the author, as we have always known him, drowning in extravagance and repetition on this sensational occasion. It is only at such a price that he is able to extend the event over six chapters of which these are the titles:

Chapter XIX: The Road to the Place of Enlightenment.
Chapter XX: The Decoration of the Place of Enlightenment.

Chapter XXI: Māra's Attack.
Chapter XXII: The Enlightenment or Abhisambodhana.
Chapter XXIII: The Hymns of Praise [sung in turn by the various
               categories of gods to the new Buddha].
Chapter XXIV: Trapuśa and Bhallika [the two merchants who
               offered the Buddha his first meal after his Enlight-
               enment].

Of these six chapters it is at once evident that the second and the fifth
are pure padding and of little interest to us. The first and the last re-
late episodes which preceded and followed the Enlightenment. The
two which remain to describe its achievement, Chapters XXI and XXII,
are really two ways of telling the same story. The two expressions "He
will destroy Māra's army" and "He will reach complete Enlightenment"
are interchangeable and constantly interchanged. We can say with
sufficient precision that the Order of monks, the *Sangha* which kept
the treatises of knowledge, was responsible for the methodical and
nearly rational account of Chapter XXII, while the numerous lay
zealots dredged up from legendary memory the dramatic phantasmagoria which is strung out in Chapter XXI. Each confirms the other, the
latter being the mythological and popular aspect of the scholastic rea-
soning by which the Master conquered the light of Truth. The Indian
artists, at a loss how to represent the psychological crisis of the Predestined One during the night of solitude, chose "Māra's Attack" as the
better subject. This substitution has everywhere met the approval of
donors.

Towards Enlightenment

LET us now follow the Bodhisattva, after his bath in the Nairānjanā
River, as he walked towards the fig tree which his whim had chosen
but which, of course, became for the zealots the inevitable one. The
short distance can be easily walked today, and it is in part outlined by
tombs of the superiors of the Hindu monastery which, after the devasta-
tion of the countryside by the Moslems, took over this sacred Buddhist
territory. At the time of Hsuan Tsang's travels it was still divided by
two compulsory stopping places indicated by monuments commemorating two episodes worthy of note. Their interest for us is as examples
of the kind of distortion popular legends fall into even when they are
based on fact. Thus we are told that Kāla or Kālika, the serpent god,

made aware of the Bodhisattva's coming by the particular sound of his footsteps, came up from the ground and predicted his imminent triumph.

The second episode is that of the Bodhisattva's coming upon a humble cutter of grass, Svastika, and asking him for some grass to sit upon while engaged in meditation towards Enlightenment.[1] According to the *Lalitavistara,* this scene gives rise to quite an exchange of words with the grass cutter Svastika, in the course of which the Bodhisattva explains patiently that Enlightenment is not acquired simply by having a fine mound of grass to sit upon. One must during the past ages have accomplished many worthy acts, attained many perfections, and received numerous prophecies. If Enlightenment could be passed from hand to hand, of course he would make a present of it to him, as to everyone. But, that being impossible, he promises to share with Svastika the recipe for salvation as soon as he has discovered it.[2]

This said, he took up his armful of grass and went on to the Bodhi tree. After having gone around it seven times, always keeping it to his right, he carefully spread the long strands of *kuśa* grass that he, son of a king, owed to the charity of a lowly man. Upon this bed of grass, purest of the pure, he sat at once in the manner of yogī, facing east—that is, looking towards the Nairānjanā, then unobscured by any edifice. With concentration he at once took a firm resolution: "Upon this seat, though my body dry up and my skin, my bones and my flesh be dissolved—without having reached Enlightenment, no matter how long and difficult to reach, I shall not stir from this seat." He did not have to go to such lengths. His studies, quickly ended, took a year; his fruitless austerities cost him six years; his complete success was to come in twenty-four hours. The following day the rising sun would shine, not upon one ascetic among many others, but upon a unique Being without equal anywhere in the world; for it is one of the dogmas of Buddhism that in a given time and universe there can exist only one Buddha.

Sambodhi

ALL we have read so far has told us at length how, coming from the night of time, a Predestined One approached little by little perfect Enlightenment; but we still are in ignorance of its nature. Because Buddhism claims to be a religion without mysteries, it owes us explanations; and, truly, it never refuses them. What made a man among men the superman, the supra-divine being that is a Buddha, is just what he discovered and which no one yet had discovered. No longer will it need discovering. It is the working of human destiny. Having done this, he has found the means of curing all our ills. There lies the secret of his exceptional grandeur, the reason for the perpetual gratitude of his disciples, the justification of the devotees' adoration. It must be said that, if such a blessing were actually given us, he that gave it would forever deserve the gratitude of the whole of humanity. The Buddha, Śākyamuni, came to show us how precarious our lot is, how fatal its end and how reckless our indifference. Impermanence, pain, and unreality became the keystones of his doctrine, and our unavoidable sufferings constitute the repeated litany of the Four Noble Truths, the premises for his preaching. This disheartening instability and emptiness of appearances is expressed in the quatrain which has become the credo of the followers of the doctrine.[3] All of this will be explained to us, but in Indian terms and technical formulas which make it hard to understand at one reading. When Menander, the Indo-Greek king, had the sage Nāgasēna elucidate the subtle meanings of the Good Law to him, he constantly asked "for a comparison" to help him understand.[4] Perhaps this is also the best way for us to seek clearly the Buddha's attitude towards the problem of destiny.

If you know bees and have stopped to watch their incessant buzzing activity, characterized by the poet Maeterlinck as "innumerable and perpetual, enigmatic and foolish flutterings"[5] which are forever repeated in an endless chain of swarms and the construction of new hives which lead to new swarms, your mind is haunted by the image of a great wheel forever turning upon itself. The same kind of spectacle is exhibited on our city streets with similar feverish as well as futile activity, for the actors will soon turn to dust. Upon reflection, we no longer know whether we are more sorry for those miserable insects or for ourselves. We wonder whether the fatality which activates them is not the same as that which also incites us to run faster and faster. So the Buddha, having freed himself from the dull resignation of his fellow men and broken the spell of instinct, was able to raise himself against the eternal new beginnings of human generations. No man has ever had a more vivid sense of the absolute vanity of the universe and the incurable misery of our destiny. None has probed from so high nor with a sharper eye the folly of this interminable dance of death, perpetually drawn into the vortex of the wheel of life—*saṃsāra*. This is the discovery that established the fundamental and durable basis for his superiority and glory. To it he owes having become the "Awakened One" among those who are sunk in the torpor of custom, and the "Enlightened One" among those resigned to live in the darkness of ignorance. In the realm of the blind he is the "Seer."

The doctrine which then will be preached by the Buddha will be a destructive menace to the empire of the master of the sensual and material world governed by desire, which is to be abolished by the Good Law. This ruler is "the first-born of the gods," [6] Kāma: Love—or if you prefer, Māra: Death; for the Indians did not wait for Ronsard to tell them that "Love and Death are the same." The Buddhist doctrine not only tends to deplete his kingdom but to starve him personally, in case you should be ignorant of the fact that gods feed on the sacrifices offered to them by men. [7]

Now it must be understood that the duel between the Bodhisattva and Kāma-Māra was inevitable, and we can see the two protagonists of the drama of *Sambodhi* facing each other. Though the outcome of their conflict was assured and the Bodhisattva's victory proved his pre-eminence over all, it brought no solution to the problem of universal salvation. It was only during the following night that, thanks to a number of judgments and arguments, the Predestined One finally opened the way to complete release from the vortex of recurring births for gods, men, beasts, spirits, and the damned. Here, it could be said, are useless words. If life is so radically bad and pain so unbearable, haven't we the remedy at hand? A collective suicide could wipe out humanity. . . . This is speaking like a European, and a materialist at that. A shrug of the shoulders would be the Buddhist's only reply. No matter how general this suicide might be, it would serve absolutely no purpose, for no one has the power to abolish at will his own *karma* [8] and consequently to escape rebirth. *Saṃsāra* does not so easily let go its prey. For death to be really a final liberation—that is, *Nirvāna* from which there is no coming back—it must have been reached through the total suppression of desire and egoism and attained thanks to the practice of all the virtues—in a word, by becoming a saint. Thus it is that the purest morality is the outcome of the most pessimistic doctrine and consequently attenuates its fundamental despair.

Māra Pāpiān

LET us not anticipate the First Sermon, for we have enough to do in trying to find our way amid the confusing descriptions given us of the *Abhisambodhana.* Having caught a glimpse of the profound reasons which separate the Bodhisattva and Māra, it is important for us to know the latter's complex personality. First of all, he is a great and powerful god who reigns above many others in the sixth sphere, and his empire extends to all lower levels including the earth and the various strata of Hell. He controls all the spheres of desire, sensual pleasures, and their painful consequences. As the master of this material universe, the sovereignty of which is his *raison d'être,* he sees to it that it reproduces itself constantly, for that is the only means of duration which beings and things have in this world of ours. That is why he is called "Kāma," which means "Love." But as it is axiomatic that everything which is born must perish, and this world is so constituted that each being feeds upon and subsists at the expense of others, he is also Death, and the Buddhist texts prefer to call him Māra. As both a productive and a destructive power, he takes on in turn the aspects of Love and Death, being the Spirit of Life. And because he is the spirit of life, in the eyes of the monk he becomes the spirit of evil. But he is a versatile spirit with many facets—the mythological god of a long-term but transitory world; the metaphysical Being which must persist in his being; in humanity he is the life force; in man he becomes natural instinct. Thus it is due to him that the world goes on, but because of this he is the born enemy of the monk who has come to condemn desire and love and to claim that he has found the way for man to escape from rebirths and successive deaths. That is why the Buddhist texts constantly brand Māra with the epithet of Pāpiān (literally, "the Worst").

Our intention is not to become the devil's advocate but simply to point out that Māra had a legitimate argument. First he wished to defend his kingdom, which the Bodhisattva proclaimed he would destroy, but he also wished to preserve the right of action, of ownership, the right to happiness, the right to love, to marry, to have children, perpetuate the family and so carry on the cycle of earthly life. A frightful cycle of ephemeral joys, illusory happiness, and a perpetual succession of lives furnishing new causes for sorrow and death, contended the monk. Perhaps he in turn was right, but let the whole of humanity become part of the Buddhist Community and in one generation the whole earth will be depopulated. Who will dare to say that after the extinction of human thought there will be nothing lacking in the universe? The Buddha's contemporaries did not fail to see this practical result of the Master's doctrine. Soon the people of Magadha were heard to murmur that "Gautama the Ascetic has come to preach the extinction of the families." [9] So Māra was not the only one to protest, and he might well plead not only that he was representing the most legitimate interests of the individual but that he was defending social solidarity. This solidarity he contrasted with the egotistical laziness of the begging monk, whose sole concern was his personal salvation. With the hope of making the Bodhisattva refrain from his vain austerities, Māra said to him, "What living man had best do is to live. It is in living that you will practise goodness." [10] This is a most judicious remark but one that will have no effect on a foreordained verdict. For the Buddhist ascetic, as for the whole monastic community, the spirit of love can only be the devil.

The Conflict Between Māra and the Bodhisattva

WE have followed the Bodhisattva since the preparations for his birth and we have investigated the nature of Māra; nonetheless we feel barely able to read and understand the confused accounts that are given us of their conflict. First, we must remember that the Bodhisattva was absolutely alone, sitting with empty hands in his lap on strewn grass at the foot of a tree. Not only had his five companions abandoned him as a false prophet, but the gods, who had been hovering in the background, prudently left at the approach of the conflict, only to return later for the proclamation of a victory to which they did not contribute. Secondly, we already know that this struggle preceded the attainment of Enlightenment. All the texts and even the two adversaries agree upon this: Māra knew that he had no chance of success against a complete Buddha, and the Bodhisattva therefore wanted the conflict to take place before the outcome became inevitable. According to the *Lalitavistara* he even sent a sort of challenge to his rival in the form of a light ray from his *ūrnā* (the characteristic sign between his eyebrows) which reached Māra in his celestial palace.[11]

The first scene is the only one that truly deserves the name of

"Māra's Assault." Alarmed by the imminence of the Enlightenment of his sworn enemy, the worldly sovereign called forth his thousand sons and generals and decided to mobilize his army. This army was incredibly horrible, being composed of most repulsive monsters with hanging tongues, bared fangs, eyes of burning coals, deformed bodies, some without arms and others with a thousand arms, some headless and others with a thousand heads or even with the heads of ferocious beasts, and so forth. There were also specters, spirits (*prētas*), ghosts, devils both large and small, gnomes, giants, kobolds, or trolls—in effect, the traditional horde of demons whether Eastern or Western. Human imagination has its own conventions, even when it comes to the invention of nightmare figures. Spitting out serpents and wearing garlands of skulls, dragging mountains and brandishing trees, gathering clouds and hurling thunderbolts, all these revolting creatures threw themselves upon the defenseless monk with horrendous cries. His earlier merits, plus his attitude of universal good will, created such a zone of complete protection around him that he laughed at his aggressors while not a hair on his body was disturbed. In vain did Māra try to spur his troops on, and even the arrows of his marine monster lost their sharp points, and spontaneously were covered with flowers. For this reason the classical Kāma became "the god with flowered arrows." Finally, weary and discouraged by the uselessness of their efforts, Māra's dark hosts fled as do a band of jackals when a lion growls, or a flight of crows among which falls a stone. And so the account closed with this striking picture: "Māra, the Demon, sad, discouraged, his heart bleeding from a secret wound, reflecting as he drew lines upon the ground with an arrow: 'Gautama the Ascetic will destroy my empire.' "

This scene does not lack in grandeur and shows plainly the effect of popular imagination when given an epic theme apt to call into play the resources of traditional beliefs. We could find proof of this, if necessary, throughout the Orient from Gandhāra to Java and from Ceylon to Tibet, for it is thus that the Buddhist imagery represented this episode and through it the attainment of Enlightenment. But theologians, turned loose upon the finest of epic subjects, made hash of it.

Among a confusion of platitudes and contradictions in the three texts a second version is found in which the moralizing influence of the monastic order took over from the devout laymen's taste for fables and mythology. A conflict was still at stake, but this time it was not an armed one but rather a competition for moral victory between the Bodhisattva and Māra. Each one contested that his merits were superior to those of the other. The monk insisted that in his case it was not a unique sacrifice that had given him authority but innumerable sacrifices made during past existences, when he had given up everything—his possessions, his hands, his feet, his eyes, his blood, his head—and these without any objective but the salvation of human beings, and even now their liberation was his one aim. Unfortunately, in his solitude, he had no witness to confirm his claims, while his adversary had a multitude of partisans. Because of this Māra shouted, "You are defeated!" But the Bodhisattva answered, "O Demon, this earth, impartial mother of all, is witness." [12] And reaching down with his right hand in the gesture so often represented in Buddhist iconography and which has remained the symbol of attaining Enlightenment, he touched the earth with the tip of his fingers.

At once there were six earthquakes and a sound like that of the gong particular to the Magadha resounded. Then the earth, not content to behave in the Indian manner, had recourse to that of Greece: "And the Great Earth, named Sthāvarā, opened the ground near the Bodhisattva and emerging halfway out adorned with all her ornaments bowed before him and said, 'It is true, O great man, it is true; it is as you say and I am the eyewitness.'" At the sight of this miraculous apparition Māra's army is said to have taken flight. The later legend, which has been retained in Cambodia, added its ingenious bit to this new theme. It must be remembered that in ancient India for a donation to become irrevocable it was necessary for the donor to pour a little water on the hands of the receiver. In the course of time the ritual sprinkling of water accompanying the hundreds of thousands of million alms made by the Bodhisattva caused the earth to be soaked and the Indian Demeter's hair became so wet that in wringing the water from her tresses she created a flood, which swept away the whole diabolical horde!

The second phase of the duel came when the Buddhist Satan became the tempter. Disappointed by his failure of extermination, Māra then turned to his daughters to seek success where arms had failed. With docility they followed their father's orders and, approaching the Bodhisattva, displayed "the magic of women." Their smiles, sighs, and all varieties of lascivious attitudes as well as exhortations for him to take advantage of the spring season failed. Though the writer catalogued the thirty-two devices used by women in such situations, he realized full well that Māra's daughters were but allegorical figures, as is indicated by their names: Pleasure, Displeasure, and Concupiscence.[13]

Attainment of Enlightenment

It is high time to put aside these fantasies, whether mythological or allegorical, and turn to reason. With the rout of Māra's army and his daughters' failure, let us agree with the theologians that all the baser instincts and evil thoughts, all seeds of sin were extracted from the future Buddha's heart and everything was ready for the marvelous flowering of *Sambodhi*. In the meantime the sun had set, but the beautiful April moon had risen and bathed in its light the leaves, the river, and the sleeping villages. Alone, the thinker was awake, more than ever determined to discover the secret of man's destiny which until then had always eluded men as well as gods. Because of his previous studies and former practices, he already knew that he would only find it in his thoughts by the strength of his intuition if his mind, made completely pure, was clear enough to reflect the universe as a faithful mirror. India has always chosen the direct method of introspection. Our immediate problem is to know how we can follow it into the mysterious arcana where microcosm and macrocosm are reciprocally mirrored and clarified. Fortunately, popular imagery has conserved an approximate representation of the world as the Predestined One conceived it. He is said to have told his disciples, "In the convent's vestibule you must imagine a wheel with five spokes. Inside the five subdivisions you will think of the five ways of rebirth—at the bottom, hell, the animal kingdom, and the region of spirits; at the top, men and gods. On the hub, Lubricity, Violence, and Stupidity in these forms—a dove, a snake, and a pig. On the circle of the felly, you will imagine the twelve terms of Production one after the other. And the whole will be held together by the claws of Impermanence." [14] If we can visualize such a wheel of transmigration as has been represented in Tibetan paintings, it will greatly help us to understand what is to follow.

13. Māra's Attack and the Enlightenment.
Gandhāra school, 2nd–5th century A.D.

14. Calling the Earth to Witness. Bihār.

The First Watch

WE are told that as a preparatory exercise the Bodhisattva, acting as a good yogī, began by successively penetrating the four degrees of Meditation and banishing all emotions as well as all intellectual operation. Thus he remained as pure spirit, cleansed of any flaw or tarnish. It was then that, thanks to the intensity of his mental effort, the veil lifted and his "divine eye," as the texts call it, opened, seeing at one glance into infinite time and space. That is exactly what he did do during the first two watches of the night. Thus we read:

> And the Bodhisattva having concentrated, purified, clarified, and fixed his thought, having freed it from all unpleasant inclination, and having nearly unburdened it of its entire *karma* and stabilized it during the first watch of the night he gathered it and stretched it to take in clearly the knowledge given by the divine eye. And the Bodhisattva, purified and superhuman, saw with his divine eye all living beings. He saw them falling to be reborn into high or lowly castes, happy or unhappy, mean or good, according to what their *karma* was worth. Oh, see those who sin by their acts, their words, and their thoughts; those who slander the worthy; who teach false doctrines. Because of their attachment to the laws of false doctrines, after the dissolution of the body they fall into an unfortunate condition and are reborn in Hell. . . .

On the other hand, the good after death went to heavenly worlds. Thus the Bodhisattva saw beings disappearing, falling, being reborn, and so forth. Such was the knowledge that came clearly to him during the first watch and from it came an intuition.[15]

Consequently, it was with a general view of the whole universe, at that time, that the Bodhisattva began. And as he contemplated it, he must have seen far more than was retained by his monastic interpreter who, in our mind, was too greatly preoccupied with the damnation of heretics, the beatification of the true believers, and his faith in the impeccable working regularity of *karma*. He showed as best he could the perspicacity and the breadth of vision with which the Bodhisattva contemplated the perpetual revolutions of the great wheel of existence, which seemed to him like those hydraulic machines called *norias*, composed of a chain of buckets (or earthenware jugs in India) affixed to a large wheel and successively filled and emptied as the wheel constantly turned.[16] It must be remembered that the contemplator in this case was a man above men who, rising above humanity, observed not only with sympathy but also with terrible lucidity the futile activity of the human anthill. We should not be afraid of being mistaken in thinking that he also discovered no beginning, no end, and no sense to the cycle of generations "which are born, grow, fall and are reborn." [17] What follows will confirm this opinion, and if the text did not say so it is because it was obvious.

The Second Watch

AFTER the Bodhisattva had explored space, it was the past that he searched during the second, or middle, watch of the night. Before his superhuman eye passed the hundred-thousands of millions of past existences—both his and others'. With lightning speed they all came back in every detail; for example, "I was here under such a name, of such a family, of such caste, etc. . . ." Thus we see the Bodhisattva exploring the past after having watched the present and then summing up in his mind the whole experience of the world. Because of the formidable and heartbreaking knowledge made possible by this superhuman gift, Gautama was now ready to face, during the third watch of the night, the supreme problem for which he has sacrificed everything in this life —namely, the extinction of suffering.

The Third Watch

LET us admire the method followed by Gautama. Born a man, it is human suffering which he first tried to cure. For this he cannot be accused of egotism, as philosophical speculation can do no better than to begin with a knowledge of self. Since Socrates, the whole Occident has been in agreement. Second, the Bodhisattva had learned from the Sāṅkhya scholars that nothing happens without cause; therefore the only way to discover the remedy for the congenital ailment that afflicts man is to undo piece by piece the mechanism of his destiny. The question being thus squarely put, the answer was not long in coming, and the formula of the Twelve Productions, which mutually condition each other, reveals [18] it to us. These appear below in their exact sequence, with a brief parenthetical explanatory statement given for each.

1. And the Bodhisattva thus thought: What unhappiness it is for him who comes to this world to be born, to grow old, to die, to descend, to be reborn. And the unfortunate fact is that no recourse is found against this great aggregate of pain, old age, illness, death and what follows. No way is known for putting an end to this great accumulation of suffering!

(Such is the initial datum: it is the existence of suffering, both avowed and proclaimed, which is summed up in two terms "old age" and "death." Its representation is found on the first of the twelve sections which are marked off on the felly of the great wheel and is of a corpse either carried to the funeral pyre or abandoned to the beasts and birds of prey.)

2. And the Bodhisattva thought: What is the cause of old age and death? When do old age and death occur? He then thought: It is when there is birth that there is old age and death: old age and death are the sequelae of birth.

(It goes without saying that in order to grow old and die one must begin by being born: "A tree cannot be cut down before it has grown." Birth is represented by a scene of a woman giving birth.)

3. What is birth due to? On what occasion is there birth? The coming into existence means birth; the occasion for birth is the coming into existence.

(*Bhava* in Buddhist speech does not mean "existence," but "becoming" or "production" or even "reproduction." For a child to come into the world he first had to be conceived. All births presuppose first conception and then gestation; that is why coming into existence is represented by a pregnant woman.)

4. To what is coming into existence due? On what occasion is there coming into existence? It is when possession has been taken that coming into existence occurs; so coming into existence is on the occasion of taking possession.

(Conception can only occur after copulation, and it is possession in that sense which is meant. Monastic prudery caused the union of the sexes to be symbolized, as in Genesis, by the picking of fruit from a tree.)

5. What causes possession to be taken? On what occasion is possession taken? When there is desire then possession is taken; so that the taking of possession is caused by desire.

(To use the language of our catechisms, there cannot be "act of the flesh" if it is not preceded by carnal desire. *Trichnā* is a good term for "sensual lust"; but since the word really means "thirst," it is represented by a man drinking but also drawing to him the half-clothed woman who is serving him refreshment.)

6. What is the cause of desire? On what occasion is there desire? It is when there is sensation that there is desire; thus, desire is caused by sensation.

(For desire to be aroused there must be a reason, and this reason can only be a sensation or perception (the two notions are not as yet distinct). Since sight is the most keenly representative of our senses, *vedanā* is foremost "visual perception." Only a woman who is seen can be desired, and that is why sensation or perception is symbolized by an arrow shot straight into the eye.)

7. When is there sensation? On what occasion is there sensation? It is when there is contact that there is sensation; what occasions sensation is contact.

(Sensation or perception can only occur when there is contact between the senses and their objects. According to Indian ideas, it is the senses which reach out to the exterior objects and then refer them to the mind. Artists usually represent contact by a human couple either sitting or standing in a close embrace. Other more prudish representations are of the plowman holding on to his plow.)

8. When is there contact? What is the occasion of contact? When there are the six sequences (each succeeding event) there is contact; contact is occasioned by the six sequences.

(It goes without saying that there can be no contact between the senses and the external world unless the senses exist: "a blind man sees nothing." These senses and their domains are six in number—five external senses: sight, hearing, touch, smell, and taste, plus an internal sense, *mānas*. They are represented by a human mask with an opening for each sense and showing a second pair of eyes for the *mānas,* or by a house with all windows open but still vacant.)

9. When are there the six sequences? What occasions the six sequences? When there is name-and-form there are the six sequences; thus the six sequences are occasioned by the name-and-form.

(The existence and activity of the senses imply the existence of a person who uses them and who, in turn, is informed by them. But a person is defined by having a form—that is, a body—and is designated by a name, with the connotations that such a word had in antiquity, when the name was taken to represent the essence of the individual. The union of these two factors, one spiritual and the other purely physical, constitutes the "personality," and thus this term can best be used to translate the composite term "name-and-form." This is represented by a passenger on a vessel floating on the ocean of existences, for the question at stake is whether he will reach the "other shore," i.e., salvation.)

10. When is there name-and-form? What occasions name-and-form? When there is consciousness there is name-and-form; thus name-and-form comes into being with consciousness.

(Personality, however impermanent in Buddhist concepts, can exist, or at least have that illusion, only if there is some consciousness of self. Since this consciousness, which differentiates the individual from the rest of the world, occurs as early as the animal stage, it is symbolized by a monkey, sometimes on a tree, sometimes not.)

11. When is there consciousness? What occasions consciousness? When the preconditions occur there is consciousness; thus the preconditions occasion consciousness.

(Each individual is born with an aggregate of physical, intellectual, and moral characteristics, which are implied in the individual consciousness and which we call by the term "heredity" or, as some say, "predestination." By the word *samskāra*—literally, "making up" or "co-efficient"—we must understand all those particular tendencies and potentialities that are called innate because they are inherited from an indefinite line of ancestors. Since these preconditions predetermine the status, the conditions, and the general orientation of each new life they are symbolized by a potter who, by molding clay on his wheel and with his hand, fashions his vases.)

12. When are there preconditions? What occasions preconditions? When there is nonknowledge there are preconditions; thus preconditions are occasioned by nonknowledge.[19]

Parenthesis on the Unknowable (Avidyā)

LET us examine the meaning of "nonknowledge," for on the understanding of the twelfth point depends the clear understanding of the whole formula. While from Number 1 to Number 11 we follow the sequence that more or less loosely links the terms one to another, the connection between Number 11 and Number 12 escapes us. We do see that the last is represented by a blind female camel obediently following her guide, who is none other than the personification of her *karma*. Even if we do know where she is being led, we have no idea of where he and she came from.

Evidently the twelfth condition, instead of having been poured in the same mold as the other ten, should have been the subject of a more complete commentary similar to the first, thus stating the termination of the series as explicitly as the beginning. Fortunately, this explanation is given us in context, and all we know of Buddhist thought confirms it. A close reading proves that the formula called "the production of mutual dependence" brings together, not abstract concepts, but concrete realities or at least an establishment of facts. We must insist on this point, which is essential. To insert in the series any general idea would be as radically contrary to its spirit as to its contents, and that is why to construe *avidyā* as "ignorance," which is the usual translation, is to denature, and even block, as by the insertion of a foreign body, the whole workings of the sequence. The way the Bodhisattva proceeded is fortunately clearly expounded as a whole. Taking suffering as a constant and undeniable fact, he tried to trace back step by step the source of this evil. But the moment came, as it always does, when the human mind reached its boundaries and came upon the unknowable. From this basic Unknown—the "Unseen," as the pundits always say, or the Invisible, as we say—spring those accumulated preconditions from the past that determine the modality of each new personality. Since the individual inherits this legacy from the past unknowingly we shall use the term "unknowableness" for *avidyā*—being sure that what this means is not an idea but a *fact,* and even a fact of common experience. This fact is that no one knows whence come the urgent, if not irresistible, tendencies that determine one's present existence and lead to the perpetuation on earth of "old age and death."

Thus the formula with its twelve links becomes more and more intelligible but still gives rise to metaphysical questions, which the Master refused to answer. As a result of his silence, the problems thus left fell into the hands of theologians whose discussions brought about the most contradictory solutions.

In the presence of such confusion we can do no better than to listen

patiently to the voice of ancient tradition. We shall concede that, if the
Buddha did not know all there was to know, he at least may have had
and given the impression that he knew all that was necessary, for he
discerned both what was important to know and what was of no sig-
nificance. In all circumstances he behaved on this point with complete
integrity and answered with sincerity and clarity. No intimation of
charlatanism is to be attached to him. As the Son-of-Mālunkyā said to
him crudely, "When one is ignorant of something, it must be admitted."
And that is just what the Blessed One did. He, too, saw that human existence is only a fugitive light between two black mysteries—we emerge
from the invisible past only to be plunged into the unforeseeable future. Here the Bhagavad Gītā echoes the Buddhist texts: "Imperceptible
in their beginning, perceptible only in the middle of their course, living
beings and things again escape us at the end. What good does it do to
complain?" [20] The Predestined One avoided all speculations in this area
and reproved them as being pernicious and an obstacle to an attainment
of the most urgent concern to man: his "liberation."

So we are told over and over that "the Buddha elucidated and taught
only that which could lead to the appeasement of passion, to serenity,
wisdom and Nirvāna." His attitude was absolutely clear to all who
listened to him. He never recognized suffering as having an educative
value or as having any source of merit. Never did he accept it as a trial
imposed by a superior will; nor did he ever endow it with blessed
compensations in a happier world. He accepted suffering as it came,
and took it for the evil that it was, and he was only concerned with
finding the means of preventing its future recurrence. But he never
claimed to know its final cause, or that of any of the elements constituting our conception of the universe; nor did he pretend to suppress it by special grace and in accord with his personal will. He may
not have, even as the first among men, distributed happiness among
his disciples, but he discovered the series of conditions that engender
and inevitably propagate suffering. It was now left to him to mull over
his discovery in order to find where the root of the evil lay, and then
he would be able to prescribe a line of moral conduct that would gradually bring wretched mortals the alleviation of their misery. What
more could they wish for?

The Third Watch (Continued and Ended)

WE can now go back to following step by step the development of the Bodhisattva's thought. At no time did he pretend to construct a rational system of deductions, each following the other in a causal sequence of abstract ideas. Logic in that epoch had not yet evolved that far. He simply followed his way noting as he went the important stages of the journey made significant by each new fact encountered, whether physiological, psychological, or mixed. All he cared was that it be a fact of universal and constant experience. Step by step he advanced until the time came when he could no longer see the way. If he could not push his investigation further, he could at least verify its results by following it in reverse order. The true purpose of a roadway, once it is open, is to make traveling in both directions possible. So the formula of the Twelve Productions can be recited in two directions, and the establishment of facts that mark the way will remain the same and their order will be invariable in both directions. The viewpoint alone will change and, with it as he proceeds, the traveler's point of view. To re-ascend from suffering, through all the conditions which cause it, to the unknowableness of its last origin, is to proceed in an exploration which aims, above all, to satisfy intellectual curiosity. To descend along the same course, from unknowableness to suffering, may be to act as a moralist who, sighting the origin of evil, discovers its remedy. That is just what was intuitively revealed to the Bodhisattva. We shall now give only a résumé of the many variations he executed on this theme.

First of all, he took in reverse order the series of the twelve conditions: "Because of (or depending on) unknowability preconditions are established—consciousness, personality, senses, contact, sensation, desire, union, conception, birth, old age, death, sorrow, suffering, distress, and despair: this is 'the origin' of 'this great complex of sorrows.'"

Then another intuition came to him and he again followed the series, but this time in a negative form and first in ascending order: "In the absence of what is there neither old age nor death? By suppressing what are old age and death suppressed? Without birth there is neither old age or death; and it follows that, by suppressing birth, old age and death are suppressed." And so it follows: "Without birth there is no coming into existence . . ." until "Without preconditions there is no unknowableness." All this was not pure tautology, for after each "next origin" of each condition he came to know its suppression.

To better express the content of this new datum, he went over the formula a third time—in the negative form but now in descending order: "In the absence of what are there no preconditions? What has to be suppressed in order to bring about the suppression of preconditions? In the absence of unknowableness, no preconditions are necessary; by suppressing unknowableness, there is then suppression of preconditions" and so forth, until "By the suppression of birth it follows that old age, death, sorrow, sadness, suffering, distress are suppressed; in this way this great aggregate of pain is suppresed." Again he had taken a further step: after each origin in turn, after the suppression of each condition, he had found "the way" to its suppression.

All that remained for him to do was to proclaim, to his great satisfaction, the result of his successive discoveries: "And this is how the Bodhisattva having brought together in his mind these unheard-of concepts became aware of knowledge, sight, science, intelligence, goodness, wisdom, and this intuition came to him: I, who am here, at this moment, I know what is," and instantly he recited the series of conditions to the final conclusion:

> Here is suffering and here is the origin of suffering, here is the suppression of suffering; here is the way which leads to the suppression of suffering. All this I have come to know as it is. And this is how the Bodhisattva in the last watch of the night, at dawn, due to his wisdom, having surveyed in one sweep of his thought all that a man, a great man, a superman, a bull among men, a champion among men, a lotus among men, the first of men, a leader of men, etc. can know, understand, reach, see and clearly imagine—became enlightened by the supreme and complete Enlightenment.[21]

Having at last reached the ultimate extent of his cogitations and sacrifices, he became that unique being without equal: a Buddha. A cry of triumph escaped him, and the *Lalitavistara* even had him show off his magical powers by performing an act of levitation. This was a sign of victory recognized by the gods, and they immediately hastened forth to shower him with so many celestial flowers that a mound of

them rose to his knees. A whole chapter of the *Lalitavistara* is devoted
to the compliments bestowed on him by the divinities.

The question that faces us now is this: Was there here really cause
to claim a miracle? That Buddhism is a great religion and that the
formula of "mutually dependent conditions" is its basic dogma no one
can dispute; but it must be admitted that such as it appears in as literal
a translation as possible, this formula seems, at first sight, of almost
childish simplicity. As we have said before, it is in no sense a logical
deduction of abstract concepts, implied one within the other. It is nothing more than a list of ascertained facts, brought together in as loose as
diverse a fashion by a certain link of reciprocal dependence made absolute only by their order. Of course, to ascend from one fact to the next
and determine its succession took not only the strength of character
necessary to face facts but also high-mindedness, which made possible
the contemplation of their development—"as from the top of a mountain people's activities can be seen in the valley." The ability to make this
sequence proceed back and forth in both directions gave the Bodhisattva
all the clarifications he felt was necessary for the attainment of his initial
aim. This seemed to be a diagnosis of the course to be followed to arrest
the disease based on its development. Still, the critics, both Asiatic and
European, found it hard to admit that the Bodhisattva, in all his wisdom, had only achieved a sequence of truisms.

It is, of course, obvious that we would not die if we had not been
born; that we would not be born if a couple had not united; but for
this union there had to be desire, and desire could not occur without
perceiving its object. In turn, sensations presuppose senses, their contact
with the external world, and a psycho-physical organism animated by
a spiritual conscious principle, which comes forth completely molded
from an unknown past. All this makes sense and its statement is accessible to any intelligence. But the scholars took pains to make it obscure in order to make it seem more profound. The rich variety of
meanings in Sanskrit served their purposes, and each chose whatever
fitted in best with his philosophical speculations or moral principles.
Eventually the twelve conditions were presented not simply as depending one upon the other but as engendering one another. The most disconcerting complication was that, instead of proceeding—as the Master
had originally done empirically—from results to their causes, the scholars attempted to progress logically from causes to effects. Since the en-

gendering of the series within the framework of one existence gave rise
to confusions, it was imagined that the formula had to take in three
successive lives of one individual. This gave rise to the new interpretation:

I. *Ignorance* (1) becomes a primary cause of the obscurity from
which arise the preconditions (2), the heritage of prenatal *karma*.
II. These, in turn, produce (in the embryo) the awakening of consciousness (3), which produces (in the fetus) individuality (4), which produces (in the newborn) the senses (5), which produce (in children)
contact (6), which produces (in adolescents) sensation (7). (It should
be noticed that up to this point, in the course of the present life, only
effects of the past have been noted. But the following numbers will
begin acting as causes to prepare for the future.) Sensation arouses desire (in the young man) (8), which produces (in the adult) attach-
ment to things of this world (9), which throw (adult man) into the
various activities of existence (10). III. *Karma* accumulated by these
activities produces in turn a (new) birth (11), which then produces
old age and death (12).

In short, with the use of many parentheses, sense can be made of
the formula taken in reverse, and even the two ends can be pretty well
brought together, since it is necessary to re-establish the perpetual cycle
of the Wheel. The Mahāyānic sects later invented even more subtle
combinations between the various links.[22]

Aśvaghoṣa, both philosopher and poet, did most to fully restore the
true development of his Master's thought. He, too, preferred to have
the Predestined One begin by contemplating in his mind "as in an un-
tarnished mirror" what he called, as we have done, "the cycle of the
wheel of the world," circling under the implacable drive of *karma's*
whip. He, too, had him unravel the series of occurrences, which in their
invariable order spell out the successive stages of all human destinies.
He also had him at the same time discover the three qualifications
characteristic of this becoming which knows no beginning or end, no
primary or final cause, no destination or creation. At the sight of the
unending whirl of rebirths the future Buddha at first found himself
overcome by a feeling of great compassion for all beings, who, regardless of their category, are fatally afflicted with suffering. After passing
in review all the miseries that attend the life and death of all beings,
without hope of happiness, whatever region of the universe may be

theirs, the divine eye of the Bodhisattva perceived that the sorrowful cycle of all existence was without stability and support. It is most understandable that, coming upon the enigma of the world, as we all have, he refused to attempt solving the mystery of its origin and its end. It was enough to have perceived its painful futility. The fundamental insubstantiality of what, for lack of a better term, we may call the elements of our inner life and the external world; the irremediable impermanence of all the possible combinations formed by these fugitive factors, which depend one upon the other; the pitiful unanimity of all beings in their suffering—these are the three experimental evidences which arose from the spectacle of life and imposed themselves upon the penetrating intelligence of the Bodhisattva. They remained, as we shall see, the three principal ideas of his doctrine, the unending theme of his discourse. Those among his biographers who recognized that the formula of the Twelve Productions, in spite of its naïveté, contained the seed of the Good Law saw clearly, and thus dated perfect Enlightenment from its conception.

CHAPTER VII

THE FIRST SERMON

ENLIGHTENMENT came to the Bodhisattva as dawn broke and, due to a rare privilege, our age will have seen the coming of a Buddha. The end of his evolution, which took thousands of years, finally came in our epoch. But even a perfect Buddha does not furnish the undeniable proof of his perfection until the day he begins to preach his doctrine or, in Indian terms, "when he sets the Wheel in motion." Thus, the First Sermon spoken by the Master assumed particular importance, and in chronological order it became the third Great Miracle. The Nativity was the first; the Enlightenment, the second; and the Final Decease, the fourth. The place when this event occurred became the site for the third of the Four Great Pilgrimages. Consequently, a special chapter would seem in order.

The Days Following Enlightenment [1]

THAT the Buddha had the right to enjoy in peace the happiness of the final achievement of his ascension was not disputed, and Buddhist tradition gave its approval. The length of time for this respite, which first started with seven days, came to be extended to seven weeks. [2] For forty-nine days the Blessed One rested and enjoyed his felicity. This beatitude was to be his sole subsistence. Of course it has been recalled that Jesus, after his baptism in the Jordan, was taken by the Holy Spirit into the desert, and there he fasted for forty days and forty nights. In theory, nothing could be more similar, in practice, nothing could be more different.

The Buddhist texts are not in agreement on the number of weeks which separated the *Abhisambodhana* from the first meal taken by the Master, or on how they were spent. This is due to the fact that the authors did not follow the same version of the *mahātmaya* of Bodh Gayā; or else, brimming over, they wished to insert some prodigious inventions. These variations need not worry us, for we have learned to guess their purpose. We know from Hsuan Tsang and we have seen with our own eyes, thanks to the archaeological diggings, that the narrow enclosure of the "area of Enlightenment" was crowded with monuments, practically touching one another, all supposed to commemorate some miraculous episode. Those which recalled each of the seven weeks were among them.

According to the general testimony, the first weeks were spent in beatific immobility or in health-preserving walks. To begin with, the Blessed One did not move from his seat: "As it is the rule for kings not to leave for seven days the place of their coronation, so it is for Buddhas when they have been consecrated to remain in contemplation for seven days, without uncrossing their legs." [3] As a compensation the Master is said to have spent the second week walking back and forth on a promenade still venerated by the devout. North of the Bodhi tree, Cunningham dug up its vestiges—a small brick walk about one yard high and wide and sixteen long. Hsuan Tsang reported that the Buddha could only take ten steps each way (the Chinese step is twice ours). Except at both extremities each of his footsteps was marked by a lotus flower, of which there were eighteen in all. Naturally, the *Lalitavistara* could not be content with such a restrained promenade, so the Master's first outing (which according to this account filled the fourth week) took him to "the Ocean of the East and to that of the West"—that is, from the Bay of Bengal to the Gulf of Oman—and back. Agreement between the texts and the monuments returns in regard to the sanctuary of the "Unblinking Look," for it is from there that the new Buddha is said to have contemplated fixedly, without even blinking an eye, the Bodhi tree. As he had done during the first week, he continued to repeat: "It is here that I became enlightened with the supreme, the perfect and complete Enlightenment; it is here that I put an end to the immemorial suffering of birth, old age, and death." [4]

Amid the monotonous accounts of these dull activities and litanies, one episode stands out in surprising relief. During that week the weather was unusually cold and rainy. The serpent king, Muscalinda, saw his opportunity and was equal to it. Leaving his underground abode, he enveloped the body of the Blessed One seven times in his folds and spread his great polycephalic hood above the Buddha's head. While thus completely sheltering the new Buddha from the rain and the cold, the serpent felt throughout his many coils a sense of well-being theretofore unknown to him. When the week was ended and good weather returned, the *nāga* king uncoiled himself from around the Master. Then, resuming his human form, he bowed low at the Buddha's feet and, after circling three times around the holy figure, withdrew to his abode. The representation of the savior of the world embraced by a serpent and enjoying a peaceful beatitude in spite of a raging storm is most strange to us, but is completely Indian in feeling. It appears among the sculptures of Amarāvatī, but it is Indochina that has given it its finest form.

All our sources seem to find it necessary to slip into their accounts of the seven weeks a repetition of the scenes of the Temptation, both utterly useless and misplaced. The *Lalitavistara* alone has known how to bring back the theme of Māra's encounter in a novel way. It was known, and Māra was aware, that his only chance for success was to have the new Buddha go directly from Perfect Enlightenment to Nirvāna, which was its inestimable reward. If he did so, the Evil One's kingdom would lose only one member and consequently would not be threatened. Māra therefore approached the Buddha and made one wish (which was granted some forty-five years later): "May the Blessed One enter *Parinirvāna; this is the time for the Blessed One to enter *Parinirvāna.*" But to these words the Predestined One answered:

I will not enter Parinirvāna, O Evil One, before I have taught well-informed monks to be intelligent, wise, skillful, learned, and only when they have completely grasped the meaning of the doctrine and are capable of turning their own understanding upon themselves and of miraculously teaching the Law, after having justly refuted eventual heretics and establishing their own point of view. [This same statement is repeated in regard to nuns, zealots both masculine and feminine, and the three other groups which, with the monks, form the Buddhist Community.] I will not enter Parinirvāna, O Evil One, as long as I have not renovated in this world the tradition [of the three jewels] Buddha, Law and Community.[5]

Māra, once more rebuffed, found nothing better to do than to step aside and, taking his usual pose, draw lines on the earth, this time only with a stick. However, his three daughters tried to console him by bringing to him the captive Buddha. In vain he tried to warn them of their folly, but the beautiful celestial nymphs dared to use their charms on the Buddha as they had once before on the Bodhisattva. This time their impudence could not go unpunished, and they found themselves transformed into old and decrepit hags. Only their sincere penitence and the Master's infinite forbearance brought back their pristine beauty.

The one thing the author forgot was that the Buddha was supposed to have remained absolutely silent concerning his future intentions.

The First Meal After Sambodhi

THERE still remained a sixth and a seventh week to account for and this was done by taking the Master from the banyan tree of the goatherd to the Tārāyaṇa tree. The end of the forty-nine days was drawing near and the Master had only fed on his felicity. The physical being of even the most enlightened of men requires food. Tradition has it that the honor and merit of giving Śākyamuni his first meal fell to two simple merchants who were passing by. They were members of the third caste, to which belonged the woman who gave him his last meal before *Sambodhi*—the young village girl, Sujātā.

The texts attach equal importance to the two repasts between which the attainment of Enlightenment occurred. The first broke the fast of six years of austerity; the second, that of the seven weeks of pure felicity. Since a little of the supernatural is often part of the simplest act, the gods were given the opportunity to provide the Blessed One with the bowl in which he would be allowed to receive his food. We must recognize that, by the very fact of his Enlightenment, the Buddha found himself instantaneously and spontaneously ordained a Buddhist monk and consequently subject to, in advance, the rules he later imposed on the members of the Order.[6] The statutes of the Order state that a monk cannot accept an offering from hand to hand but only if it is put into a begging bowl, one of the few utensils he is allowed to own.

The Blessed One, it may be recalled, had thrown into the river the gold container in which Sujātā had served him the rice cake, after he had eaten. He now found himself empty-handed and would have been greatly hampered if the deities nearest the earth—namely, the Four Guardian Kings—had not immediately brought him the necessary alms

Photo Bulloz

15. Nāgarāja: The Serpent King after Resuming his Human Form.
Mathurā, 1st–2nd century A.D.

16. First Sermon in the Deer Park.

(Left) The Buddha Represented by a Pillar with the Wheel of the Law. Sānchī Stūpa, 1st century A.D.

(Below) The Same. Ayaka frieze, 3rd century A.D.

Copyright Archaeological Survey of India, Government of India

Courtesy of John M. Rosenfield

bowl. This bowl, of course, was to be the one he used on his daily
rounds of begging and the one to be venerated after the Ultimate
Death. This myth holds a grain of truth, for the Buddha did in fact
use a begging bowl, which (authentic or not) public veneration conserved a thousand years or more after his death. This is another example
of the mixture of truth, probability, and fiction in history. Sanskrit poets
claim that the beautiful wild goose is able to separate milk from water;
and one could ask what historian has the secret for sorting from such
mixed data the fabulous from the real and the exact amount of each.
Possessing no such talisman, let us follow the texts as they bring us the
various episodes of our story.

Two rich merchants, the brothers Trapuśa and Bhallika, are about
to come on the scene for a brief but unique appearance, bringing with
them a large caravan of five hundred ox carts. At the head of these were
two pure-bred bulls, guided by the touch of a stalk of blue lotus or by a
garland of flowers. Coming from the Utkala country (today the district
of Ganjām in southern Orissā) they were headed northward, probably
through Gayā, to the great markets of Rājagṛha and Vaiśālī. Since it
was necessary that some extraordinary occurrence should warn them of
the nearness of the Master, either the bulls refused to go ahead or the
carts became mired, so that confusion spread throughout the caravan.
But whether or not they were guided by a kindly deity, they soon came
upon the Blessed One sitting beneath the Tārāyana tree, shining like
the rising sun with the splendor of his recent Enlightenment. Completely reassured by this sight, they said to each other, "This is a monk
who eats at certain hours [the rule being that monks ate once a day,
just before noon], have we something for him?" Some answered,
"There is a sweet dish made with honey and some peeled sugar cane."
The two merchants approached the Buddha and, bowing to the ground
before him and circling around him three times, said, "May the Blessed
One do us the kindness of accepting our offering of food . . ." This
was the moment for a miracle.

This came to the Predestined One's mind:

"It would not be seemly for me to receive this offering in my hands.
What did the former Buddhas use to receive alms?" And he knew
that it was a bowl. At this moment, realizing that it was time for
the Predestined One to eat, the Four Great Kings from the four

cardinal points rushed forth to offer golden bowls: "May the Blessed One do us the favor of accepting these bowls of gold." "These bowls are not suitable for a monk," and with this thought the Predestined One did not accept them.

Without being discouraged, the divinities persisted in offering him bowls fashioned from the six other precious materials (silver, jasper, crystal, amethyst, sapphire, and emerald) or even from the whole seven. Each time the Buddha refused. At last the four gods resigned themselves to bringing him, "each in his hands," an alms bowl made of stone, such as is prescribed by the monastic rule. Let us keep them for a moment immobile in that hieratic pose: two on each side of the Master, who was seated under his tree with his right hand raised in a welcoming gesture. As such they were posing, without knowing it, for the representation of the third Great Miracle. This offering of the four bowls and Māra's temptation provided the artists of Gandhāra with the only scenes which they felt able to use as the representation, or at least the evocation, of the *Abhisambodhana*. The two scenes were used interchangeably according to the donors' desires, and are visible to us today on the many votive *stūpas,* whose square bases are used to represent, one on each side, the Great Miracles. None will be surprised to find that the highly dynamic episode of "Māra's Assault" was eventually far more popular in Buddhist Asia.

The third scene with which we are confronted is as follows. Again the Buddhist canon exerts its influence. The Buddha reflects that four bowls are too many and only one is needed, so he receives from each of the gods one bowl and, holding them in his left hand, one atop the other upon his lap, he welds them into one. The *Lalitavistara* has him do this simply by the strength of his will, but the *Mahāvastu* more prosaically thinks that he caused the bowls to fit into one another by pressure from his thumb. Thus the four bowls became one, but on it the rims of the other three were always to be seen.

The Chinese pilgrim, Fa-hsien, who found the Buddha's alms bowl in Peśawār being held in great veneration, noted that the original four different edges could easily be seen. Twice a day the precious relic was exhibited before the faithful, probably placed on a throne and protected by a dais such as is shown on a number of the bas-reliefs from Gandhāra. The offerings received from this veneration were sufficient to care for a monastery of seven hundred monks. But all the glories of this world are transitory, and when Hsuan Tsang came through Peśawār more than two centuries later, the "monastery of the Bowl" had fallen into ruin and the sacred container had vanished before the Hephthalitic invasion. Remaining written descriptions and monuments give us an idea of its shape, much like the large hemispherical wooden vessel used by Buddhist monks today. If the search for a rational explanation of miraculous events in legends were not a vain pursuit, it would be easy to find in the grooves left by the carver's gouge the origin of the encircling edges that are always shown on the bas-reliefs.

In the texts the fourth scene, the encounter with the merchants, was directly joined to the first, and at Gandhāra and Ajantā that is how things are represented. While the men of the caravan are busily working to get their carts out of the mire, the two merchants, their offering in hand, approach the Master with a great show of respect. The meaning of the story is to let it be known who were the first men to offer the new Buddha the first gift of food, and thereby to establish the prototype of the faithful layman. They are thus creating a precedent.

Later, when the Predestined One or one of his monks was a guest of some devout persons, it was the rule that in return the hosts receive an edifying speech. This worthy custom could not have been initiated too early, and that is why the Buddha did not feel free of obligation towards the two merchants until he had spoken some gladdening words to them. One of the characteristic qualities of the Master's teaching is that it was always adapted to meet the level of the mind and the spiritual need of the recipients. He gave first proof of this by sparing the kind merchants the recital of the metaphysical truths he had just discovered. Instead, he recited a magical formula suitable to each cardinal point and called upon the presiding deities to ensure a safe journey to bipeds and quadrupeds, day or night, regardless of the direction traveled.

The *Lalitavistara* ends the story there, but other accounts feel that one good deed calls for another. These merchants were pious, and they were rich, and it was up to them to give concrete proof of devotion.

The most meritorious of benefactions was either the erection of a sanctuary or the establishment of a monastery for the Order, but as the Order had not yet come into existence, the Master gave Trapuśa and Bhallika some cuttings from his hair and nails and they erected one or two *stūpas* over these offerings once they were back in their own land.

But what was this land? Caravans often trekked great distances, and sometimes they even exchanged their ox carts for a ship or vice versa. Thus, when the Good Law was brought to countries beyond India, the newly converted countries found in the legend of the two merchants proof that their faith in Buddhism went back to the time of the Buddha. According to the place of origin attributed to Trapuśa and Bhallika, the Buddhist influence went with them to the northern region as well as to that near the southern waters. Even before crossing the Hindu Kush Range, Hsuan Tsang found traces of Buddhism around Bactria.[7] He might have encountered Buddhism in Ceylon or Burma, had he gone that far; and the great pagoda of Shwe Dagon in Rangoon prides itself upon having kept Buddhism alive.

The Request

AGAIN we are not surprised to find ourselves confronted by two different versions of the same story, one completely rational, the other seemingly confused by myths. These accounts reveal the two halves of the Buddhist church: the monastic Order, as seen in its relatively rigid framework, and the loose mass of lay believers. According to the monks, the Master was at first hesitant to preach a doctrine that the common people might neither understand nor accept, and it was only his compassion for suffering humanity that overcame reason's selfishness. The zealots, however, believe that it was largely the gods' entreaties that won him over.

It is a rule that nothing happens in the life of a Buddha which has not already happened in the life of his predecessors or will not happen to his successors. It must be understood that each new Enlightened One hesitates before communicating to the profane the truth of what he has just discovered. There are two reasons for this—one intellectual and one moral, both of them judicious. The doctrine, we are told, is profound and thus requires an extreme concentration of mind in order to be understood. And since it insists upon the extinction of all desire, it therefore demands utter control of oneself and of one's passions. How can the average man be expected to understand the doctrine's principles and to practice its dictates when he is the prey of his constantly recurring desires, the plaything of his inattention? The latter would discourage his weak spirit, and the former would be beyond the capacity of his intelligence. Thus the preacher would waste both time and energy. "Better remain silent and not worry."

And so it was that the first impulse of the most eminent of sages was to relax and follow the course of least resistance. But was humanity, caught in the constant whirl of rebirths, to be refused the chance of escaping from this infernal cycle?

This was the time, if ever, to call in the divinities, and what better advocate for such a saintly cause could be found than Brahmā, the most spiritual of all Indian gods. To him was given that important role, not to the royal warrior, Indra, as in the scenes of childhood. True, when Brahmā believed his first attempt rebuffed, he did call upon his old companion, and upon myriads of other divinities as well. All came in their ceremonial attire, with "their cloaks draped over the left shoulder," to plead with the Buddha.

The artists, always in league with the donors, were happy to comply with important representations of the Request, matching the images of the Instigation, with one important difference. In the former the central throne is occupied by the Buddha, while in the latter it is by the Bodhisattva. Whether the compositions are crowded or reduced to two protagonists, it is always Brahmā, known by his hair, who occupies the place of honor at the Master's *left;* while "Śakra, the Indra of the gods," is now pushed to the other side, for the representations had to follow the rules of etiquette.

Whether the gods believed or not that their requests, three times repeated, convinced the Buddha, it was still quite another consideration that touched him. When contemplating a lotus pond, we may note that some flowers are still quite immersed while others rise well above the waters. Still others, obscurely trying to reach the light, are close to opening on the surface. Contemplating the world with his divine eye, the Buddha understood that human beings fall into three categories: those who have sunk irremediably into error, those who already have reached the truth, and the others who still float between error and truth. For the first there is no hope (at least for the present, for we should despair of no one and nothing) of bringing them out of the darkness of their ignorance or their false beliefs. The second group need no help, for they have helped themselves. But there is still the in-between group, uncertain, hesitating between the true and the false, and wavering between good and evil. These will be either lost or saved, depending on whether or not they hear the Good Word. It was for the love of them that the Buddha resolved "to set the Wheel of the Law in motion."

The Choice of an Audience

ONCE the Buddha's resolution was made, its execution knew no delay. But in order to preach there had to be an audience, and the question was: "Before whom will the new Buddha deliver his first sermon?" Various suggestions seem to have been made, but the Blessed One's mind turned towards the five disciples who recently had abandoned him when they saw him give up his austerities. With his magical eye he saw them, living in a hermitage near Benares, and he immediately decided to join them. At least this is how tradition has it established. It is evident that these five souls, avid for new revelations and accustomed to meditations of a philosophical and religious nature, would be best suited to understand the doctrine and most likely to be lost if it were not communicated to them. But it is surprising to find the Buddha being made to take a journey of nearly one hundred leagues on foot after a long fast, without allowing him to speak a word about his new discoveries. And it is even more surprising to note that he was to come back to Bodh Gayā from Benares almost at once. One can only wonder whether the Benares sermon was really the first or simply the first to win him converts.

On the Road to Benares

AT all events, we shall accompany our hero on his way to the famous holy city, which is on the boundary of the orthodox regions of "the Middle" and the poorly Brāhmanized areas of the East. Because of this, Benares was probably a rendezvous for inventors of new religions. We should note the curious fact that the journey was to be remembered, as told in legend, by two episodes that began or ended with a rebuff to the Buddha. The first of these incidents came about on the short run of around seven miles between Bodh Gayā and Gayā. The Predestined One passed an *ājīvika,* a mendicant monk like himself but belonging to a sect that was to remain one of the most violent rivals of the one he intended to establish. Upaka (for we know his name) started a conversation by complimenting his colleague upon the freshness and purity of his complexion as well as upon the serene quality of his entire appearance and then asked: "Who is your master?" Śākyamuni answered, "I have neither master nor equal: I am a perfect Buddha." This reply aroused surprise and his questioner cried, "Surely you will not pretend to be a saint?" The Blessed One answered, "I am a saint, being Supreme Teacher of the world."

More and more surprised and, using the terms of his community as well as that of the Jaïns to designate a savior, the man continued, "Surely you will not pretend to be a *Jina* (a Conqueror)?" and Śākyamuni declared himself to be the Conqueror, for he had conquered all perverse inclinations. Upon hearing this the other simply asked him with the usual Oriental indiscretion: "Where are you going, reverend Gautama?" "I am going to Benares to enlighten the blindness of the world and to set the Wheel of a new Law in motion." "Very well, Gautama," and having thus spoken the *ājīvika* continued on his way towards the south and the Predestined One towards the north.[8]

Here was slight success! The questioner, instead of being moved by the Buddha's words and following in his footsteps, turned his back on him and continued on his way in the opposite direction. The importance of all this is that, at that very spot, Śākyamuni for the first time proclaimed from his own mouth and before another man his new and supreme dignity as well as his well-defined aim to save the world. This is what the faithful found important, and the place where those memorable words were spoken was thought worthy of a special sanctuary; this in turn kept the memory of the episode alive. Little does it matter that the *ājīvika* did not understand his privilege.

We know through the Singhalese tradition what became of him. In the southern region where he was going he fell in love with a girl of the lower class. After winning her by going on a hunger strike, he became crushed by work and by outrageous abuse from his wife and in-laws. Not knowing which way to turn, he suddenly remembered the young and beautiful religious whom he had once met near Gayā. He started northward again and asked for the Buddha wherever he went. Finding him at last, he became converted and was received into his Order. So all ended well, and this extra bit of history sufficiently proves the two things that were important to bring out—namely, that

Upaka was still blinded by his passions when he met the Master, and
that the privilege of having received his first confidence meant that he
should not die before being saved.[9]

Let us come back to the Buddha, whose road we are now able to
follow. The distance between Gayā and Benares is little more than a
hundred and thirty miles in a general westerly direction, but we are
told that the Predestined One was walking towards the north. The texts
even believed they knew the names of his first stopping places and of
the more or less mythical hosts who each night offered him bed and
board. However, there is agreement on only one point, which is that
on the fifth or sixth day he reached the Ganges. Since he could walk
only about fifteen or twenty miles a day, the distance covered represents
the one hundred miles between Gayā and the large river, on the condition that he went due north. If the Master had taken the normal westerly direction, he would have had twice as many stops before reaching
the bank of the Ganges. The texts, our only valid guides—and valid
only to the extent that they are—suggest that the Buddha took a wide
detour, going from south to north across Magadha to quickly join the
highway, the trunk road of that time, which followed the northern
shore of the riverway of Hindustan. Therefore, he crossed the Ganges
at the point where he was to cross forty-five years later for the last
time and where the future imperial capital of Patnā was to be built. It
was only later that he turned due west, and this sharp turn doubled
the length of his journey. Evidently this itinerary across a land that
he already knew had its advantages or attractions for him, and, as we
know, time is of no moment in the Orient.

As a matter of fact, the Predestined One had to cross the Ganges,
for it is on the left bank that Benares, facing the rising sun, also rises
with its many palaces and temples joined by majestic stairways. Here a
new affront awaited him. At that season the mighty river, swollen by
the melting snows of the Himālayas, flows like a torrent, and both
paddling and swimming across are impossible even when holding onto
a cow's tail. The Buddha consequently sought the ferryman and asked
to be taken across. When asked in turn for his fare, the Master was
obliged to admit that he could not pay. We need not fear to repeat it:
the savior of the world, the Teacher of men and gods, did not own one
cent. For all practical purposes, he was only a begging monk. In view
of the ferryman's refusal, the Buddha decided to forego the rule, which

he is supposed to have imposed on himself as well as on other monks—
that is, to refrain from exhibiting any magical power—and with one
leap in the air he betook himself across the Ganges.[10] Almost at once
King Bimbisāra was apprised of the event, and he issued an edict that
thenceforth all holy men, no matter what their sect, need pay no ferry
tolls. This detail settles for us the place of the ferry station on the right
bank of the river as being in the kingdom of Magadha.

We have no evidence that Indian artists tackled this picturesque episode, but the Javanese sculptors of Borobodūr did justice to it. They
represented the river, stocked with fish and turtles, flowing between
wooded banks inhabited by wild animals. In the foreground is the boat
used as a ferry, connected to the bank by a board. The Buddha, already
on the other side with two other monks of a Brāhmanic sect, is being
admired by them for his supernatural power, while the ferryman,
seated by his wife, is sunk in despair at his overwhelming mistake. He
cannot forgive himself for having allowed his greed to let slip the
chance, which may never come again, of acquiring the extraordinary
merit capable of getting him to heaven by showing kindness to a man
saintly enough to have crossed the Ganges dry-shod. By missing the
opportunity of this lifetime he has at the same time compromised his
future existences. So overcome was he that he fell to earth unconscious,
the texts tell us—behavior which is not surprising since fainting is a
common practice among heroes of Indian tales and novels.

The Place and the Prologue of the First Sermon

SINCE it would have been unseemly for the Buddha to overdo the use of
his magic powers, he resumed his journey on foot and finally came to
the outskirts of Benares. Perhaps he, too, exclaimed, "Hail to Saintly
Kāśī!" as do today's pilgrims, for the ancient name remains in their
memories. As is the rule, he waited until morning to enter the city.
Having done his begging, taken his bath, and eaten his meal, he did
not loiter but went straight to the hermitage where the group of five
disciples had retired. This place is known to us and today is called
Sarnāth, about four miles north of Benares. It is still distinguished by a
large elevated *stūpa,* which bears its old name abbreviated to "Dha-
mekh" (from "Dharma rājikā," indicating that it was due to the religious devotion of Dharma rājā or the "King of the Law," which was

the name Emperor Aśoka acquired because of his zeal for building Buddhist sanctuaries).

The perseverance of the Archaeological Administration of India has brought to light many sanctuaries and monasteries near Benares, and the dates for them cover a fifteen-hundred-year period, for the area was not devastated by the Moslems until the end of the twelfth century. The numerous art objects, architectural fragments, bas-reliefs, and terracotta statues brought up during the patient diggings have been installed in a beautifully designed local museum. The justly celebrated lion capital from the Aśoka column erected near the commemorative *stūpa* ranks first in the exhibition, which continues with fine Buddha images of the Gupta period and ends with works of more recent times. The date of the later building, credited to Queen Kumara, *devī* of Kanauj, goes back to the twelfth century. However, Buddhists have found the way to this holy site, and through their devotion a new sanctuary has been raised.

The monasteries of ancient India, like those of Cambodia today, consisted of small huts scattered across the landscape and used as individual cells by the monks. The texts and inscriptions call the ones used by the Buddha "Perfumed Cabins." Because Sarnāth was the first hermitage that housed the new Buddha, today's devotees feel justified in calling their edifice the "Magistral Cell of the Origins" and thus tradition, long interrupted, now continues before our eyes.

If we are to believe the names of this holy area and the tales, which attempt to explain its holiness, this characteristic would greatly antedate Buddhism. Some accounts indicate that the presence of deer could mean that the site may have been a forest area reserved for the king of Benares' hunt. Others evoke the fantasy that *rishis* had made these woods close to Benares their favorite retreat.

As to the deer's importance, an easily found expedient was to transform the king of their herd into an early incarnation of the Bodhisattva. Because of hunting by the king of Benares, there was great useless bloodshed; so the king of the deer made a pact with the king of men by which he would furnish daily one gazelle for the latter's table in exchange for the latter's promise not to hunt. The deer's fate was settled by drawing lots, and one day the lot fell to a doe heavy with young. None but the Bodhisattva would take her place, so he spontaneously came and offered himself up to the court's cook. Of course when the cook caught sight of the noble animal, the knife fell from his hand. The king, learning the whole story, at once came forth from Benares and, overcome with admiration for such self-sacrifice, declared that all deer should go untouched. In spite of the demands made by the peasants, whose crops the deer were destroying, he refused to revoke his edict, and that is why the *Mahāvastu* sometimes writes "The Protection of the Deer" instead of "The Deer Park." [11]

The touching tone of the fable and its purely Indian character is easily recognized, but even more moving and remarkable is its later echo in history. Emperor Aśoka, at the beginning of his conversion to Buddhism, set forth in his first edict the following:

> In the past in the kitchen of his Gracious Majesty, "the Favorite-of-the-Gods," hundreds of thousands of animals were killed daily for the table. Now, beginning with the composition of this religious edict, only three are killed for that purpose, two peacocks and one deer, and even the deer not regularly; from now on not even these three will be killed.

Where else but in India could such an official text be found, dating back over twenty centuries at that?

This edifying account was necessary if we are to understand the variety of names for "The Deer Park," where the Buddha first set the Wheel of the Good Law in motion. All these names designate the same spot; and since the religious buildings or their ruins had not yet taken the place of the trees, we can easily imagine that the scene was much the same as that of a princely park of the Rājputāna in our time. There, too, groups of monks (*sādhus*) install themselves without a by-your-leave, and there is nothing the Mahārājā can say about it. Some take shelter under the buildings; others set up small tents; and all go about their affairs peacefully, doing their chores in the open: cutting wood, cooking rice, bathing or rubbing themselves with ashes, reading or meditating, and sometimes practicing such austerities as standing immobile in unnatural poses, lying on spikes, or sitting between the five fires. Such was the life already being led by the Master's five former disciples in the company of many other ascetics. They lived in a hermitage open to all, knowing nothing of the one they had seen fit to abandon forever. Suddenly he appeared, coming towards them, and all their antagonisms were aroused. It is better to let the text speak for itself:

Thus the Five of the Fortunate Group saw from afar the Predestined One coming towards them and having seen him they plotted
among themselves: "Here is the ascetic Gautama approaching—
that slacker, that greedy one, that fallen one. . . . None of us must
go to meet him nor rise before him nor help him with his cloak
and his begging bowl. We must offer him neither food nor drink,
nor, after having pushed forward a stool for his feet, say to him,
pointing to vacant seats, "Here, Reverend Gautama, are vacant
seats; if you wish, do sit down." One of them, Ājnāta Kaundinya,
did not approve of this but said nothing. As the Predestined One
moved nearer to the place where the Five were and as these felt
ill at ease, each on his seat, the desire came over them to rise. As a
bird in a cage placed over a burning fire feeling the heat of the
fire has only the desire to fly away, so, as the Predestined One came
before the Five of the Fortunate Group, they were feeling ill at
ease on their seats and wished to rise. And why was that? Because
in the whole realm of living beings there is none who at the sight
of the Predestined One does not rise from his seat. So as the Predestined One drew closer to the Five . . . , as these felt unable to
withstand the majesty and splendor of the Predestined One, they
were thrown from their seats and all, breaking their agreement,
arose. One stepped forward towards him, another took his cloak
and alms bowl, another brought forward a seat, another brought
a stool, and still another brought water to bathe his feet, and they
said, "Welcome, Reverend Gautama, you are welcome, sit down,
here is a seat ready for you." So the Predestined One sat on the seat
prepared for him and the Five . . . , after having exchanged with
the Predestined One various friendly and agreeable words, sat beside him.[12]

The conversation began with the usual compliments addressed to
the Buddha on the serenity of his face and on his clear complexion. But
he, making the best of his advantage, thought only of preparing his
companions for listening to and understanding his Law. He gently
reprimanded them for their familiarity and forbade them to use the
common expression of "reverend" when addressing him. No longer
was that title worthy of him, for, having the means to be free from
death, he had become the supremely Enlightened One—the Buddha.
If they would only listen to him, be taught by him, they in turn would
soon learn that their goal had been reached and their aspirations ful-

filled. "There will be no rebirth for them." Without waiting any longer
to prove that he was omniscient, he showed them that he had read as in
an open book the feelings in their hearts as he came towards them a
minute before. Embarrassed, repentant, and subdued by his prestige,
the Five were ready to hear him and become converted to the Good
Law.

The First Sermon: Setting the Wheel in Motion [13]

WHILE these preliminaries were going on, night came, a beautiful,
clear moonlit night. During the first watch the Predestined One remained silent; during the second watch he held a friendly conversation;
it was only with the coming of the third and last watch that he at last
began his real sermon. With a shrewd sense of the prejudices that were
still in his five listeners' minds, he began with a justification of his having given up the excesses of asceticism. His sudden interruption of his
austerities had been due, not to a passing weakness, but to a firm and
thoughtful resolution:

> There are two extreme ways into which the religious must not fall.
> What are these? One is the life of pleasure given over to enjoy-
> ment; such is a lowly course, gross, vulgar, unworthy and empty,
> which does not lead to salvation. The other is a life of austerity
> given over to maltreating the body; such is a painful course, useless
> and which leads nowhere. Avoiding both extremes the Predestined
> One discovered and teaches the middle road which leads to peace,
> to knowledge, to Enlightenment and Nirvāna.

A brief commentary may not be amiss here. The Buddha seemed to
be concerned only with clearing up the unfortunate misunderstanding
that came between himself and his former colleagues; but, in truth, the
canonical text had a double aim. The laxity of the monastic rule of the
Buddhist Community was one of the constant criticisms made by rival
sects, and it was most important to put the refutation of this criticism
in the mouth of the Predestined One at the very beginning of his
preaching. It was also useful to warn the neophytes in advance of the
considerable role, in both the theory and the practice of the Good Law,
of the displayed predilection for the "middle way."

Pushing this critical point aside temporarily, the Master immediately went on to expound what has always been considered by his faithful the heart of his doctrine. We have already witnessed above the genesis of his discovery; but this time it was not presented as if it were arising in his mind, nor did he begin anew the construction or analysis of the series of the Twelve Conceptions reciprocally conditioned. The new formula, which the texts unanimously attributed to him (and there is nothing to prove that, barring some minor interpolations, he was not its author), assumed a didactic and mnemonic turn suited to the use of catechumens.

Defining in turn and in technical terms the existence, origin, the suppression and handling of evil, the Master stated in four propositions the therapy for human suffering. However, it should escape no one that the first two arguments are important in pointing up the two essential links—suffering and desire—while the two that follow limit themselves to stating the result of his pondering over the chain of sequences first in reverse order and later in the negative. So the doctrine has not advanced.

One: "Here is the noble truth of the origin of suffering: birth is suffering; old age is suffering; illness is suffering; death is suffering; being united to what one does not love is suffering; being separated from what one loves is suffering; in short the whole make-up of our being is suffering." [14]

Once more our starting point is the existence of suffering (*duḥkha*). It is clear that the word initially signifies human suffering in its many forms—physical as well as moral pain—but will end by meaning the evil of living, metaphysical evil. What we have translated by "the make-up of our being" is expressed in technical terms by "five aggregates, 'heaps' (*skandha*)," which in coming together constitute the mosaic of mosaics, which is in fact our illusory, transitory, and miserable personality. The old term "name-and-form" made distinct the physical and mental elements within us. The Buddha came upon these as already vaguely formulated and catalogued in an increasing order of subtlety, depending on whether they belonged to the senses (pleasure, pain, sensations), to the intellect (ideas, concepts), or to the will (tendencies, impulses, volitions)—all finally coming forth in the consciousness of self. By this is meant the universal but ridiculously erroneous feeling that leads each of us to believe that he is *someone,* a substantial and durable entity, placed at the center of the world and distinct from it. It was this most tenacious and morally pernicious illusion in particular which the Buddha decided to combat.

Two: "Here is the noble truth on the origin of suffering: it is thirst which leads us on from rebirth to rebirth with its procession of pleasures and passions seeking here and there its satisfactions: the thirst for pleasure, the thirst for life, the thirst for power."

"Thirst" is nothing more than desire, lust, concupiscence; in short, an avidity for enjoyment which is born without end of its own satisfactions ("such as trying to quench thirst with salt water"). This thirst is at the origin of all our sins as well as of all our torments. The text names only three kinds but, subdivided by the scholiasts, they become a hydra of a hundred and eight heads, each of which inflicts a biting wound on poor humanity.

Three: "Here is the noble truth about the ending of suffering: it is the extinction of this thirst by totally extinguishing desire, banishing it, rejecting it, breaking its bonds and suppressing it."

The first two truths have retraced for us the picture of human life, constantly perturbed and damaged, harassed without end by that insatiable sting of desire. But, as it is written, nothing exists that does not have its opposite. The obverse of illness is health; and the antithesis of sorrow, of worry, of agitation in the human condition is the state of calm, of quiet, of perfect peace—which is called Nirvāna. Let us not speak in this connection of pleasure or joy, of happiness or beatitude, since that would be to fall back in the domain, and under the domination, of passions from which we must liberate ourselves completely. Obtaining this supreme peace of mind is possible, if not easy. Complete extinction of desire by separating us from worldly considerations will *ipso facto* free us from human misery. What more could be wished? What does one who is overcome by his burden ask for if not to be rid of it once and for all? And should it not be enough for one who suffers to be shown the way of allaying his suffering? We are coming to that.

Four: "Here is the noble truth which leads to the abolition of suffering: it is the Noble Eightfold Path, namely—the Right Views, the Right Aspirations, the Right Speech, the Right Conduct, the Right Livelihood, the Right Effort, the Right Mindfulness, and the Right Meditation."

After the statement of evil, the diagnosis of its origin, and the prognosis of its antidote comes the prescription for the cure; and this is within the means of all people of good will, bringing forth nothing new except perhaps in its ending. The commentaries on them also would indicate that the rules for morals are everywhere the same. The Right Views (1) are naturally the orthodox Buddhist views as opposed to the false ones of various other sects. Right Aspirations (2) are the firm intentions of following the path of abstention, of good will and mercy—in short, not to sin in thought. Right Speech (3) and Conduct (4) do away with sinful words as well as sinful ways. By Right Livelihood (5) one can avoid such cruel means of existence as that of being a butcher or a huntsman because of the bad *karma* these inevitably store up. Right Effort (6), or application, as contrasted with indolence and laziness, is the vital energy with which one can stifle all wicked tendencies and re-enforce the good ones. Right Mindfulness (7) or *smriti,* literally meaning "memory," is the faculty not merely of remembering things and concepts but also of keeping alert and in full possession of one's faculties so as to control one's acts, feelings, and thoughts. Finally by *samādhi,* meaning "concentration," appeal is made to the most ecstatic meditations, well known to all Indian *yogīs* but quite different from our pious exercises.

Such are the "Four Noble Truths" or, as could be said, the Four Truths of Noble Souls, or the Four Axioms of the Pure and the Four Dogmas of the Saints. As such, they remain the keystone of the Buddhist catechism. Though the ancient texts make no mention of it, the Buddha deliberately adopted a medical pattern for his doctrine and its application. He first defined the illness that he wished to cure, then he revealed its cause, and, having envisioned its cessation, he prescribed the remedy. Beyond this, nothing troubled him. It remained for the patient to recover from this illness not, as the Brāhmans pretend, by corporal austerities or ritual offerings, but by following a mental discipline that conforms to the directives of a doctor who is both expert and compassionate. The Buddha wished to share his own experience with those who were suffering—having awakened, he wished to awaken them; his thirst quenched, he wished to quench theirs; having found peace, he wished to bring them peace.

The complete cure, absolute Nirvāna, takes a long time—many years and possibly many successive lives of awareness, restrictions, and continual constraints. The course may seem rigorous and slow in producing its salutary effects. But what is all-important is that its efficacy seem certain to those who believe in the transmigration of deeds (if not of souls) and who place their faith in the holy triad of the Buddha, the Law, and the Order.

The Other Side of the Doctrine

WHEN the Blessed One thus set up the Four Strong Pillars of the Good Law for the first time, the "Five of the Fortunate Group" according to the texts, "were delighted to hear him" and, successively, Kaundinya first, all understood it. For this they could not claim much merit. The Master had quickly shown them the way to salvation and, this being the essential point of the doctrine, they could be converted without fear and become ordained monks, even though they still had far to go be· fore penetrating the secret of the doctrine.

Within each of the three great philosophical systems of India knowl· edge is increased on each of two very different planes; on that of com· mon experience, not transcended by the ordinary mind, and on that of esoteric truth, which is the exclusive attainment of the initiates. The limited anthropocentric formula of the Four Noble Truths presents little more than the pragmatic and moralizing side of the Buddha's thinking. It still remains for us to learn from his lips that we are all easy prey to an insidious illusion. Our salvation will become certain only the day we learn that an inescapable impermanence surrounds all phenomena—psychic as well as physical, painful as well as happy—and that the basis of all things is that they have no basis.

So we come to those concepts which the Master himself declared difficult to understand and of such an abstruse nature that he hesitated to incorporate them in a sermon. It is true that they demand a certain skill in the manipulation of abstract ideas, for, although the idea of a world in motion and lacking in stability is not foreign to us, we must make a marked effort in order to conceive it, as well as ourselves, as having no substantial and durable existence. Such, however, is the fundamental thesis of the Good Law and that which has brought on the criticism that it is pure nihilism. This is unfair, as has been demon· strated by T. Stcherbatsky, for the notion of "vacuity," elaborated on at length by Buddhist sects, should be understood not as "nothingness" but as "relativity."[15] There is no doubt that this principle goes back to the teachings of Śākyamuni, for it alone confers unity as well as originality on his whole system. Whether or not he listed interminable *dharmas* or "norms"—understood as the elements or final factors of the world of appearances, the items without link in the states of our consciousness— does not matter, for he did fix the laws of their fugitive appearances. Also his prime concern was apparently—like that of a compassionate healer—with the application of his doctrine to mankind; he left to future theoreticians the task of adapting it to the whole of the universe. Contrary to the teachings of the Vedas or to the rationalists, the Buddhists refuse to claim finding any real substance or any entity beyond the phenomena of experience. As Paul Oltramare [16] expresses it, "While the Vedānta asserts the existence of the being and denies the becoming and the Sāṅkhya asserts both the being and the becoming, the Buddhist denies the being and retains the becoming." Such theoretical divergences were bound to bring forth equally different conceptions of salvation. The Vedāntist wishes for his soul only "non-duality" and reabsorption into the Great Whole, of which it is a particle momentarily separated. For the Sāṅkhya the ideal, on the contrary, is the total isolation of the spirit—its utter freedom from the bonds by which a possessive nature holds him. The Buddhist's goal, however, is "cessation," the pure and simple abolition of the painful course of *saṃsāra*. By turning over to his disciples, as the fruit of his studies and meditations, the double watchwords of "emptiness" and "suppression," the Buddha became, as far as we are concerned, the leader of one of the three great systems of Indian thought.

Here we can only briefly sketch this doctrine, which is especially difficult for people like us to penetrate, brought up, as we are, on spiritual ideas that are really only the heritage of poorly purged animistic superstitions, bequeathed to us by our uncivilized ancestors. Again a comparison may be helpful. An Occidental faced with the identification of a river will first give it a name and trace its course, thus giving it an apparent individuality among all rivers. This first step is of the practical nature of experimental research. On the philosophical side, he will note, as did Heraclitus in the past, the constantly changing character of the ever flowing waters. But it will be difficult for him not to consider the banks as a solid and permanent frame. This is the beginning of disagreement with the Buddhist. In his eyes, not only are the constantly flowing waters made up of a plurality of appearing and disappearing phenomena, but the banks, which shape their course and which temporarily confer upon them a semblance of reality, are no less impermanent than they. That is not all, and the Greeks have already said it: It is not possible to bathe twice in the same river. To go further, the bather who comes back today to bathe at the same place is not the same man he was yesterday. Just as the river is nothing more than the passing of millions of separate drops of water between ever changing banks, so what we call "self" is nothing more than a flux of conscious states passing through a psycho-physical organism, whose only stability is the existence it acquires from them.

In short, the molds through which our perceptions of things flow are no less of an illusion than the perceptions themselves. The formative elements, formations and forms, finally fade away in the same mirage. Expressed in technical terms, the *samskāra* are no less impermanent than the *dharma*. Experience teaches us that there is a kind of link between things, and to explain this the Buddha stated that between these multiple *dharmas,* each one distinct and momentary, there exists a law of causal dependence which orders them in a continued series. And it is this very continuity which, deceiving the ignorant and the stupid, causes them to stumble into the worst error, namely the belief in the true existence of a personal self.

Once this heresy has been disposed of, everything becomes as clear in the disciple's mind as it was in the Master's system. He then knows himself to be only the unreal and impermanent location of a fleeting series of mental phenomena—the only ones that really count. Not only is he always in a state of transformation, as an embryo, a child, an adult, and an old man, but at no moment of his life does he remain the same person he was the moment before. It then becomes nonsense to wonder if the individual who is reborn is the same who died or another. Being an entity, he is nothing more than "a bit of history," to borrow a phrase from the biologist Le Dantec.

Once a man has learned this and has become convinced of the impermanence and the unsubstantial character of his self as well as of the world, the futility of desires as well as the emptiness of their objects will become obvious. Then the selfish passions that hold this transitory person fast to the cycle of *samsāra*—to the Great Wheel of Rebirths, which is forever turning in the background of these concepts—will spontaneously release him. Once these attachments have lost all their power to hold him, there will emerge the possibility for him to put an end to the flux of the *dharma* by following the only remaining one among them, which is unconditional, impassive, and immutable— namely, Nirvāna.

All this holds together with great coherence, and as soon as these ideas took hold in the various schools of thought it was this concentrated theory that best served the objectives of Buddhism and the Good Law. The new credo can be found engraved on votive offerings in this famous stanza: [17]

> Of all the things that proceed from a cause,
> The Buddha the cause hath told;
> And he tells too how each shall come to its end,
> Such alone is the word of the Sage.

Here is the expression of what could be called the fifth great truth, that of universal emptiness. What is important for us to remember is that this new credo was derived from the coordinated Formula of the Twelve Productions, as were the four propositions. The two aspects of the formula are quite distinct, depending on whether one is seeking the alleviation of evil or is interested only in the reciprocal interplay of causal dependences. Thus the needs of the intellect may be just as well satisfied as those of the heart.

It was up to the five disciples, thanks to the above, to understand the principle that ordains the evolution of all phenomena and at the same time to catch sight, through the transitory character of the self and the world, of the only chance available for an escape from its painful mechanism. To help them do this, the Master tirelessly hammered out his comments on the original formula, starting with either of these points of view. While the four propositions of his inaugural sermon set forth the practical application of the formula, the above stanza in proclaiming the universal contingence of causes and effects briefly summed up its spirit. One was the moral aspect and the other the metaphysical, but the latter was practically unheard by the Blessed Group of the five early converts. The first of the Four Noble Truths barely touched, in passing, upon the composite nature of the five heterogeneous aggregates whose ephemeral combination is the cause of what we call our personality. A second sermon was soon to clarify this in great detail. Successively the Master asked without fail concerning each of the five *skandha:* "Is it eternal or perishable? It is perishable. Does what is perishable cause pain or pleasure? It causes pain. Can what is perishable, painful, transitory be considered mine, be what I am, be my self? Evidently not, Master!" And thus it became clear that there was no self.

Though the First Sermon spoke of only the Four Noble Truths, which were in themselves new enough, the Master repeated them three times to ensure a better understanding by his five listeners. Each truth was expounded in turn, each had to be understood; each was fully understood. And because there were four in number, the Wheel of the Law, set in motion by the Blessed One and by no one before him except his Buddha predecessors, is said to have "turned three times" and in "twelve ways."

The Symbolism of the Wheel

IT seems important to give some explanation concerning the symbol that the Buddhists adopted to indicate and to represent figuratively the preaching of their Master. We already know that the wheel was the first of the seven Jewels of the Universal Monarch or *Cakravartin,* "the one who sets the wheel in motion." It also must not be forgotten that the Bodhisattva might have become the sovereign of the universe, had he not preferred to conquer a spiritual empire. For the Indian, the wheel as symbol for the universe would serve just as well as symbol for the spiritual empire, and so the "setting of the Wheel of the Law in motion" became a synonym for the First Sermon insofar as it brought a new moral order into the world.

The metaphor, of course, rapidly took on a concrete representation, and at the precise moment of the First Sermon the *Lalitavistara* had a special Bodhisattva bring Śākyamuni a beautiful wheel set with precious stones and with a "thousand light rays" radiating from its hub. Miniature reproductions were soon to be sold as *ex-votos* or mementos by vendors in the Deer Park. Aśoka, conforming to the quickly established custom, had this same symbol crown the column put up by him on the site of the First Sermon. The ancient school of Indian sculptors in turn represented the First Sermon by a wheel set on a throne between two oriflammes. Later, when the Indo-Greek school placed the Buddha on the throne and surrounded him with the Group of the Five, it continued the tradition by having him rest his hand on the wheel with or without a deer on each side. The monks were already represented in Buddhist garb, thus indicating that with the setting of the Wheel of the Law in motion, the Order had been founded. From then on the holy triad of the Buddha, the *Dharma,* and the *Saṃgha* was complete and was ready to help towards salvation all who had faith.

Would that it had ended there; but the slope of symbolism is frightfully slippery, and just as the idol usurps the place of the god, so the concrete object is substituted for the idea for which it stands. Such became the fate of the Wheel of the Good Law. One wonders what the Buddha, the enemy of all superstitions, would think of the modern prayer wheels and prayer rattles.

CHAPTER VIII

THE FIRST CONVERSIONS

I T has been written that the Buddha, in attaining his degree of perfection, had done all that was required of him.[1] Having achieved
detachment from terrestrial things, he was under no obligation to take
part in the activity that surrounded him during the few remaining
decades of his life. It was as if he had mysteriously gone through the
unsilvered looking glass of perfect saintliness and no longer belonged
to this world. Thenceforth, nothing could disturb his serenity. His
charity consisted only of receiving alms, which were a source of infinite merit for his benefactors. His triumphs were without peril and
his compassion free of sorrow. This transcendental passivity is constantly
seen in the scenes of his life, and the Indian school of art was able to
represent many of his miracles simply by indicating his presence by a
symbol. When the Indo-Greek school finally made his person the central figure in its compositions, it was in hieratic attitudes and with the
serene immobility of the idol he was destined to become.

The same is true of the texts as of the figured monuments, but the
writers, being obliged to preserve chronological order, were not able to
achieve quite the same effect. The author of the *Lalitavistara,* feeling
that his task ended with that of the Master, ended the biography of the
Buddha just after the First Sermon. Fortunately, all our sources do not
go dry at the same time. The *Mahāvagga* related in great detail the
resounding conversions obtained in the Magadha, when the Master
was in the prime of his supreme Enlightenment. The *Mahāvastu* and
the *Abhiniṣkramana Sūtra* did likewise and even gave us ample detail
concerning the Buddha's first visit to his native city. Finally, the *Nidāna-
Kathā* did not end before recounting the acceptance of the Jētavana
offering. According to all evidence, the history of his last year, as that of

his early years of teaching, seems to have remained sharpest in the memory of his Order.

It is not astonishing that the first three of these texts, which claim to be part of the Scriptures concerning the monastic discipline, gave so much space to the biographical details of the Buddha's life. They wished to have the monastic rules that controlled admission to the Order go back to the Buddha. As we have seen, the fact of his Enlightenment automatically caused the Blessed One to become a monk, and it had to be so in order to give him the right to ordain others. It also goes without saying that the first ordinations, carried out by the Master himself, acquired in time a miraculous character. It would have been enough for him to extend his hand and let fall from his lips the traditional formula: "Come, begging monk, and practice the religious life to end suffering," and the neophytes, whether one or a thousand, instantly lost all the external marks of their previous condition and found themselves clothed in monastic robes, with heads shaved and begging bowls in hand—"in every way similar in their bearing to monks ordained one hundred years ago." [2]

Later when conversions became far too numerous and the sphere of influence spread to all of Central India, the Buddha was obliged to extend to members of his Order the right and duty of recruiting their own members. At first he would have thought it sufficient for the admission of monks as well as lay believers to use the formula of the "Three Refuges." Each would simply have to repeat three times, while respectfully squatting on the ground, "I place my trust in the Buddha, in the Law (*Dharma*) and in the Order (*Saṃgha*)." But the candidate as a *bhikṣu* must already have had his head shaved and must be dressed in the three garments of the monastic robes, and after that he had acquired "his leave of the world."

Soon the Buddha, for all his omniscience, learned from experience the necessity of making admission into the Order more difficult.[3] Since then it has been required of the neophyte, before complete ordination, that he be at least twenty years old, that he have spent some time as a novice, and that he be presented to a chapter of no less than ten monks by a responsible spiritual director of at least ten years' experience. The monks before whom he appeared were expected to put him through a question period according to certain rules. We need not worry over these liturgical details, for all the investitures that we are to review, from that of the first five disciples to that of the five hundred young Śākyas, whether magically achieved or not, were carried out by the Master himself. It was only when it came to his son Rāhula and his half-brother Nanda that he preferred to have his disciples carry out the usual rules for the novitiate of the first and the ordination of the second.

The Benares Conversions

LET us then follow the thread of our story to the point where it will snap in our fingers. We left the Buddha in the Deer Park busy with the indoctrination of his five former colleagues. All the texts agree that Kauṇḍinya was the first to understand and Aśvajit the last to grasp the meaning of the doctrine. The Pāli tradition early gave the latter a modest role in bringing about the conversion of the two Great Disciples. As for Kauṇḍinya, the alertness of his intelligence was responsible for his being called the "Knower." This implies that he was the "Knower of the Good Law." It is also thought that he outlived the Master and that fifty years after his ordination he took part in the Council of the Elders, supposedly at Rājagṛha, which was held for the purpose of defining the canon of the Scriptures immediately after the death of the Blessed One. When they came to the *Sūtras,* Ānanda began to recite that of the Four Noble Truths and that of the Impermanence of the Self—the very ones that Kauṇḍinya had heard the Master preach for the first time in the Deer Park. Overcome by the emotional impact of his early memories, the old monk twice fainted.

Legend, always alert in gathering in all data, remembered that there was someone admirably suited to become one of the early converts: the nephew of the great *rishi* Asita. He had promised his dying uncle that as soon as he learned of the Buddha's Enlightenment he would hasten to hear him. To do so became all the easier for him, for he had entered a Brāhman order near Benares. Converted at once and becoming known as Mahā Kātyāyana, he became one of the great Buddhist missionaries. He is said to have spread the doctrine throughout western and northern India and even into the heart of the Pamirs.

The story of the conversions also mentions another figure who had good reason to watch out for the coming of the new Buddha. This was the king of the serpent jinni, Ēlāpattra.[4] This *nāgarāja* lived on the way to Taxila, traveling towards the Indus, in a marvelous bubbling spring with a considerable flow of water. Today its location is called Hasan-Abdal, and Hindus and Moslems, for once in accord, continue to venerate this spring under the invocation of the *guru* Nānāk, and its Sikh guardians jealously keep the area free of the impurity of tobacco smoke. We should know that at the time of the Buddha Kāsyapa, the immediate predecessor of our Śākyamuni, Ēlāpattra was one of his monks who was condemned to be reborn as a *nāga* in punishment for an impatient gesture. This consisted in angrily brushing off a cardamom leaf from his forehead when it disturbed his meditation. He was only to be absolved from this punishment by the next Buddha, and therefore he lost no time in coming to the Deer Park to seek release. Some say he came as a tremendous many-headed reptile, others claim as a Brāhmanic novice still with damp hair and hands.[5]

The older tradition did not hold by these ancient fantasies. Among the many inhabitants in Benares a large number, suffering from what has been called *mal du siècle,* were desperately trying to find an answer to and a remedy for the inexplicable miseries of the human condition. They hoped to find both in the assurance and peace of a new religion. Being in the throes of the same spiritual agony from which the Buddha had victoriously emerged, these seekers were ready for his doctrine. The first and most famous of his lay converts was the son of a rich banker of Benares whom the texts call Yaṣa, Yaṣaṣ, or Yaṣodeva. We even know about his anterior birth.

His father, distressed because he had no children, at his wife's instigation, turned to the jinni of a large Indian fig tree who was known to satisfy all requests made to him. The would-be father promised to build the jinni a temple in exchange for the satisfaction of his wish; but the sterile wife threatened to chop down the tree in case of failure. The poor sylvan spirit found himself in a quandary, for the request was beyond his powers; but he knew women to be vindictive as well as superstitious. So he in turn sought help from Śakra, the Indra of the gods, who reassured him. There happened to be among the Thirty-three a *dēva* who was reaching the time of rebirth, as was made evident by the signs on his person. As long as he had to "fall," he might just as well be reincarnated in the womb of the banker's wife. After some hesitation, this came about and the birth took place in the banker's family amid great jubilation, and the child was brought up in the midst of luxury and pleasure. His spirit, which had already been purified, did not allow him to become mired in this voluptuous existence, the vanity of which he soon perceived. Many experiences similar to those of the Bodhisattva were attributed to him and he, too, left home under cover of darkness.

Śakra, remembering the promise he had made to Yaśas before re-birth, then led him to the Buddha's retreat on the far side of the river Vānārā. The exalted young man forded the river and fell at the feet of the Master.⁶ The costly sandals that he left on the other bank of the river were a clue to his distressed family, who were looking for him in order to bring him back home. The prestige of the Buddha, however, had its effect on the parents as well as on the boy, and once they had become lay disciples, they could not decently oppose their only son's ordination, no matter how hard it was on them. This sensational con-version started a whole train of others. First Yaśas' four intimate friends followed his example, and soon the contagion spread to fifty of their companions. The disciples who immediately became saints now numbered sixty.

The rainy season being barely ended, the Buddha bade his sixty monks to go forth, each on his own, and preach the Good Law to the people, and he addressed them thus:

> O monks, I am liberated from all human and divine bondage and you too are liberated. So start on your way and go forth for the good and the happiness of many in compassion towards the world, for the benefit, for the good, and for the happiness of gods and men. Do not go two by two on the same road. Preach the Law which is charitable in its beginning, in its middle, and in its end; preach its spirit and its letter. Extoll in the plenitude of its purity the prac-tice of the religious life. There are those who by nature are not blinded by passion; but if they do not hear the Law preached they will be lost—those will become converted to the Law. As for me, I shall go to Urubilvā, the town of the army's chief, in order to preach the Law.

Our sources vary in placing the next magistral catch on the part of the new savior either in Benares or on the way to Urubilvā. There he converted in a body thirty young merrymakers who had formed a kind of club for their own enjoyments. One day they went on an outing in the country and brought along a courtesan for the one unmarried mem-ber of the group. As they were disporting themselves in the bath this unscrupulous woman gathered up their adornments and fled. When they realized what had happened, they ran here and there looking for the culprit—and ran right into the Buddha. Of course they asked if he had seen the thieving woman. His answer might have fallen from the lips of Socrates: "So, what do you think, young men—is it better for you to go in search of this woman or in search of yourselves?" No more was needed to settle their destiny. The Master's voice caused them to turn within themselves, and, giving up their happy frolic, they listened patiently to his indoctrination. So there were thirty more monks, but we are not told what became of the twenty-nine wives they so rapidly abandoned.[7]

The Urubilvā Conversions

THE reason for the Buddha's return to the site of his Enlightenment so soon after the Benares conversions was that he dreamed of an even more miraculous catch of souls. He must have known as soon as he came to Urubilvā that there were in the neighborhood at least three important orders of Brāhmanic anchorites, directed by three brothers who were said to be descendants of the great *rishi* Kāśyapa. The members were recognized by their large mop of hair and by their garments made of bark. They lived in huts built of branches on the edge of the jungle, with their novices and their flocks. Thanks to these, they were practically self-sustaining and, withdrawn in the forest, they practiced their sacrifices, studied, and meditated in their own way. They thus formed a sort of colony or a Brāhmanic outpost in a country still poorly Aryanized. Their austerities, their complicated rites, their mythological and cosmogonic traditions, along with their literary and grammatical knowledge of "the perfect language" (Sanskrit), had quickly brought them popular veneration.

The feat of converting members of this colony to the new doctrine seemed in itself a most difficult one, for the Buddhist negation of the self and the "Being-in-itself" was in complete opposition to their own theories. Success with them would mean a brilliant achievement for the future of the Good Law. The Blessed One came back to this area as if carried on the wings of his recent victories. Sure of himself and convinced of his mission of salvation, he began his conquest, but did so in a most subtle manner.

He started by settling in the enemy's camp. The oldest of the brothers, Kāśyapa of Urubilvā, a very old man, could do no more than welcome the Buddha to his hermitage; but soon he perceived the young monk with the shaved head, already popular with the villagers nearby, to be a dangerous rival. Legend admits that the contest between the two became very severe and that the Buddha was forced to make use of all his ability. His triumph over the obstinate pride of his old adversary was achieved only by recourse to miracles—thirty-five hundred of them, said the Pāli texts; five hundred, said the *Mahāvastu,* more conservative than usual. Happily, none of these texts described or even enumerated them all; and the pictorial artists' selections, made from among the most spectacular of them, help us to recognize those that, having remained in the people's imagination, are worthy of our attention.

The fervor of the writers and, following them, of the ancient artists is particularly spent in depicting the comic variations on the theme of "the bewitched hermitage." It does no harm to be amused at the expense of one's adversaries! Sometimes the anchorites' few pieces of furniture or household equipment became invisible just as they were needed; at other times the ceremonial accessories for the sacrifice refused to be handled. Or the wood from the woodpile would not let itself be split or the holy fire to be lit, or the offering would not leave the spoon—then, suddenly, all would become normal again. Each time the Brāhmans were fairly certain that these phenomena, not at all amusing in their eyes, were due to magical power that the "Ascetic Gautama" was able to exert, even at a distance and without any show. But still they persisted in believing themselves to be stronger in magical powers and more eminent in saintliness than their mystifier. Consequently, something more than these childish pranks had to be performed in order to curb their pride, and a sensational miracle was in order. It is, however, important to note that the form of this decisive miracle is different in the two great Buddhist traditions, the Northern and the Southern. For one it took the form of fire; for the other, water.

Both recognized the prodigious feat, but they were not in agreement as to its importance. The Buddha asked Kāśyapa's permission to sleep in the hut in which the sacrificial fire was kept burning, and the old man warned him most sincerely against taking such a risk, for the place was haunted by a wicked dragon that was feared by all. Śākyamuni took no heed of this wise counsel, and as soon as he went in the hut the *nāgā* entered and a terrible struggle ensued. Smoke against smoke appeared, fire against fire, so that the whole structure seemed to go up in flames. In the end the supernatural power of the Blessed One overcame the reptile's fury, and the Buddha's triumph, according to the *Mahāvastu,* won over all the anchorites. The Pāli texts, however, beginning with the *Mahāvagga,* believed that still another miracle was necessary to complete the conversion. The second event, which was completely ignored by the *Mahāvastu,* went as follows:

That same year an unusual thunderstorm broke over the countryside, bringing in its train such torrential rains that the Nairānjanā rose and flooded the hermitage, which was near its bank. Worried over the fate of his guest, old Kāśyapa, showing great kindness, took to a rowboat in search of the Buddha and found him walking with dry feet amid the turbulent waters, undeniably demonstrating the superiority of his supernatural powers.[8] This time the old Brāhman was won over and bowed his tousled head at the feet of the young Tonsured One. All his disciples followed his example.

There are still millions of people to whom these tales are articles of faith. What is bewildering to us is the lack of agreement between the texts, and we again turn to the figured monuments for clarification. In fact the central Indian school and that of northern India treat the motif of the fire in an equally picturesque manner. At Sānchī, as in Gandhāra, we can see the flames coming out of all the openings of the hut, which looks as if it is burning up, while the old anchorites seem stricken with horror and the novices rush forward with jugs of water to put out the fire. But it is only on the Greco-Buddhist bas-reliefs and in the account of the *Mahāvastu* that the Buddha, in person, presents to the distressed Brāhmans the serpent quietly coiled inside his alms bowl. It is in vain that you will seek in the whole Gandhāra repertory the water episode, and the reason for this is as peremptory as it is technical. Never did the Indo-Greeks attempt to represent a river in sculpture. Consequently, they did not try to give a figured representation of the violent overflowing of the Nairānjanā, and it seems most probable that the absence of an image caused the miracle to be forgotten, first in the oral accounts and later in the written stories of the northwest. At least the *Mahāvastu's* silence corresponds to the omission found in the imagery of the north. However, it was child's play for the ancient Indian sculptors to represent running water by a few wavy lines with fish and aquatic birds among them. That probably is the reason why the artists of the eastern door of the great *stūpa* at Sānchī are in complete accord with the *Mahā-vagga* in representing the miracle of the flood on the façade of the left-hand jamb of the doorway.

Another item indicates the influence that the figured monuments had on the context of the legend. As faithful interpreters of popular and therefore simple ideas, the bas-reliefs usually represent the three Kāśyapa brothers side by side—at Sānchī in their rowboat, and in Gandhāra in front of a bowl from which emerges a cobra's head. And yet the *Mahāvagga* definitely stated that the eldest Kāśyapa, of Uru-bilvā, and his five hundred disciples were the first to be converted. With the enthusiasm of new converts, they threw all their accouterments and Brāhmanic utensils into the river, and it was upon seeing these familiar objects floating in the water that the other two brothers, the river Kāśyapa and the one from Gayā, realized that some extraordinary event had occurred at their elder brother's hermitage. Greatly alarmed, they immediately set forth, one with his three hundred disciples and the other with two hundred, and it was then that they, too, became converted.

When the *Mahāvastu* had the thousand anchorites and their three superiors becoming converted at once, it is clear that the writer's inspira-tion was a result of the artists' repeated representation of that scene. However, he was unwilling to sacrifice the picturesque detail of the Brāhmanic material from the hermitage floating downstream on the Nairānjanā, and for that purpose he invented a nephew for the three Kāśyapas. It was explained that he lived further down the river with two hundred and fifty disciples and, when they, too, joined the others above, it brought the total number of converts to twelve hundred and fifty. The ease with which these figures were increased makes one be-lieve that they had already been amplified in the *Mahāvagga* by the last two additions.

The Rājagṛha Conversions

It is admitted by all that the new Buddha, less than a year after his *Sambodhi* and in that very area, had won a spectacular and difficult vic-tory. The fact that a Brāhman order had been converted en masse and had become a Buddhist Community was no small achievement, but that in itself created certain difficulties. To have uprooted hundreds of sedentary beings not only from their false ideas and their futile rites but from their residences and their flocks and provisions as well, and to have turned them into wandering, begging monks, presented the problem of feeding this hungry troop.[9] Neither the village of Urubilvā nor the neighboring hamlets, nor even the town of Gayā, could undertake that task for long. So tradition realized that it was necessary for the Buddha to take his band of new disciples to the capital of Magadha, alone rich enough to supply daily food without difficulty. Of course other reasons were given: the need for the new Buddha to show the inhabitants of Rājagṛha his superiority over the old Kāśyapa and also to keep his promise to King Bimbisāra, supposedly made seven years earlier.

King Bimbisāra

No longer was it as a young and unknown ascetic in search of a master that Śākyamuni returned. He was now the leader of a sect, followed by hundreds of disciples; and the respect paid to him in public by the eldest Kāśyapa was enough to ensure popular devotion. All this was worthy of special honors and we can be sure that the biographers did not let this chance for elaboration slip by. As faithful observers of ascetic rules, the Buddha and his retinue stopped in the royal park outside the walls of Rājagṛha. The *Mahāvastu* claimed that all the city's inhabitants, led by their monarch, went forth to greet them. There followed an extremely useful and interesting list of all the social classes as well as all the working corporations that made up the population of such an Indian capital more than two thousand years ago. Of course a general conversion crowned the demonstration—an unusual item and probably invented later.

The *Mahāvagga* began in a much simpler fashion. The royal visit was carried out according to the rules of protocol and ended with an invitation to dinner at the palace for the following day. The Pāli texts, in turn, organized a triumphal procession on this occasion. Acting as drummer was Śakra, the Indra of the gods, who had descended from his heaven in the shape of a Brāhman novice to sing at the top of his lungs praises to the Blessed One.[10] The rest of the account happily followed a more historical form:

So the Blessed One went to the palace of the king of the Magadha, Seniya Bimbisāra. Having gone there, he sat down with the Bhikkhus

17. The Buddha Preaching.
Sārnāth, 5th century A.D.

18. Conversion of Kāśyapas (the Flood).
Sānchī Stūpa, 1st century A.D.

who followed him on seats laid out for them. Then the king of
Magadha, Seniya Bimbisāra, with his own hands served and offered
excellent food, both hard and soft, to the fraternity of Bhikkhus with
the Buddha at its head. When the Blessed One had finished and
cleansed his hands and his bowl he sat down near him. Sitting near
him the Magadha King Seniya Bimbisāra thought, "Where may I
find a place for the Blessed One to live in, not too far from the town
and not too near, suitable for going and coming, easily accessible for
all people who want [to see him], by day not too crowded, at night
not exposed to much noise and alarm, clean of the smell of people,
hidden from men, well fitted for a retired life?"

And the Magadha King Seniya Bimbisāra thought: "There is the
Veluvana [Bamboo Grove], my pleasure garden, which is not too far
from town and not too near, suitable for going and coming. . . .
What if I were to make an offering of the Veluvana pleasure garden
to the fraternity of Bhikkhus with the Buddha at its head?"

And the Magadha King Seniya Bimbisāra took a gold vessel [with
water in it, to be poured over the Buddha's hand]; and dedicated
[the garden] to the Blessed One [by saying], "I give up this Veluvana pleasure garden, Lord, to the fraternity of Bhikkhus with the
Buddha at its head." The Blessed One, after having taught, incited,
animated, and gladdened the king of Magadha, Seniya Bimbisāra,
by religious discourse rose from his seat and went away.[11]

And thus for the first time the wandering group found itself the
proprietor of a residence (*vihara*) where the traveling *"Bhikkhus"*
would always be sure of finding shelter. In the Bamboo Grove at
Rājagṛha the Blessed One was to spend the following rainy season,
and where during his long teaching career he frequently came back
and stayed for lengthy periods. Soon he was to have, as we shall see,
similar resting places on the edge of most large cities of Central India.

Two Great Disciples

THE most important event that occurred during the Buddha's first sojourn in Rājagṛha, according to general agreement, was the coming of
two great disciples, Śāriputra and Maudgalyāyana. The texts give
ample space to these eminent figures, who were to become among the
members of the Order "the first of those who have a penetrating intelligence" and the other, slightly less elevated, "the first of those who
have magic power."

Upatiśya, called Śāriputra after his mother, and Kolita, called Maud-galyāyana after his clan, came from villages near the capital. Both came from important and rich Brāhmanic families, and together, as friends since childhood, they had brilliantly pursued studies fit for "kings with-out crowns." Their future seemed assured as socially successful. But one day as they attended a large gathering, half pilgrimage and half fair, Śāriputra was struck by the thought that in one hundred years nothing would be left of that multitude, and the indifference of all those people, faced with death and yet bent on pleasure, puzzled as well as sad-dened him. He had little difficulty in sharing with his friend Maudgal-yāyana this profound sense of the vanity of worldly life. Both entered religion under the guidance of Sānjaya, son of Vairatī. His amoral skepticism, however, repelled the two youths, and they decided to seek a better director. Their lucky star, or previous merits, led them to the Buddha, the only Master worthy of them.

Let us turn to the texts themselves—one Pāli and the other Prākrit—for their versions of this occurrence, for the difference in detail will serve to confirm their fundamental accord. The *Mahāvastu* had Śāri-putra meet the Kāśyapa's invented nephew on the road to the capital; while the *Mahāvagga*, believing that the original group of Five had come to join their Master at Rājagṛha, entrusted the role of informant to the least gifted of them, Assajit (or Aśvajit).

From the Mahāvagga (*Pāli Spelling*)
I-23

1. At that time Sañjaya, a paribbāgaka [wandering ascetic] resided at Rāgagaha with a great retinue of paribbāgakas, with two hundred and fifty paribbāgakas. At that time Sāriputta and Moggallāna [two young Brāhmanas] led a religious life as followers of Sañjaya the paribbāgaka; these had given their word to each other: "He who first attains to the immortal [*amata*, i.e., Nirvāna] shall tell the other one."

2. Now one day the venerable Assaji in the forenoon, having put on his under-robes, and having taken his alms-bowl, and with his kīvara on, entered the city of Rāgagaha for alms; his walking, turning back, regarding, looking, drawing [his arms] back, and stretching [them] out was decorous; he turned his eyes to the

ground, and was dignified in deportment. Now the paribbāgaka
Sāriputta saw the venerable Assaji, who went through Rāgagaha
for alms, whose walking [etc.], was decorous, who kept his eyes
on the ground, and was dignified in deportment. Seeing him he
thought: "Indeed this person is one of those Bhikkhus who are the
worthy ones [arahats] in the world, or who have entered the path
of Arahatship. What if I were to approach this Bhikkhu and to ask
him: 'In whose name, friend, have you retired from the world? Who
is your teacher? Whose doctrine do you profess?'"

3. Now the paribbāgaka Sāriputta thought: "This is not the time
to ask this Bhikkhu; he has entered the interior yard of a house,
walking for alms. What if I were to follow this Bhikkhu step by
step, according to the course recognized by those who want something."

And the venerable Assaji, having finished his alms-pilgrimage
through Rāgagaha, went back with the food he had received. Then
the paribbāgaka Sāriputta went to the place where the venerable
Assaji was; having approached him, he exchanged greeting with
the venerable Assaji; having exchanged with him greeting and
complaisant words, he stationed himself at his side; standing at his
side the paribbāgaka Sāriputta said to the venerable Assaji: "Your
countenance, friend, is serene; your complexion is pure and bright.
In whose name, friend, have you retired from the world? Who is
your teacher? Whose doctrine do you profess?"

4. [Assaji replied]: "There is, friend, the great Sāmañña Śākya-
putta, an ascetic of the Śākya tribe; in His, the Blessed One's name
have I retired from the world; He, the Blessed One, is my teacher;
and His, the Blessed One's, doctrine do I profess."

"And what is the doctrine, Sir, which your teacher holds, and
preaches to you?"

"I am only a young disciple, friend; I have but recently received
the ordination; and I have newly adopted the doctrine and discipline. I can not explain to you the doctrine in detail; but I will tell
you in short what it means."

Then the paribbāgaka Sāriputta said to the venerable Assaji:
"Well, friend, tell me much or little as you like, but be sure to tell
me the spirit [of the doctrine]; I want but the spirit; why do you
make so much of the letter?"

5. Then the venerable Assaji pronounced to the paribbāgaka
Sāriputta the following text of the Dhamma: "Of all objects which

proceed from a cause, the Tathāgata has explained the cause, and He has explained their cessation also; this is the doctrine of the great Sāmañña."

And the paribbāgaka Sāriputta, after having heard this text obtained the pure and spotless Eye of the Truth [that is, the following knowledge]: "Whatsoever is subject to the condition of origination is subject also to the condition of cessation." [And he said]: "If this alone be the Doctrine [the *Dhamma*], now you have reached up to the state where all sorrow ceases [i.e., Nirvāna], [the state] which has remained unseen through many myriads of Kappas [world-ages] of the past."

6. Then the paribbāgaka Sāriputta went to the place where the paribbāgaka Moggallāna was. And the paribbāgaka Moggallāna saw the paribbāgaka Sāriputta coming from afar: seeing him he said to the paribbāgaka Sāriputta: "Your countenance, friend, is serene; your complexion is pure and bright. Have you then really reached the immortal, friend?"

"Yes friend, I have attained to the immortal."

"And how, friend, have you done so?"

7-9. "I saw, friend, the Bhikkhu Assaji, who went through Rāgagaha for alms [etc.]. But I will tell you in short what it means."

"Tell me much or little as you like, but be sure to tell me the spirit [of the doctrine]; I want but the spirit; why do you make so much of the letter?"

10. "Then, friend, the Bhikkhu Assaji pronounced the following Dhamma sentence: 'Of all objects which proceed from a cause, the Tathāgata has explained the cause, and He has explained their cessation also; this is the doctrine of the great Sāmañña.'"

And the paribbāgaka Moggallāna, after having heard [etc., as in paragraph 5, down to the end].

I–24

1. Then the paribbāgaka Moggallāna said to the paribbāgaka Sāriputta: "Let us go, friend, and join the Blessed One; that He, the Blessed One, may be our teacher."

[Sāriputta replied]: "It is on our account, friend, that these two hundred and fifty paribbāgakas live here [as followers of Sañjaya], and it is we whom they regard; let us first inform them also of our intention; then they may do what they think fit."

Then Sāriputta and Moggallāna went to the place where those paribbāgakas were; having approached them, they said to the paribbāgakas: "Friends, we are going to join the Blessed One; that He, the Blessed One, may be our teacher."

[The paribbāgakas replied]: "It is on your account, Sirs, that we live here, and it is you whom we regard; if you, Sirs, are about to place yourselves under the spiritual direction of the great Sāmañña, we all will place ourselves also under the direction of the great Sāmañña."

2. Then Sāriputta and Moggallāna went to the place where the paribbāgaka Sañjaya was; having approached him, they said to the paribbāgaka Sañjaya; "Friend, we are going to join the Blessed One; that He, the Blessed One, may be our teacher."

[Sañjaya replied]: "Nay, friends, do not go; let us all three share in the leadership of this body [of disciples]."

And a second time Sāriputta and Moggallāna said [etc.]. And a third time Sāriputta and Moggallāna said [etc.]. [And a third time he replied]: "Nay, friends, do not go; let us all three share in the leadership of this body [of disciples]."

3. But Sāriputta and Moggallāna took with them those two hundred and fifty paribbāgakas and went to the Veluvana. But the paribbāgaka Sañjaya began, on the spot, to vomit hot blood from his mouth.

And the Blessed One saw them, Sāriputta and Moggallāna coming from afar; on seeing them he thus addressed the Bhikkhus: "There, O Bhikkhus, two companions arrive, Kolita and Upatissa; these will be a pair of [true] pupils, a most distinguished auspicious pair." [12]

From the Mahāvastu (*As Translated by Foucher*)

So the reverend Upasēna having dressed himself in the morning, having put on his cloak and taken his alms bowl he started out towards Rājagṛha to beg for his food. And the religious Śāriputra caught sight of the reverend Upasēna at a distance coming towards him with a charming way of coming forward and backward, of looking ahead and in back, of extending and withdrawing his arms, of wearing his robes and carrying his bowl as a worthy man who has accomplished his task, with his talents all turned inward, with his spirit meditative, strong, in conformity to the Law, his eyes fixed on the ground at the distance of a yoke before him. And having seen him he felt his soul made completely serene: "In truth the bearing of this monk is attractive; I must absolutely speak to him."

And so the religious Śāriputra approached the reverend Upasēna and, having come close, after having exchanged courteous greetings and a friendly conversation was engaged he remained beside him. Standing beside him the religious Śāriputra said to the reverend Upasēna: "Is your Lordship a master or a disciple?" "I am only a disciple, O reverend." "If it is so, what doctrine does your master teach? What does he preach? And how does he teach his disciples the Law? What do his precepts and his instructions consist in? You must explain it all to me." "I am not learned: it is only of the spirit of the doctrine that I can talk to the reverend." At these words the religious Śāriputra said to the reverend Upasēna:

"It is the spirit which interests me; why attach such importance to the letter?

"It is he who understands the spirit who reaps its benefit,

It is by the spirit that he realizes the price
And we too, after having absorbed
During many days all this collection
Of futile texts and words,
We have each time been previously disappointed."

After these words the reverend Upasēna said to the religious Śāriputra:

"After having shown the phenomena are from a cause the Master indicates its cessation." And then, in truth, the pure and unclouded vision of the Law came to the religious Śāriputra on the spot as he stood there.

And then having understood the Law and rejected the false doctrines, his expectations fulfilled, his doubts dispelled, his thought softened and made active, all his being bending towards Nirvāna, he said to the reverend Upasēna: "Reverend Upasēna, where does your master reside?" "The Master? In the Bamboo Grove, in the field of Kalanda." And having thus spoken the reverend Upasēna continued on his way to the city of Rājagṛha to beg for his food.

The religious Śāriputra went to where the religious Maudgalyāyana was; and the latter saw him coming from a distance with a fresh complexion the color of the lotus and a completely serene morale; and having seen him he said to him: "Fresh and clear is Śāriputra's complexion and his morale is completely serene. Would it be that you have discovered the absence of death and the way leading to it? As a full-blown lotus the material of your robe is fresh and clear and your morale is appeased. Have you somewhere been granted the absence of death, that an aura twice as brilliant radiates from your person?"

"The absence of death, reverend Maudgalyāyana, I have found as well as the way which leads there! He who, say the books, manifests himself as rarely as the flower of the *Ficus glomerata* in the forest, the Buddha, this mass of splendor, He has manifested himself, He, the torch of the world."

At these words the religious Maudgalyāyana said to the religious Śāriputra: "What is the doctrine of the Master? What is his sermon?" To these words Śāriputra answered Maudgalyāyana:

> "The phenomena which are born of a cause,
> The Predestined One has told of the cause,
> He has also told of its cessation:
> Such is the doctrine of the Great Sage."

And then, in truth, for the religious Maudgalyāyana, on the spot, such as he stood the pure and unclouded vision of the Law came to him. And then having understood the Law and rejected the false doctrines, his expectations fulfilled, his doubts dismissed, his thought softened, his thought active, and all his propensities seeking Nirvāna, he said to Śāriputra. "Where does the Master reside, O Reverend?" "Reverend, the Master resides in the Bamboo Park, in the field of Kalanda, among a great community of monks, with twelve hundred and fifty monks. Let us go and find the Master in the Bamboo Park after we have invited Sañjayin, and before the Blessed One we shall practice the religious Life." To this Maudgalyāyana said to Śāriputra: "Let us go straight from here to the Bamboo Park; why bother to go and see that false doctor, Sañjayin?" "Not at all, O Reverend Maudgalyāyana; Sañjayin has not failed us; for it is because of him that we left home."

And so both having gone to the hermitage, they invited Sañjayin, saying: "Let us go to the Blessed One, the great Teacher, to practice the religious life." At these words the religious Sañjayin said to them: "Do not go to the Ascetic Gautama to practice the religious life. I have here five hundred disciples who belong to me: you will guide half of them." "The Law and discipline are well taught by the Blessed One. With him success is in sight and all veils are lifted. We have had enough of waiting in vain for the satisfaction of our aspirations." And so after having invited Sañjayin, they left his hermitage and went towards the Bamboo Park and the five hundred religious went with them while Sañjayin cried out: "It is not one or two or three or four, it is the whole five hundred that Upatiśya takes with him!"

And the Blessed One in the Bamboo Park turned to his monks and said: "Prepare seats, O Monks, for the religious Śāriputra and Maudgalyāyana are coming with a procession of five hundred to practice the religious life near the Predestined One. They will be among my disciples the head pair, the fortunate pair; one the leader of those with great intelligence; the other the leader of those with magic powers." [13]

Legend of course, took to heart the duty of confirming the Buddha's words. With satisfaction he is presented between these two pillars of his spiritual empire, bidding them at times to accomplish delicate missions. When he discussed increasingly difficult problems with the congregation, Śāriputra was the only one capable of following and completely understanding his thought. As to Maudgalyāyana, he ascended and descended at will to the many heavens and hells, bringing back data that enabled him to make innumerable converts. Neither was to outlive his Master (tradition would have it that neither wished to), and in time both retired to their own villages to die.

Their precious relics—real or spurious—were distributed among the monasteries of Buddhist India as the new religion expanded. Emperor Aśoka's pilgrimage would not have been complete if, after the places made holy by Śākyamuni's stay, he had not also visited the *stūpas* of the two great disciples. The Chinese pilgrims found their cult established in numerous monasteries, and reliquaries bearing their names were found among the excavations at Sānchī. It should be noted, to the credit of Buddhist thought, that Śāriputra was recognized as superior to his prestigious brother and even Maudgalyāyana was the first to proclaim that wisdom ranked above magic.

Mahākāśyapa

AŚVAGHOṢA went on to tell of the conversion of the great disciple, Mahākāśyapa.[14] He, too, was the son of a very rich Brāhman of Magadha, and it is said that his father was second only to the king in the number of his servants and the size of his property. This child, who had come late, showed at an early age the most utter contempt for the goods of this world as well as an invincible distaste for pleasures of the flesh. Against his will, he was married to a beautiful young girl from Vaiśālī, but happily he discovered that she shared the same dislike for gross sensuality, and for twelve years they lived together in complete chastity. In a spirit of austerity they slept apart on the low beds prescribed by religious rules. One night the husband saw that a black snake had come into their room and was dangerously near his sleeping wife's hand, which was touching the floor. Quickly he grasped her arm and, rudely awakened, his wife accused him of having had unchaste thoughts. Thereafter they decided to give up their rigorous endeavor and to separate in order that each might enter the religious life.

At first sight the Buddha and Kāśyapa felt that they understood each other. It is even said that the Master exchanged his cloak for that of his new disciple and asked him to share his seat. Thus was established ahead of time the reason for Mahākāśyapa's eminent role the day after the Buddha's death. A later tradition, trying to extend his functions of maintaining the Good Law, attributed to him the right of transmitting the Buddha's powers to his successor, Maitrēya. Mahākāśyapa is said to have remained in a state of ecstasy inside one of the Magadha hills awaiting the reappearance of the Buddhist Messiah so that he could place upon him the monastic cloak of Śākyamuni.[15]

Popular Reactions

So many important conversions were bound to increase the prestige of the new Order in the eyes of the people. The notable examples of so many highly placed religious or social figures who gave up the secular Vedic culture and adopted the diametrically opposed doctrine, taught by a young and barely known monk, had two simultaneous effects: increased preaching on the part of the new leader and numerous new conversions. Though the latter were often from unknown families, people were troubled by what they felt was a general social disruption. We have already mentioned this discontent, which spread among the inhabitants of Magadha due to the epidemic of religious vocations, caused by the young Śākya. Tradition has preserved the memory of this conflict in two stanzas.

The *Mahāvagga* gives the following account:

At that time many distinguished young Magadha noblemen led a religious life under the direction of the Blessed One. And the people were annoyed, murmured and became angry: "The Sāmañña

Gotama causes fathers to beget no sons, the Sāmañña Gotama causes wives to become widows and families to become extinct. Now he has ordained one thousand anchorites and then the two hundred and fifty followers of Sañjayā and these many distinguished young Magadha noblemen are now leading the religious life under the direction of the Sāmañña Gotama." And when these people saw the Bhikkhus they reviled them with the following stanza:

"The great Sāmañña has come to the Capital of the Magadha people;
He has converted all the disciples of Sañjayā
Who will be the next to go?"

And the Bhikkhus heard those people who were annoyed, murmured, and became angry; and they told this thing to the Blessed One. [He said to them] "These rumors, O Bhikkhus, will not last long; they will last only seven days; after seven days it will be over. If people revile you, answer them with this stanza:

'The great heroes, the Predestined Ones
Lead men by the true Law;
Who will murmur at the wise
Who lead men by the power of the Law?' "

Then the people understood and the noise lasted only seven days, and after seven days it was over.[16]

And in fact, what was there to be said? The Buddha forced no one, and the Order was already closed, not only to the very ill and to criminals, but to all whose conversion would cause harm to third parties, such as young children, slaves, men in the king's employ, and debtors who would thus find a way to avoid honoring their debts. The argument seemed to silence the people of Magadha. Nevertheless, the Buddha, although the possessor of only a small part of the truth, sincerely felt that he had it all, and this gave him the invincible strength to become the most pitiless of saints after having been the most compassionate of men. The salvation of human beings, in the way his Indian contemporaries understood it, was all that mattered to the Indian savior. His case is not unique. We need only recall the Gospel of St. Luke:

And he said unto them, Verily I say unto you,
There is no man that hath left house or parents or brethren, or wife or children for the kingdom of God's sake,

Who shall not receive manifold more in this present time, and in
the world to come life everlasting.[17]

Just as the mendicant monk is really the only true Christian, the
bhikṣu is the only true Buddhist, and if everyone had listened to the
above reforms, human society would have been completely overthrown
and eventually destroyed. The Buddha "did not come," any more than
did Christ, "to bring peace on earth, but far more to divide families."
He gave us new, clear proof of this when he returned to his native city
after seven years with the aim of converting, willy-nilly, all his relatives.
At this juncture we can easily see the truth in a humorous statement
made by an Irish missionary in India. In reply to a question in the catechism: "Who are the Saints and the Martyrs?" the answer came back:
"The saints are the saints, and the martyrs are those who live with the
saints."

The Conversions in Kapilavastu

WE shall again try to reproduce the oldest account we can find of the
conversions in Kapilavastu, disengaged from ornamentation applied
later. While the Blessed One, in the plenitude of his perfection, was residing in the Bamboo Grove in Rājagṛha, his renown reached his compatriots, the Śākyas, and it aroused their desire to see him again. As
usual, they turned to Śuddhodhana, and the good king, always kind to
their requests, decided to send his son an urgent invitation. Udāyin,
son of the court chaplain and a former playmate of the Master, was
chosen to carry the message. Chandaka, the faithful horseman, could
not be forgotten, and he has often been associated with Udāyin's first
overtures.[18] No sooner had they reached the Buddha than he urged
them to convert. Neither one had the slightest inclination to do so, but
having received official instruction to conform in every way to the
former prince's desires and also thinking this would in no way be final,
they decided to accept. They saw no barber ready to shave their heads
nor monastic robes prepared for them, but they had not reckoned with
the Blessed One's magic powers. The five words of the ritualistic formula that he pronounced transformed them into properly equipped
monks on the spot.

Later versions thought it entertaining to have the king successively dispatch nine of his ministers with their retinues to his son, each time with the same result: in the immediate presence of the Blessed One they and their suites became converted and promptly forgot everything pertaining to the outside world, including their mission. Only Udāyin remembered, and he told his former playmate that he had come with the hope of bringing him back to Kapilavastu. With the help of divine intervention from the Śākyas reborn in heaven, the Buddha was brought to a kindly acceptance. So it was that at the end of seven years he turned his thoughts and his face towards his native city.[19] Udāyin, not letting a moment slip by, induced the Master to take advantage of the autumn season, the best for traveling, when it is neither too hot nor too cold. Finally the Buddha started on his sixty-day journey with sixty stopping places between Rājagṛha and Kapilavastu.

In the early texts we find an episode that seems to have some authenticity. King Śuddhodhana had not yet forgiven his son for the "Great Departure," which had caused the cruel disappointment of his dynastic expectations. Of course he started out, as is seemly, to welcome the Blessed One but, meeting on the way some monks coming to beg in the city, he could not stand the idea that his heir, the prince, had become like them. After ordering these mendicants not to come before his eyes, he had his four-horse chariot return to the palace. Was it on his part a forewarning of what a spiritual cyclone the Buddha's coming was to let loose upon his people? At any rate, it was now the Buddha's turn to send Udāyin as an emissary to the king with the task of making him understand that it was as honorable to be the father of a Savior of the world as of a Universal Monarch. It was only after having been thus appeased that Śuddhodhana organized a procession similar to that of Bimbisāra in the past, to welcome the Master who, according to the rules, stopped on the outskirts of the city in the Banyan Grove. From that point on, the texts are again in accord.

The Buddha was not unaware of the fact that no one is a prophet in his own land, that most of the Śākya nobles had known him as a child, and, what is more, that he was going to come face to face with his father. But he also knew that a Predestined One may not rise, much less bow, before anyone, for he who accepted such an excessive honor would have his head fly into seven pieces. How to solve such a difficult question of protocol on the one hand and terrible sanctions on the other? Obviously he could only resolve the problem by manifesting his magical powers. This he did by creating a magic platform as high as a palm tree, upon which he walked back and forth to the amazement of the Śākyas. Before such a prodigious feat all can bow, and Śuddhodhana himself "adored his son for the third time."

This scene was represented two thousand years ago in great detail on one of the panels of the eastern archway of the great *stūpa* at Sānchī. There can be seen the procession, with chariots, horses, elephants, guardians, and musicians leading; the inhabitants at their windows watching; others winding their way through the tortuous streets of Kapilavastu and out of the city to the hermitage of the Banyan Grove. The king and the court have stepped out of their chariots and are all looking up with hands joined and eyes glued to the airy platform of the invisible Buddha.

The texts even credit the Buddha at this time with the twin miracles of water and fire that later will ensure his victory over the heretical masters. And to add a touching note, Queen Mahāprajāpatī, who had lost the power to cry since the departure of her nephew and adopted son, recovered it while bathing her eyes with the water that had flowed over the Blessed One's body.

Śuddhodhana

AT once the ice was broken between father and son and they engaged in friendly conversation. Still unhappy, the king made much of the painful contrast between the life his son might have led and the one he was leading. He also pitied him for having to walk barefoot, for sleeping on a hard bed, for being without a perfumed bath, without fine clothes, without adornments or gold utensils, without guards, musicians, or women. The Buddha took up each of these points in turn and quietly showed the king that a sage can be happy in the absence of all these luxuries and that the religious state has its own compensations. This dialogue, prosaically treated by early writers, was taken up by the eleventh-century Kashmiri poet Kshemēndra, whom we quote:

> The father speaks: "You who spent delightful nights in beds glistening with the high-lights of silks, on the terrace of a crystal palace, how can you now sleep on the bare forest ground with the rough half-grazed grass stubs left by the deer's tooth?

"You who drank from gemmed cups beverages as pure and fresh
as the moon, ah, how can you now drink from the pond in which
buffaloes and elephants, maddened by the heat, have wallowed and
made the water bitter and dark with their filth?
"How is your throat bare of its necklaces . . ."

and so it went, and the Buddha answered:

I need no more the royal parasol, having the trees of the forest;
my friends are the animals in the woods; my pleasure bed is the
earth; my clothes are made of whittled-down bark of trees; my private purse, the contentment from little; my favorite queen, the compassion for the poor . . .[20]

It must be explained that the justification for all this was the
thought that never before had there been such a spectacular gap as the
one between the Master's princely and luxurious youth and his present
condition as a mendicant monk. After the family exchanges came the
inevitable sermon, and before taking his leave the father invited his
son and the whole community of monks to come to the palace for
their one daily meal. Perhaps he wished to spare himself the shame
of witnessing his son begging for his food in the city streets; but it actually meant that he was bringing into the family's fold a most disrup-
tive element under a most benign appearance.

It would seem that there was no hesitation in putting the Buddha
in the most delicate situation imaginable for a man who had removed
himself from the world. Here we find him having to face all his family:
father, adopted mother, wife, child, half-brother, uncles, cousins, childhood friends—in short, everyone he had left that night long ago without so much as a good-by. What was going to be his attitude? The answer of the canonical texts is easily perceived: His coming back was an
act of pure compassion and his converting them to his Law his most
sincere way of showing them his affection. The truth is that Śuddhodhana was the most recalcitrant convert of all. He continued to resist
conversion long after his three brothers and "myriads" of Śākyas had
embraced the doctrine, and it was only much later that he decided to
give the park where his son had already settled to the Order. It was only
in the more recent texts that Śuddhodhana was brought gradually
through the four degrees of saintliness. In spite of this, the oldest tradition attributed to him an amazing kind of religious conscription. He

requested of all the noble families under his rule that those who had two or more sons turn one of them over to the Buddha to become a monk. His aim, we are told, was to constitute for the former prince a following more worthy of him. It is also possible that in so doing he felt that he could prevent the complete disruption of families, starting with his own. It was made clear that, in accord with the terms of the decree, his second son Nanda (the Master's half-brother) and the Buddha's own son Rāhula were automatically exempt. But the implacable Savior was not to be hampered by any worldly rules, and the ordinations of Rāhula and Nanda are justly the two most noteworthy episodes of the "return to Kapilavastu."

Rāhula and Nanda

IN the case of Rāhula, ordination was rapidly expedited. As women like to believe in what they hope for, Yaśodharā had never given up hope of winning back her husband. The texts and bas-reliefs portray her adorned with all her jewels and pushing in front of her the fruit of their union, then aged six. She had coached the child to ask his father for his inheritance. Yaśodharā had in mind the kingdom, but the Blessed One, who knew better, took her at her word and did not refuse his son the Truth. Since blood will tell, the child would not "leave the paternal shadow," and he was taken to the hermitage, where his father had him ordained by his two great disciples. Yaśodharā was left with her vain hopes and her jewels, much to the grandfather's sorrow.

There was still one more hope for his dynasty and that rested on the "beautiful Nanda." If it was true that Nanda was to marry the prettiest girl in Kapilavastu, be anointed heir apparent, and move to a new palace—on that very day—then his imperious half-brother broke up three festivities at once. To accomplish Nanda's abduction, the Predestined One stooped to a ruse. The kindly Nanda, seeing him beg in the street, left his fiancée and rushed to take his half-brother's alms bowl from him. He returned it at once full of delicacies. The Buddha, with design, refused to accept the bowl, and the poor prince, out of politeness, carried the bowl back to the hermitage.

There, monks overcame him, had a barber shave his head, and then tore off his adornments and clothes in order to put on monastic robes. But even so Nanda's heart had not changed, and this gave the monks a chance to ridicule him for regretting the loss of his beloved. In vain he attempted to escape from the monastery, and in the end the Buddha took him, clinging to the hem of his cloak, to Indra's heaven to cure him of his lovesickness.

As they flew through the air they first saw a female monkey on top of a tree burned in a devastating forest fire; the unfortunate creature had miraculously escaped death, but she was badly burned and her skin was torn and bleeding. Then without transition they came upon the ornamental nymphs of the heaven of the Thirty-three. Upon seeing these celestial beauties, Nanda had to admit that there was as much difference between the nymphs and his fiancée as between her and the female monkey. So he resigned himself to accepting the religious state with patience in the hope that the merits thus acquired would allow him to be reborn in such charming company. As everything becomes known, and especially in a convent, soon Nanda became known as the "lover of the nymphs" until at last, through sheer will power, he was able to rid himself of the vain and passing fascination of feminine beauty. It is easily understood that this anecdote was of abundant inspiration to Indian artists and writers.

The Śākyas

It would seem that a contingent of five hundred young Śākya aristocrats came more or less voluntarily before the Buddha to become disciples. They were richly adorned and when the barber Upali was called upon to shave their heads, they gave him their jewels, for which they no longer had any use. As a result, the poor artisan from a lowly caste became rich, and yet he seemed unable to enjoy his newly acquired wealth. Instead, either because of the irresistible influence of example or because of the "maturation" of his previous merits, he could only dream of becoming a monk himself. According to Buddhist doctrine, his humble birth was in no way an obstacle, and the Buddha agreed to the ritual of instantaneous ordination. The result was that when the five hundred young Śākyas, who in the meantime had gone back to take leave of their parents and friends, came back to the hermitage for their own ordination, they found that Upali, though much their inferior in caste, had become their superior in religion. This meant that they owed him honor and respect. It was not without some difficulty that the Blessed

19. Gift of Anāthapiṇḍāda (Covering the Ground with Gold and the Presentation). Bhārhut Stūpa, 1st century A.D.

20. The Return to Kapilavastu (the Buddha Represented by a Tree).
Sānchī Stūpa, 1st century A.D.

One got them to curb their pride and to bow before the feet of a former servant, for each took his rank in order of his seniority, the only hierarchy allowed by the original Order.

Whether or not the facts given by the legend are to be trusted, a question certainly arises: Did the Buddha's sublime compassion have a beneficent effect on the city of Kapilavastu or did it, on the contrary, act as a scourge? He is said to have carried off the flower of its youth, and if the Śākyas, who in the past were invincible warriors, became impregnated with the Buddhist ideas of nonviolence, these facts may have combined to make them an easy prey to their neighbors. Whatever the cause, the city was eventually destroyed and drenched in the blood of its inhabitants. That catastrophe ended the Kapilavastu cycle, and the truthful testimony of Fa-hsien tells us that as early as the fourth century A.D. the whole region had returned to jungle.

The Gift of Jētavana Park

THE sinister events just mentioned were still the future's secrets when the Blessed One was escorted from Kapilavastu to Śrāvastī in a festive and joyful mood. This move came as a result of an invitation that the Buddha, while near Rājagṛha, had received from a very rich merchant of Kosala. The latter was called Anāthapindada, or "The Incomparable Almsgiver." Having come to Magadha on business, he stopped at the house of an associate and there he met and heard the Master. He then became a lay follower, and with the enthusiasm of a neophyte he begged the Blessed One to honor Śrāvastī, his home town, with his presence. Before giving his promise to do so, the Buddha asked if there might be a hermitage nearby for himself and his monks, and when assured that there would be he had the Great Disciple Śāriputra go with his new zealot to ensure that all would be according to the rules.

The choice of Anāthapindada and the Master's emissary fell on the most beautiful park of the region. It belonged to Prince Jēta, or Victor, and he refused to give the land up, "unless," he said in jest, "it be covered with gold coins." The merchant agreed and, emptying the family treasure-house, covered all the ground with goldpieces. But in order to preserve the shade he made an agreement with the owner not to cover the land on which the most beautiful trees—mangoes and sandalwood—were standing. The prince's spontaneous contribution caused the hermitage to be named: "The Jēta Park, hermitage of Anāthapindada."

Located near the Buddha's native land, in a fertile plain but in sight of the high, snow-capped Himālayas, this beautiful park became one of his favorite residences. There he spent at least twenty-five periods of retreat, which took place every year during the rainy season. Thus the name of the park often appears as the heading for numerous sacred texts, and its donation became a subject found on all ancient Buddhist monuments.

It was to this beautiful park that the Buddha was escorted with great pomp when he arrived in Śrāvastī, and he was full of appreciation for its charm and beauty. Where, in the past, the great of the land had come to enjoy themselves, monks in yellow robes now went to and fro, settling down in separate little huts in the shade of the trees. The Bhārhut artist thought he should represent in advance the "perfumed cabin" that the Buddha was to sanctify by his presence, and he actually named it so on the margin of the sculptured medallion. There it was that the Blessed One led the day-to-day existence that we shall soon describe; there, also, he received the lay faithful who came from everywhere to call on him.

Even today, due to the Indian Archaeological Service's success in bringing the place to light, pilgrims come to worship at this site. At the time of Fa-hsien the countryside, as we have said, was deserted; but nature, indifferent to human calamities, had retained the transparency of the waters and the luxuriance of the lotus flowers and their leaves. The beauty of the site, however, instead of giving pleasure to the travelers, only awakened nostalgia for the past and sharpened the melancholy of their exile.

> They had come [Fa-hsien wrote] at the peril of their life and they now found themselves in a foreign land. Of those who, with the same aim, had, as they had, crossed one after the other so many countries a few were dead, others had returned home; and they, now, while looking with their own eyes upon the place where the Buddha had once lived, but where he was no longer visible, had their hearts torn by regret.

We understand the pathos and share it.

PART THREE

Minor Cycles

CHAPTER IX

DUTIES OF A BUDDHA

UNTIL NOW, not only have we watched step by step the progress of the future Buddha towards Enlightenment, but we have also followed the peregrinations of the Perfect Buddha in quest of his early disciples. His goal having been reached, he, and we with him, could do no more than tread the same ground or at best go round and round within the same circle. No new creative idea came in any way to reorient his life and he found himself personally condemned to repetition.

What does remain to fill in the interval of about forty-five years between the settlement of Jētavana and approaching death? Some bits and pieces, found in the lengthy sacred Buddhist texts, which, though they are really quite numerous, are always incidental and too often obviously invented. They constitute a considerable collection of disconnected anecdotes, at times insipid, at other times picturesque and witty but lost in a sea of homilies. The impression gained from the interminable readings, so full of repetitions, is much like the one made by the immense Ganges valley, where the Predestined One preached. Covered by dust during the dry season and by a green coat when the rains come, it remains flat and denuded, with only an occasional group of trees indicating a village. Similar to those leafy islands scattered over the monotony of that great land, both so gentle and so sad, numerous episodes stand out against the gray background of the Buddha's preaching career. How could it be otherwise when it is said that in the course of his nomadic life he encountered all varieties of beings, from the damned to gods, and all human conditions, from pariahs to kings and Brāhmans? Out of this vast experience grew a wealth of morality tales, from his past lives as well as his present one, amusing or, more often, pathetic —but always aimed at edification. We must confess that it is not edification we are now seeking but selection and classification, which will throw light upon the behavior and the psychology of our Buddha.

We have found that a chronological arrangement of the various scenes and episodes is impractical and that the social classification of their actors is no help, so we turn toward a possible geographical approach. This has already proved most useful for our study, and it corresponds in full to one aspect of Indian mentality. A quick survey of the mass of compiled reminiscences makes them appear grouped, much as planetary systems within a diffuse nebula. The centers of these groupings are the holy cities of the eight pilgrimages, Śrāvastī, Sānkāśya, Vaiśālī, and Rājagṛha.

Daily Life

THE great commentator of the Pāli canon, Buddhaghosa, carefully traced, from the texts that he knew better than any one, a succinct description of the way the Blessed One's daily habits were viewed by people of his time (fifth century B.C.).[1] He rose early, we are told, as is the custom of Indians as well as of people given over to the meditative life. These early moments stolen from sleep gave him time for meditating and for casting his divine eye over the whole of the universe. In due time he dressed to go out and, taking his alms bowl in his hand, he set forth to beg for his food, just like the simplest of his monks. It is recalled what a scandal this was thought to be in his native city. Upon returning to the monastery, he washed the dust off his bare feet, ate his one daily meal before noon, and, while waiting for the members of his congregation to do likewise, sat on the doorstep of his cell. This time was reserved for his spiritual "sons," for their exhortation, their instruction, and their moral guidance. To those who wanted it he gave a suitable subject for meditation, such as the ten objects of disgust and the thirty-two impurities in the human body, followed by more and more elevated and abstract subjects, for this was a religious exercise *par excellence*.[2] Afterwards each monk could withdraw to spend the hot hours of the day as he wished, usually sitting at the foot of a tree in semi-somnolence. This was the hour, if we are to believe the texts, for the demon of the flesh to lurk about, the very same feared by our monks. During that time the Buddha took his afternoon nap, "lying on his right side like a lion," but it was understood that his state lay between sleep and wakefulness so that he never lost the trend of his thought.[3] When the sun's rays became less intense and the temperature dropped, then came the public meeting, open to all and sundry and frequented by the curious as well as the faithful. Once this was over the Buddha bathed and rested a bit.

With the peace and quiet of evening falling on the hermitage, he again belonged to the disciples, and instruction as well as conversation were carried on far into the first watch of the night. More lenient than some of the commentators, we happily let the Buddha have a few hours of sleep instead of having him spend the second watch receiving the divinities and the third divided among a walk, a short sleep, and early morning meditation and contemplation.

It is important to note that Śākyamuni personally accepted and authorized his monks to accept dinner invitations in the homes of his lay faithful of all conditions. On such days the morning begging for food was omitted, and the first talk with his disciples was replaced by a sermon to his hosts. The above routine, of course, could only be followed during the sedentary periods, spent in the groves near the large cities. When traveling, the monks spent much of their time, after the morning begging tour, covering the day's run and looking for shelter.

The Quest for Food

How did the Buddha carry out his round of begging for food? The rules of his Order tell us explicitly that the Master's way was the right one.[4] Not only did he have to be properly robed, dignified in his bearing, contemplative in thought—as we have already described the begging monk—but he must not go directly to the house of a rich lay faithful where he was sure to receive a copious offering of good food. He had to start at the beginning of the street or the market place and go from door to door so that no occupant would be deprived of the opportunity to acquire merits through charity. He also had to have an understanding with his brothers, so that they did not place too great a burden on the same families by repeated demands. As the bee gathers honey without injuring the flower, so must the monk obtain food. Furthermore, he was not to utter thanks or requests—he simply had to stand immobile and silent, with eyes lowered, waiting for the right moment. If it became obvious that nothing was forthcoming, he must go on his way without a word or a look of reproach. Still less, if he possessed some magic power was he to demonstrate it in order to gain some exceptional present. In short, he had to be content with whatever was spontaneously offered, and he always had to accept any offering given with a sincere heart. Of this the Blessed One had given the example one morning when he was begging in a street in Rājagṛha. A child who was playing, as all children do, making mud pies, came to him and lovingly deposited a handful of sand, in lieu of flour, in the great Sāmañña's bowl. The Buddha not only accepted the gift but also predicted that the little boy would be reborn as King Aśoka in recompense for his alms.[5]

Buddhaghosa did not fail to repeat in connection with Śākyamuni the cliché, contained in all sacred texts, that the Predestined One's quest for alms was always attended by special miracles. As soon as he entered a city an enchanted atmosphere reigned—a gentle rain settled the dust before him, birds and animals welcomed him with song and joyous cries, celestial music was heard, and the earth became level under his feet. Alerted by these signs, the inhabitants hurried to bring him their offerings.[6]

However, there were dark sides to this rosy picture. Sometimes in the "Brāhman villages" Śākyamuni and his disciples had to face the stinginess or even the antagonism of the inhabitants. Of course Māra, the great king-turned-devil, was responsible for this, stooping to harden the minds and hearts of people against his sworn enemy and his monks. Sometimes they also met hostile dogs, which, as is well known, have never liked beggars carrying sticks. As a matter of fact, in time the equipment of wandering monks included a long stick with which to ward off biting dogs. This same stick also served to hold a few rings, the tinkling sound of which heralded the coming of the monks. The Buddha himself was never in need of this particular instrument. His coming was always noticed and the following story will show how he dealt with dogs.

One day at Śrāvastī, upon coming to a fine house, he was met by the furious barking of a white dog, the absent proprietor's pet. The Buddha fixed the animal with his eye and said, "Will you stop showing off!"[7] Instantly the dog, lowering his head and, with his tail between his legs, sadly retired to a corner. When Suka, the master, returned, he asked the servants, "Who has hurt the dog's feelings?" "The Buddha,"

they answered. At once the owner hastened to Jētavana to rebuke the
Blessed One, but the latter quickly silenced him by telling him that his
dog was none other than the reincarnation of his proud and stingy
father. If he needed proof of this, he only had to ask the animal to reveal the place where, as a man, the former had hidden the treasure he
had refused to turn over to his son, even when he was dying. No sooner
said than done and Suka, having become richer as well as convinced,
invited the Buddha to dinner.

Invitations

WE have already read about several of the dinners to which the Buddha
and his monks were invited, but we should know something of the
ritual connected with these functions. First, an invitation was addressed
to the Master and he accepted it "by his silence," and it always included
his suite of disciples. On the morning of the event, some representative
of the host came to the hermitage and told the Blessed One that all was
ready and for him "to take his time." This gesture proved that the invitation was genuine and afforded the host the opportunity to learn how
many people were to be fed.[8] In due time the Buddha and his companions arrived at the house of the faithful layman. Seats had already
been set out for the guests but they brought their own bowls, for it
must not be forgotten that they were honorable "outcasts." Had they
not brought their alms bowls, the host would have had the obligation
not only of providing a great many utensils but also of destroying them
after the feast, for they would automatically have become impure.

As soon as the guests were seated, the master of the house and his
family served them but did not eat with them. Some of the Gandhāra
bas-reliefs show us small individual tables set before each guest. Members of the Order were permitted to eat meat and fish on condition that
the creatures were not killed before their eyes and only for them.[9] All
food as well as condiments or sauces must be placed in the bowl itself.
After the meal, all utensils had to be washed, as well as every right hand,
which had scooped up the contents. When all this washing up was over,
the hospitable family came and sat at the Buddha's feet and listened
piously to the short but necessary allocution, through which "he taught,
encouraged, exhorted, and gladdened them." This was his way of thank-

ing his hosts, and once that gesture was made, he rose with his following and returned to the monastery, for no yellow robe was to be seen
abroad between noon and the following sunrise.

Such was the usual protocol but of course there were variations,
since people with small houses did not wish to be deprived of the means
of bettering their conditions of future rebirths by performing the worthy
service of feeding monks. This was done by sending word to the
monastery in the morning that on that day ten or twenty of its occupants would not have to seek their food and that it would be brought
to them there.

There was also the problem of providing food for the Buddha and
his monks or *bhiksus* during their constant journeys, which sometimes
took them through sparsely populated and sterile lands. We are told
that in such cases "the country people, after loading carts with stores of
salt, oil, rice, and hard food, followed the Community of monks with
the Buddha at its head, saying, 'When our turn comes we shall serve
them a meal . . .'"[10] At times these people even took with them a herd
of cows so as to furnish the monks with fresh milk daily. It can easily
be understood that frequently groups of beggars—beggars by necessity,
not by virtue of their vows—would follow the religious caravan and
feed on the leftovers.

Devotion is a fine thing but it must not go astray, else it can lead to
crime. The new sect excited jealousy among the older ones, for it naturally depleted their original groups of faithful laymen. The Buddha
alone, we are told, with his innate sense of what was right, always asked
the neophytes to think clearly before transferring their allegiance to
him and also to continue their charitable acts towards the rival whose
place he was taking. This, however, was not true of the heterodox sects,
which did not hesitate to defend their prerogatives by most evil means.
If we are to believe our sources, Purāna, the superior of one of these
groups, which lived entirely naked, schemed with a layman from
Rājagrha to do nothing less than bring about the death of the Buddha.
He persuaded his devotee to invite the Master to dinner and to dig a
deep trench, such as was used to trap wild animals, in front of his door.
At the bottom were put burning coals and across the top thin branches
covered over with matting. Although he had guessed the evil intentions of his host, the Buddha accepted the invitation and came with his
retinue, but at his approach the burning ditch became a lotus pond

with the flowers forming a bridge under his footsteps and those of his following.[11]

While still in Rājagṛha, the Predestined One predicted to an occasional donor who favored the naked ascetics that his pregnant wife would give birth to a son. The heterodox group, eager to prevent at all costs the fulfillment of their rival's prediction, exerted enough influence on their stupid zealot to make him use abortive measures which caused his wife's death before delivery. Her body was carried to be cremated, and the ascetics were already feeling triumphant when to their confusion there appeared from the mother's funeral pyre a handsome little boy.[12]

Visitors

SUCH tales as the above indicate the type of devotional deceit of which the various sects accused one another, and it gives us a better understanding of the snares daily placed in the Buddha's way by his adversaries. Since the late-afternoon meetings at the hermitage were open to all who wished to come, there was no way of protecting the Master from the machinations of those who wished to lower his prestige before the public. Tricky questions were asked as well as slanderous accusations made. Of these we shall speak later. But one day a heterodox sophist stood before the Master, sitting among his listeners, and he held a sparrow hidden in his hand. He defied the sage to tell him if what he held in his hand was alive or dead. Whatever the answer, the sophist proposed to prove it false, either by smothering the bird or by letting it fly away. But that was the kind of game the Buddha would not enter into, knowing well that he would lose face.

It is thus easy to see why the Master, before entering into a controversial discussion, would always ask his opponent whether or not he was ready to argue in good faith and to keep the debate on the objective plane of ideas. Such was, we hasten to say, the usual state of mind of his Brāhmanic disputants. From the doctrinal point of view, they were the furthest removed from the Buddha, but because of their secure social position they had no reason for using deceitful procedures in discussion. As for the Buddhists, proud of having a prince as their founder, they proclaimed with serene inconsistency that the noble class was superior to that of the Brāhmans—and then went on to preach a doctrine that claimed birth rights to be of no value whatsoever, since all men, except their Master, were born alike. On their side, the members of what has been falsely called the priestly caste surely took account of the fact that Śākyamuni, under his monk's cloak, was still of noble parentage. Thus, a mutual respect was established between him and the scholars of the Brāhmanic schools. This, however, did not lessen the number of sharp disputes that arose between them, with pungent exchanges of words.

It is often said that history only concerns itself with the activities of the great folk of this world, but the fault is not so much that of history as of humanity's servile attitude. We should not then be surprised that the ancient sculptors of Central India should have so often represented the Buddha being received by the kings of his time. Bimbisāra, King of Magadha, had from the time of his conversion remained a faithful friend; and his son Ajātaśatru,[13] after criminally replacing him, also sought in the Blessed One's conversation an appeasement to his remorse. With the other great monarch of Central India, Prasenajit, King of Kośala, the Predestined One maintained courteous if not friendly relations.

Royal visits to the Buddha always followed a rigid formula. It was the monarch who took the first step. Preceded by musicians, surrounded by courtiers, and followed by guards, he advanced in his chariot as far as the road permitted, then continued on foot. At the entrance to the hermitage he stopped with his retinue and removed the five precious insignia of his rank: "diadem, parasol, sword, fly-whisk, and sandals." When he came before the Buddha he prostrated himself at his feet—a gesture that clearly acknowledged the superiority of spiritual eminence over temporal power. But according to Indian ideas the act in no way implied the humiliation of the royal personality.

At the outskirts of all independent cities governed by oligarchs, such as Vaiśālī, Kuśinagara, and so forth, the same ceremonies were repeated over and over as the indefatigable founder of the Good Law made his journeys. Tradition has it that such a show of deference even cost Prasenajit his throne. Having left his five insignia in the hands of his minister while conferring with the Buddha, he then found that his untrustworthy courtier had hurried back to the city and had Prince Virūḍhaka crowned in his place.

It has been written that a visit to the Buddha and his monks was a "supreme blessing," but it must be remembered that for the Buddha these constant callers might have become tiresome. In spite of his great patience he admitted the fatigue that came with the long lines of visitors and the daily public meetings. Because of this, when at the Bamboo Grove in Rājagṛha he liked to withdraw once in a while to the rocky hills, which are one of the picturesque elements in the Magadha plains. There he could meditate in peace. However, nothing prevented the guides of the region from inventing all sorts of tales concerning this rather simple activity as they pointed out the Master's retreat.

The majority of the daily visitors naturally were the lay faithful, mostly shopkeepers of the bazaar or the market place. "Accompanied by their wives, dressed in their finest clothes, bearing in their hands flowers, perfumes, and other offerings," they came, as we would say, "at vespers" to return his call of the morning. They came for various reasons: some simply to hear the Master's sermon or ask for his advice, others with a petition or an invitation. There was also the curious crowd, coming from afar to see with their own eyes and hear with their own ears the great preacher whose reputation was growing daily.

Rarely did anyone fall asleep during the sermon or sit looking about, scratching himself. Every day a growing crowd of people from everywhere and of all conditions clustered around the Buddha, the common people rubbing elbows with the great and courtesans standing next to the most prudish ladies. It was understood that all could come and listen, but it was hoped that no one would leave without having been deeply affected by what he had heard. The inevitable result of the visit should be either adherence to the faith or even conversion.

Adherence and Conversion

IF we dare express ourselves without irreverence thus, the art of taming souls was the Buddha's favorite sport. He himself would have claimed that the most welcome present was bringing a man to be converted. As far as we can tell, he tackled the task with rare skill. He did not launch at once into a long enumeration of the principles and conclusions of the doctrine. That could only be done with those already prepared to receive such fare. The following shows how the Master, as a good psychologist, proceeded:

5. When . . . the noble youth, was sitting near him, the Blessed One preached to him in due course: that is to say, he talked about

the merits obtained by alms-giving, about the duties of morality, about heaven, about the evils, the vanity, and the sinfulness of desires, and about the blessings of the abandonment of desire.

6. When the Blessed One saw that the mind of . . . the noble youth was prepared, impressible, free from obstacles [to understand the Truth], elated, and believing, then he preached what is the principal doctrine of the Buddhas, namely Suffering, the Cause of Suffering, the Cessation of Suffering, the Path. Just as a clean cloth free from black specks properly takes the dye, thus . . . the noble youth, even while sitting there, obtained the pure and spotless Eye of the Truth [that is, the knowledge]: "Whatsoever is subject to the condition of origination is subject also to the condition of cessation.". . .

10. When the *setthi,* the householder, was sitting near him, the Blessed One preached to him in due course; that is to say, he talked about the merits obtained by alms-giving . . . [etc., as at the end of 5 above]. And the *setthi,* the householder, having seen the Truth, having mastered the Truth, having penetrated the Truth, having overcome uncertainty, having dispelled all doubts, having gained full knowledge, dependent on nobody else for the knowledge of the doctrine of the Teacher, said to the Blessed One: "Glorious, Lord! glorious, Lord! Just as if one should set up, Lord, what had been overturned, or should reveal what had been hidden, or should point out the way to one who had lost his way, or should bring a lamp into the darkness, in order that those who had eyes might see visible things, thus has the Blessed One preached the doctrine in many ways. I take my refuge, Lord, in the Blessed One, and in the *Dhamma,* and in the fraternity of *Bikkhus;* may the Blessed One receive me from this day forth while my life lasts as a disciple who has taken his refuge in Him." [14]

The effect of such conversations, we are told, never failed, and, like a refrain, the repeated formula of faith in the Buddha, the Law, and the Order always ended the peroration. We willingly accept this assurance, but we might well ask what it was that the neophyte undertook by the acceptance of this fixed formula. If a lay believer was involved, the undertaking was slight. Groups of devout laymen and laywomen of the type of the banker Anāthapindada and the matron Vaiśākha may have become closely associated with the life of the monastery, but naturally they were rare. On the whole, zealots of both sexes simply pledged themselves not to refuse alms to the Community of monks and to observe the five commandments of the Decalogue required of the monks: not to kill, not to steal, not to commit adultery, not to lie, and not to become intoxicated. This, after all, only means that they were to follow the usual standards of morality. The zealots were not even required to be exclusive in their charity, nor did they have to take any vows or renounce any former beliefs. This in no way could be termed a "conversion," for that word is much too strong for what was only a mental endorsement barely underlined by a loose agreement to contribute in kind according to one's means.

When "mendicant monks" were involved, it was quite another matter. Not only were they obliged to approve and praise the teachings of the Blessed One, but they undertook to follow his example completely and begged from him the favor of ordination. In time, this became less frequent and subject to greater formalities. For them, as for him, acceptance of the religious vocation meant the sacrifice of home, property, caste, and family. The Buddha's sermon at ordination took on a new intent for them. Doing away with any oratorical artifice, it did not fear becoming direct and scholastic, heavy with enumerations and repetitions, which were necessary because the monks had to depend upon their memory to retain the oral teachings of their Master. We recall that the first five disciples as well as later ones were indoctrinated by listening to a series of long repetitions of the various phases of the Doctrine and its exact terms never to be forgotten.

The Buddha and Caste

ACCORDING to the circumstances and due to "the triple prestige of either his supernatural powers, his moralistic precepts, or his dogmatic statements," [15] the Buddha daily extended and consolidated the empire of the Good Law over an ever growing number of disciples. The details of repeated adherences and conversions, of which the sources have retained names and places, cannot possibly be gone into here, and all we can do is to catch a glimpse of how the Buddha understood and practiced his ministering as savior. "Never," we are told, "did it occur to him to say, 'This man is a noble; this man is a Brāhman; this man is rich; this man is poor; therefore I shall preach to this one in preference to the other.'" As the rain falls from the sky, his word fell on all

—young and old, intelligent and obtuse, virtuous and criminal, of humble and of noble parentage—without distinction.

Even caste, that rigid mold which modern India has not yet been able to shed, did not exist for the Blessed One. Occidentals have been so impressed by this that they have tried to make of the Buddha a social reformer. No one would be more surprised than he, should he know of this travesty of his personality and his role. Why try to reform a world that is defined as an unpleasant dream? He might have paid attention to caste in the case of an invitation to dinner or a wedding, but surely not when it was a question of the religious life. Having renounced his own caste, why should the Blessed One have espoused the prejudice of the system? The following would be his personal answer:

> I am neither Brāhman nor prince,
> Nor even a bourgeois;
> I take my place with common folk
> Without a penny, thoughtful, I trudge.
> In the monk's robe, without a home I go,
> With shorn hair and soul serene,
> With no truck in human affairs
> My caste is no longer in season.[16]

Having established the principle of equality in the Order, and there only, with seniority the sole mark of rank, the Buddha simply conformed to a self-imposed rule that had for a long time been observed by all non-Brāhmanic sects. We should not ask him to be neither of his time nor of his country—much less to be of ours.

Relations Between the Buddha and His Monks

So it was from among the great bulk of the Central Indian populations, from the highest to the lowest classes, that the Buddha recruited his two categories of disciples, the lay faithful and the mendicant monks. The two were complementary, for it goes without saying that the beggars could only live in symbiosis with the donors. Of the two only the duly ordained monks had the right to be called "Śākya's Sons," and towards them Śākyamuni showed a paternal solicitude. As we have seen earlier, he shared part of each day with his fellow members at whatever hermitage they happened to be living in. He always found time to receive those who came great distances to see him during the rainy seasons, and he showed interest in their happiness and well-being, inquiring about their food as well as their spiritual comfort. The Master, as such, felt himself responsible for his disciples, and though as a "Perfect Buddha" he need not have reached out from his serene aloofness, the following excerpt indicates clearly that he did:

1. Now at that time a certain Bikkhu had a disturbance in his bowels, and he lay fallen in his own evacuations. And the Blessed One on going round the sleeping places accompanied by the venerable Ānanda came to that Bikkhu's abode, and saw him so. And he went up to him, and asked him, "What is the matter with you, O Bikkhu?"

"I have a disturbance, Lord, in my bowels."

"Then have you, O Bikkhu, anyone to wait upon you?"

"No, Lord."

"Why do not the Bikkhus wait upon you?"

"Because I am of no service, Lord, to the Bikkhus."

2. Then the Blessed One said to the venerable Ānanda, "Go, Ānanda, and fetch some water, let us bathe this Bikkhu."

"Even so, Lord," said the venerable Ānanda, in assent to the Blessed One, and fetched the water. And the Blessed One poured the water over that Bikkhu; and the venerable Ānanda wiped him down. And the Blessed One taking hold of him at the head, and the venerable Ānanda at the feet, they lifted him up, and laid him down upon his bed.

3. Then the Blessed One, on that occasion and in that connection, convened a meeting of the Bikkhu-saṃgha, and asked the Bikkhus, "Is there, O Bikkhus, in such and such an apartment, a Bikkhu who is sick?"

"There is, Lord."

"Then what, O Bikkhus, is the matter with that Bikkhu?"

"He has a disturbance, Lord, in his bowels."

"And is there any one, O Bikkhus, to wait upon him?"

"No, Lord."

"Why, then, do not the Bikkhus wait upon him?"

"That Bikkhu, Lord, is of no service to the Bikkhus; therefore do they not wait upon him."

"Ye, O Bikkhus, have no mothers and no fathers who might wait upon you! If ye, O Bikkhus, wait not one upon the other, who is there indeed who will wait upon you? Whosoever, O Bikkhus, would wait upon me, he should wait upon the sick." [17]

The Commentaries abound in stories indicating that the Blessed One constantly had to intervene in questions of dicipline. He was called upon to reprimand and scold his monks and to encourage them to act with good manners, in moderation, and even with modesty. It was extremely important for the Order not to permit behavior that might shock lay members or run counter to the long-accepted customs of what was expected of Indian ascetics. So, whether he wished it or not, the Buddha, like other leaders of religious sects, had to establish quite early a detailed set of rules for monastic life. These were concerned with correcting misdemeanors, such as negligence in proper dress and bearing, but also covering four capital sins—lust, theft, murder, and false pretensions to magical powers—which entailed expulsion from the Order.

Wicked characters making up the "Set of Six," invented purposely by Buddhist writers as a foil for the Blessed Group of Five, were brought in to commit successively all possible misdeeds and in each case there followed a new restriction. The consequent list of prohibitions set up in the "Formulary of Confession" (which was to be recited biweekly by the membership of each chapter of monks) ended by having over two hundred paragraphs. This high figure should not be too frightening, for there were compromises with the rule.

In principle, the traditional statute of ascetic life was accepted concerning only "Four Resources" (*nissaya*), which a monk had the right to ask for. In fact, it was not lived up to. In theory, the monk was to live only from alms and be dressed from rags he picked up from the trash, which he then mended; nor was he to have any other shelter than the trees of the forest and no remedies other than cows' "fetid urine." But the Buddha was tolerant about invitations, presents of clothing and blankets, shelter, and medicines. As a matter of fact, a large number of the treatises on discipline were given over to citing ways of easing the regulations rather than of rigorously enforcing them. Things not actually prohibited were considered permissible as long as decorous behavior was preserved, and this gave the faithful zealots ample leeway to spare the mendicant monks worry and privation, "which did not lead to salvation." [18]

Again we recognize the Buddha's desire to maintain the "middle-of-the-road" precept, which he had recommended as early as his First

Sermon. This was the course of wisdom, but how difficult it was to trace exactly that median line without thus exposing both flanks to the criticism of those who held extreme views. In some cases, the idea of having to conform to the Four Resources was frightening and inhibited many from entering the religious life.[19] On the other hand, members of rival sects, subjected to far more austere practices, did not fail to decry the relaxed Buddhist discipline. A well-known stanza described the "Sons of the Śākya" as leading a most comfortable life, eating and drinking well, sleeping in a good bed, and going to sleep with a mouthful of sweets. And it must be said that the rule regarding the one daily meal was not strictly observed, for it was understood that certain foods, such as sweets, did not break the fast.

The criticism came not only from evil-wishers, for even the Scriptures recognized the partial truth underlying it. We are also told how two tender parents, with their son's welfare at heart, brushed aside as too arduous the jobs of scribe, bookkeeper, and money-changer, and finally decided to have him become a monk in the Buddhist Order.[20] Even in the center of the Order a rigorist group—the head of which was soon to be Dēvadatta, the traitor—rebelled during the Master's life against his excessive lenience and insisted upon the strict application, at all times, of the Four Necessities.

Of course it was difficult to bring about harmony and complete accord within a community based on such broad democratic principles. Of the three important monastic vows in Europe—poverty, chastity, and obedience—the first two were always taken by members of Indian sects, but the third, never. Probably the reason for this, which seems to us a lack of foresight, is that in India the total submission of the disciple to the Master's word is taken for granted. In fact, as in principle, the Buddha was completely sovereign in his Order. But it is also true that the members recognized no other authority. It is easy to understand how, in an organization absolutely free of any ecclesiastical hierarchy and so widely dispersed, this sole personal bond, however marvelous, might at times become tenuous. Some of the monks, particularly the latecomers, became impatient with the Blessed One's directives, however mild; and it is said that after his death one of these recalcitrants exclaimed, "Good riddance, my friends; the Great Sāmaññā was forever telling us what to do and what not to do. Now we can do as we please!"

One obstinate rebel was sufficient to shake the foundations of the Order's organization and to reveal the impotence of the only weapons at hand. Warnings of interdiction and excommunication are of no value unless the object of such threats attaches the same importance to them as he who makes them. This facilitates the understanding of why the sin of provoking disunity was considered so base and was so forcefully reprimanded. "Altercations, quarrels, disputes, controversies, and dissensions" were to be avoided at all cost.

The Buddha and the Nuns

THE equality of castes before salvation as before suffering and death had as a corollary the equality of the sexes. Logically, there was no reason to refuse women their right to the constraints as well as to the privileges of religious life. In the most ancient Upanishads we note that the Brāhmanic circles had arrived (with restraint) at this conclusion, and the heterodox sects opened their ranks to nuns. The Buddha in time resigned himself to following their example, but we are told that it took the insistence of his aunt and adopted mother as well as good Ānanda's intercession to bring him to it. After being refused several times, Mahāprajāpatī made a final effort when Śuddhodhana died. She not only had her head shaved, like all Indian widows; she also put on monastic robes and with several princesses traveled on foot from Kapilavastu to Vaiśālī, where the Blessed One was staying at that time. Moved at the sight of the old queen, who with "swollen feet, covered with dust, moaning, and weeping" assailed the entrance to the hermitage, Ānanda took it upon himself to intercede. First he recalled to the Master's memory all that he owed to the maternal care of the petitioner. Then, having made him admit that women were also capable of attaining the four degrees of saintliness, he persuaded the Buddha to permit women "to leave the world and life in the home for life without home under the doctrine and discipline taught by the Predestined One." This was granted only on condition that they submit to eight severe rules, which placed nuns under the rigid supervision and absolute jurisdiction of their male colleagues. When these humiliating stipulations were accepted with enthusiasm, the Blessed One still scolded and murmured, "If women had not gained admission into the Order, O Ānanda, religious life would have lasted a long time; the

Good Law could have lasted a thousand years; now, O Ānanda, it will not last more than five hundred years." [21]

Much might be said about all this. To begin with, when the Buddha predicted for his faith a length of time that has been proven far too short, he was being true to his doctrine of the impermanence of things of this world. It might also be said that the prudish writers of the treatises on discipline exaggerated Śākyamuni's dislike of the fair sex. Still, we know that the Buddha was not a revolutionary and that he probably shared the old Indian idea that a woman must always be dependent upon a male member of her family: father, husband, brother, son, and so forth. What seems more serious to us is that among the seven types of wives that he enumerated—one who is like a persecutor or a thief or a mistress or a mother or a sister or a friend or a servant—the last was the one he preferred and to whom he gave first place. She would have patience beyond all endurance and submissiveness that could not be disturbed. Finally, we should listen to the supreme directives he gave Ānanda on his deathbed:

"How should we behave, my lord, in regard to the feminine sex?"
"Not to see them, O Ānanda."
"But, Blessed One, if we do see them?"
"Not to speak to them, O Ānanda."
"But, my lord, if they speak to us?"
"Keep wide awake, O Ānanda." [22]

Let us also not forget that he had become a monk and that in all countries and at all times the monastic orders have held the eternal feminine to be the devil's most dangerous of snares because the most seductive. And this has never deceived women: to fear them is to avow their charms.

The Personality of the Buddha

WOULD it seem presumptuous to try to draw from this all too short and superficial study of a considerable literature an approximate representation of Śākyamuni's long teaching career? The oldest known texts represent it as it remained in the memory of his Order for one or two centuries, at most, after his death. Truthfully, in the body of the Buddhist Scriptures we have little else besides diffuse and long-winded discourses, which could in no way be thought of as the minutes of authentic conversations which must have been not only varied but frequently extremely lively. The dried plant in a herbarium loses its color and perfume but retains its shape; much the same thing might apply to all these tales, parables, homilies, and dialogues put in the Blessed One's mouth. By the time they were first put down in writing, after having been told over and over, they must have already lost the better part of their natural spontaneity. It is only rarely that here and there against the general aridity some handsome stanza comes to life. But there remains a general pattern, and from it a sketch could be drawn of how Śākyamuni understood and filled the office of Buddha during the second half of his life.

If we could in some measure restore a sense of life to the early Buddhist writings, at least in imagination and with sound historical reasons, we should have won a point. The writers themselves invite and help us to do it by their constant allusions to the way the Buddha's serene beauty and the penetrating quality of his voice won hearts while his sharp dialectics conquered minds. And probably here, too, that demon, statistics, spoiled everything, as it often does in India. Certain that redundancy was equivalent to eloquence, the worthy scholars inflicted upon themselves and upon us list upon list of flattering qualifications. In spite of them, however, it is possible for us to discern the mysterious attraction of the Buddha, which, as we are told again and again, no one could resist.

The critic must not be too hasty to condemn this exaltation of the leader of a sect by his own followers. Its absence would lead to the loss of an appreciative understanding, now confirmed by more than twenty centuries of history—and such a history as could never have been dreamed of by the Buddha's first eulogists. There is no testimony more authentic than that brought by facts. It must now be admitted that Śākyamuni's word must indeed have exerted an extraordinarily vital influence upon his contemporaries for its echo to have traveled so far and still be heard by millions of souls. Confronted by the phenomenon of the spread and persistence of great religions, we easily acclaim them as historical miracles, but we are apt to overlook the prodigious fact of their birth—which is even more amazing and no less real.

CHAPTER X

THE FOUR SECONDARY
PILGRIMAGES

Fʀᴏᴍ the canonical Scriptures we have been able to discern a portrait of the Buddha as drawn during his long career and, though its beauty may have been enhanced by distance and nostalgia, we feel that it is still a likeness of his winning personality. From them also we can retrace the itinerary of his constant pilgrimages. The primary fact is that for some forty-five years Śākyamuni carried on his tireless preaching in the central basin of the Ganges. Though this territory is relatively limited, about half the size of France, he never left it.

Later on, as his religion spread throughout the peninsula and well into Ceylon and Gandhāra, it was inevitable that devotees in these new lands wished to believe that the Blessed One had visited their ancestors. So it was that miraculous journeys were said to have been made to the southern coast and its large outlying island as well as to the mountains of the northwest. But such stories have just as much foundation as those that would have had Christ traveling in Brittany. In order to draw a map of the region brought under the Master's religious domination, it was necessary to establish the sites of the eight cities consecrated by the eight miracles that are considered of primary importance. With the Indian's remarkable topographic memory and the help of archaeology, it is now possible to circumscribe the geographical setting for Śākyamuni's entire field of activity.

The Holy Sites

How did tradition establish these holy sites? Before we go further, we should know what is meant by a "miracle." For us Occidentals the word implies not only an act in contradiction with natural laws but also very frequently an unhoped-for cure. Because of this, many of the Occidental pilgrimages have a therapeutic as well as a religious aim. With its basic fatalism, India shares none of this concept. It would be fruitless to look in the Buddhist Scriptures for anything resembling the cure of the one suffering from hemorrhoids or the resurrection of Lazarus. Never have the early texts cited a deliberate intervention by the Buddha in the normal course of the law which regulates all destinies—namely, *karma*. What then are the miracles that his religion has chosen to commemorate? Two of them would hardly have been thought of as miracles—his birth and his death. Still, we already know that the Nativity, the Final Decease, the Enlightenment, and the First Sermon rank at the very top in the list of prodigious events.

Now we shall see that the secondary miraculous occurrences were also more or less exceptional episodes in the Buddha's life. It is true that these incidents forced him to exert, whether he wished it or not, his magical powers, and one of them is even called the "Great Magical Feat." But many of his disciples and even some of the heterodox masters were also capable of such magic. Therefore, since, in accord with Indian ideas, supernatural powers were not beyond nature, it might well be said that early Buddhism was not a religion exacting from its faithful a belief in miracles. We cannot then use the term "miracle" in its full sense, but may simply understand it as a manifestation that is out of the ordinary. This being understood, everything took place much as it does right under our eyes today. If something of an unusual nature occurs in some corner of Europe, presently a publicity committee, a group of hotel keepers, and a travel agency are organized to make a good thing of it. Such a pilgrimage racket also flourishes in India today, with rather more rudimentary means; but it was well organized in ancient times. The *Mahābhārata* and the *Purāna* are filled with advertisements of purifying baths. And if you wish to know how the commemoration of the Buddha very early took this same turn, you need only read the statement cleverly inserted in the traditional account of the Final Decease. As the Blessed One lay on his deathbed, and without hesitation Ānanda asked him for his last instructions:

> "In times past, Lord, the brethren, when they had spent the rainy season in different districts, used to come to see the Tathāgata, and we used to receive those very reverend brethren in audience, and

to wait upon the Blessed One. But, Lord, after the end of the Blessed One, we shall not be able to receive those very reverend brethren in audience, and to wait upon the Blessed One."

.   .   .   .

"There are these four places, Ānanda, which the believing man should visit with feelings of reverence and awe. Which are the four?

"The place, Ānanda, at which the believing man can say, 'Here the Tathāgata was born!' is a spot to be visited with feelings of reverence and awe.

"The place, Ānanda, at which the believing man can say, 'Here the Tathāgata attained to the supreme and perfect insight!' is a spot to be visited with feelings of reverence and awe.

"The place, Ānanda, at which the believing man can say, 'Here was the kingdom of righteousness set on foot by the Tathāgata!' is a spot to be visited with feelings of reverence and awe.

"The place, Ānanda, at which the believing man can say, 'Here the Tathāgata passed finally away in that utter passing away which leaves nothing whatever to remain behind!' is a spot to be visited with feelings of reverence and awe.

"And there will come, Ānanda, to such spots, believers, brethren and sisters of the order, or devout men and devout women, and will say, 'Here was the Tathāgata born!' or, 'Here did the Tathāgata attain to the supreme and perfect insight!' or, 'Here was the kingdom of righteousness set on foot by the Tathāgata!' or, 'Here the Tathāgata passed away in that utter passing away which leaves nothing whatever to remain behind!'

"And they, Ānanda, who shall die while they, with believing heart, are journeying on such pilgrimage, shall be reborn after death, when the body shall dissolve, in the happy realms of heaven." [1]

The traveler's insurance against the journey's risks, found in the last sentence, in no way destroyed either the authenticity of the text or the sincerity of the pious believers, who were thus encouraged to make trips to the sacred places. This ambulatory devotion may have been the starting point for Buddhist art, for undoubtedly it created a demand for ex-votos and mementos. Thus can be explained the abundance of the Nativity lotus, of *Sambodhi* trees, of Wheels of the Law, and even the mound of the *Parinirvāna* that profusely decorate the oldest monuments. Could they not be replicas of the local mementos?

Even the old habit that makers of religious objects had of representing the Buddha's miracles by such symbols was taken over by the early sculptors. The great numbers of stele and *stūpa* bases, which invariably group on their four compartments or their four sides the four great scenes, lead us to believe that their dedications with appropriate annual celebrations were considered satisfactory substitutes for making the four pilgrimages and for gaining the equivalent merits as well.

If there was complete accord on the subject of the four principal miracles and their corresponding sites, such was not the case for the other four that were to complete the list of the sacred number "eight." It is easily understood that the cities of Kapilavastu and Benares, as well as the two towns of Urubilvā and Kuśinagara, could not hope to monopolize forever the benefits and fame pertaining to the Master, but there was no agreement on a further choice of localities or events. This gave rise to competition among various cities and nearby monasteries in the Ganges Valley. Again it is to the sculptured monuments that we turn for the formula that was accepted by the artists and the donors. It was definitely agreed that pilgrims had to go to Sānkāśya to worship the memory of the Descent from Heaven; to Śrāvastī for that of the Great Magical Feat; to Rājagṛha for that of The Subjugation of the Mad Elephant; and finally to Vaiśālī for the Monkey's Offering.

In reading this list we are astonished not to find the names of three cities whose early importance is well known: Mathurā, Sāketa, and Kauśāmbī.[2] It is true that the first of these remained outside of the Buddha's itinerary in spite of its great religious zeal, which was later revealed by its many foundations. But that was not the case for the other two, whose outskirts boasted of Buddhist hermitages where the Master often resided. Probably Sāketa, Kauśāmbī, as well as Prayāga and the heart of Central India, were still too thoroughly Brāhmanized for the Buddha's doctrine to meet with the same success that it had in northern Kosala, the Tirhut, and the Magadha. Let us also not forget that Sāketa, also called Ayodhyā, was Rāma's holy city; just as the "Mathurā of the Gods" of Ptolemy was Krishna's. As for Kauśāmbī, capital of the Vatsas, the reason would seem to be that its king's relations with the Buddha remained distant.

The Miracle of Sānkāśya

SOME say that it was during the sixteenth year after Enlightenment that the Buddha decided to go up to the Heaven of the Thirty-three Gods, where his mother Māyā had been reborn, and teach her the Good Law. So he mysteriously disappeared from the earth and came back only three months later, on the day of the full moon in October, near the town of Sānkāśya. His ascension, which was considered rather commonplace and within the power of others, was barely noticed. The Descent, however, was quite another matter. It became an occasion of great pomp and took place on a triple stairway made of precious materials and specially built by the gods. The Buddha descended between Brahmā on his right and Indra on his left against a sky entirely peopled with divinities singing his praises and showering down flowers. At the bottom of the steps his principal disciples and a crowd of his faithful were waiting for him.[3] Very early the episode was represented in a kind of triptych but with the panels arranged vertically. The uppermost one shows the sermon among the gods; the middle one shows the descent; and the lowest panel shows the resumption of teaching, with the Buddha giving a special examination to the members of the Community, using questions of increasing difficulty. The next-to-the-last question can only be answered by Śāriputra, and only Śākyamuni can give the answer to the final one.

This, in brief, is the account of the miracle of Sānkāśya, and our first reaction is that there never was such a miracle. The four Great Miracles have a historical basis, and the three other secondary Manifestations can retain under cover of fiction the memory of actual occurrences. Here, however, we find not the slightest bit of truth or verisimilitude. It is all pure fantasy, and only those who have faith can believe. Even the scene picked for this myth arouses suspicion. All the old texts agree on Sānkāśya, and there are good reasons for believing that it was the town today known by the ruins of Sankissa, where there are still some traces of Aśoka.[4]

A look at the map is enough to point up how removed this site is from the other holy cities. It is far off to the west between the Jamnā River and the Ganges, that is, right in what was the Brāhman's "Land of the Middle"—quite distinct and distant from that of the Buddhists, situated much farther to the east. Another item to consider is that if we were to start on a tour of the eight pilgrimages we would find that our wanderings, with this one exception, would take us through marshy country, so that in our mind Buddhism would become closely associated with marshes industriously divided for the cultivation of different cereals. Sankissa, on the contrary, is found right in the middle of a wheat-growing plain, where water is found only deep under alluvial layers. This leaves the traveler incredulous, not only about the miracle itself but about its completely alien site.

A rational explanation of a myth is always vain, but we can at least attempt to seek the reasons for the invention as well as the location of this one. On the first count there is no hesitation: has it not been written that it is an essential duty of any Predestined One to "establish his father and mother in the truth" and thus ensure their salvation? [5] It would be difficult to admit that Śākyamuni had failed in this obligation towards the one to whom he owed seeing the light of day for his last existence. And since Māyā, as a reward for this, had been promoted to the rank of a male divinity and reborn in Indra's heaven, it was fitting that her son should use his magic powers to visit her. (This was the idea of early Buddhism; later it was found easier and possibly more pathetic to have Māyā come down to earth in her original form.)

A second demand of protocol was that a brief visit would have been unworthy of such a holy task, and the least the Buddha could do was to spend one of the inactive rainy seasons with her. (Again, in passing, it should be noted that this three-month absence furnished an edifying as well as satisfying explanation for the origin of the Buddha's images, when these were at last created and their cult allowed. It was in order to lessen the pain of such a long separation from the Blessed One that such and such a king ordered from his sculptors the first statue representing the Master—the likeness of which was guaranteed by the fact of its having been executed while he was still alive. Some astute theologians, embroidering upon this, found the occasion an excellent one to have the Buddha preach the final text of the *Abhidharma* during this heavenly retreat.)

Finally, when it was time for the Buddha, his duty fulfilled, to return to earth, why should his host Indra—as well as Brahmā, who had come down specially from his superior level—not escort him down with their divine cohorts? All of this follows naturally enough, but it takes more than a sequence of customary incidents to warrant the scenic effect created by legend. All versions come back to the memorable spectacle of the Descent by means of the triple staircase. The sculptured representations make a great thing of this stairway, and even Aśoka's piety led him to imitate the gods. Though his construction was only of cut stone, it was still to be seen by Fa-hsien and Hsuan Tsang in the traditional place. Nevertheless it remains for us to explain the incongruous spectacle of this religious edifice as well as its geographic location.

If there is the slightest chance of recovering a secret lost for such a long time, it will be on the site itself. So we start crossing the great plain of the Ganges in early November, with a blue sky overhead, winding our way between fields of millet, of sugar cane left from the previous summer, and of new winter wheat. The horizon is hemmed in by groups of mangoes, hiding the villages; here and there antelopes, peacocks, and blue pigeons dot the landscape. The only prominent feature of this flat landscape is the large number of earthen ramps rising from the ground and overlooking the wells at the other end. Coupled oxen patiently go up and down these ramps with a clocklike regularity, bringing up water from the wells in large leather containers.

After seeing over and over the profile of these inclines of about thirty degrees against the sky, we cannot help but wonder whether they were not responsible for the location of the "Descent from Heaven" in precisely that area. By facing one of these with three rows of stone steps side by side we would have the perfect *santa scala* attributed to Emperor Aśoka. All that is needed to complete the restoration is the traditional group of the Buddha between his two divine acolytes at the top of the monument.

The Śrāvastī Cycle

By rights the Sānkāśya miracle should really follow the Śrāvastī one, but in our haste to have done with the former we did not hesitate to reverse their order. Not that the Great Magical Feat is in itself more easily believed, buried as it is under all the fictitious embellishments that popular imagination has heaped upon it. What we do discover under all the artificial ornamentation is the unquestionable rivalries between the Buddha and the leaders of other existing sects. The episode given particular importance is part of a cycle surrounding the inevitable competition for alms. Legend never tired of blackening the reputation of the heterodox sects by showing how they tried to ruin the Buddha's reputation in the eyes of the population and thus starve him as well as his Order. In all fairness to them it must be added that in so doing his adversaries were fighting for their own lives.

The story of the woman novice Cincamānavikā is a clever tale showing the lengths to which the opposition would go to destroy the Master's moral reputation. She was frankly asked by the leaders of her heterodox sect to use her wiles to dishonor the monk Gautama, who was then at the Jētavana hermitage. After several months of discreditable machinations, which seemed to be bearing fruit, the hoax was discovered, by the help of Indra's intervention, and the wicked Cincamānavikā was swallowed by hellfire.[6]

The same tale was later on taken up again, with the beautiful Sundari as the lure. Her lot was equally fatal, for the instigators had her throat slashed and her body hidden in the Jētavana hermitage near the Blessed One's cell. This time the hired murderers revealed the plot, the Buddha remained innocent, and the guilty ones were punished.

The Great Magical Feat

IT is time to turn to the miracle of which Śrāvastī was once most proud, being the site for its public veneration. We need not be troubled by the fact that Hsuan Tsang and Fa-hsien, whose attention was diverted by the abundance of "saintly vestiges," barely mentioned it in passing, for some relatively old texts not only proclaimed its importance but named it as one of the essential acts to be carried out by every Buddha.[7] The conflict between the Predestined One and the leaders of the religious communities antedating his seemed normal to those writers in view of the vital competition underlying it. But their way of treating it was to attribute to heterodox hostility, the lowest of motives, and the use of genuinely criminal means in order to gain their own ends. The writers hardly ever referred to higher dissensions bearing upon differences in the doctrine and the discipline. But when they did, their analysis of their adversaries' philosophical ideas was of such a ridiculous nature that these became inacceptable to sensible people.[8] Good faith has never been the guiding principle of polemics! Wordy battles are an Indian trait, since the most ancient antiquity and the

Brāhman as well as the Buddhist annals resound with the echoes of formidable public discussions. These were often held on the initiative of a king and even in his royal presence.

It would seem as if the legendary accounts condensed into one sensational "colloquium" all such verbal bouts in order to give the Blessed One a chance to overcome his rivals all at once. That such a rapid and complete triumph should be accomplished without some miracle was not to be thought of, even by the believers. And, to be sure, prodigious happenings were heaped one on top of the other as the edifying versions of the event succeded one another. Just as under the ridges of Saheth-Maheth the observer can detect in superimposed piles of texts the layers belonging to different epochs that little by little have been overlaid on the original earth, so here we have the rewritten versions that have come from an original common source. The oldest of the accounts is the one which interests us particularly, for it is the only one that allows us the slightest possibility of retracing even a shadow of the ancient activities. But even so, it may not be useless to examine the way a Great Magical Feat is completely fabricated.

To begin with, we might try to broadly restore the legend and to try justifying within reason the basis for it. We need no longer go over the origins, either material or doctrinal, of the conflict. Concerning the heterodox scholars, there is always the favorable impression that their number remains at six. Not only is this very reasonable, but it means that the names, once established, remain the same. As the last one on the list has been identified as the founder of the flourishing sect of the Jains, his historical identity confers on his colleagues a sufficient stamp of reality. On the other hand, the choice of Śrāvastī is explained in the most plausible fashion. Leery of the friendship between Śākyamuni and Bimbisāra, King of the Magadha, the heterodox counted upon the impartiality of Prasenajit, King of Kosala. Later it was said that the occasion of the great intellectual tournament was known. It was remembered (quite naïvely) that, following a brash demonstration by Pindola Bharadhvāja, the Buddha had forbidden his monks to engage in any supernatural public displays. This rule would have placed the Master in a position of inferiority, had it included him, and the heterodox immediately took advantage of it in the hope that it did. So they challenged him to a public competition. But just as a royal edict does not apply to the king himself, a prohibition concerning disciples is not binding upon their leader, and thus are the false prophets caught in their own snares.

Let us not try to assign motives but let us identify the scene where the actors are gathering. It is most precisely set between Śrāvastī and the Jētavana, thus in neutral territory, to the west of the road which led, and still leads, from the southern gate of the city to the eastern gate of the hermitage—about one hundred and fifty steps north of the latter. There King Prasenajit (to be replaced later in the account by Viśvakarman, the architect of the gods) had built a huge lecture hall for this occasion. It was still represented at the time of the Chinese pilgrims in the shape of a temple sixty or seventy feet high. Inside was a seated figure of the Buddha, facing east, just as he was during his eloquent dialectic refutation of his adversaries' criticisms and objections. Thus established in its essential characters the scene does not exceed acceptable limits. On a Bhārhut bas-relief, second century B.C., a king carefully labeled "Prasenajit of Kosala" is leaving his own city in a chariot in the direction of a large structure sheltering the "Wheel of the Law," the accepted symbol of the Master's victorious sermon. It is difficult to imagine what better means, written or representational, the Buddhist tradition could have used to establish the authenticity of the principal Śrāvastī miracle than this practical and direct approach.

But where and when have simple truths satisfied popular devotion? That the Blessed One should have won out due to the invincible power of his statement was obvious, but was it not also necessary for an event of such importance to be accompanied by some remarkable demonstration? This is the point upon which the Northern and the Southern traditions split, though both were working in the same direction. For the Northern Buddhists the Great Feat became and will always remain the "Miracle Under the Mango." On this spectacular occasion the Buddha performed a miracle that even today Indian conjurers try to imitate with a mango seed. While the latter bring forth in a few minutes a tiny growth hidden in their bag of tricks, the Blessed One caused to rise to the skies a full-grown mango, covered with blooms and fruit and buzzing with bees. And under its spreading branches he took his place. This is the way he is still represented in Indochina or in Ceylon on devotional chromos. The north gate of the great *stūpa* at Sānchī carried such a sculptural representation as early as the first century B.C. On the other hand, the Northwestern legend much pre-

21. Four Secondary Miracles.

(Left) The Great Miracle of Śrāvasti. Gandhāra, 2nd–3rd century A.D.

(Below) Sankasia. Return of the Buddha from the Trayastrimsat Heaven. Bhārhut Stūpa, 1st century A.D.

Fogg Museum, Harvard University

22. (Four Secondary Miracles, continued). (Left) Subjugation of the Elephant Nalagiri. Amārāvatī, 2nd century A.D.

Fogg Museum, Harvard University

(Opposite) The Offering of the Monkey at Vaiśālī. Sānchī Stūpa, 1st century A.D.

Copyright Department of Archaeology, Government of India

ferred to have two aquatic jinn bring forth an enormous lotus "with a thousand petals and the size of a cartwheel" upon which the Buddha sat in the teaching posture—a pose that has remained characteristic of all Gandhāra representations of the Great Miracle—at least of all the seated ones.

Thus we find that over the original verbal victory the varnish of the supernatural has been applied, and many successive applications appear which make any accurate study difficult. The Master's words became linked with more and more spectacular manifestations of his super-natural powers. The "Twin Miracles" were called in, consisting of the Blessed One's gyrating in the air, causing streams of water or shooting flames to surge forth from his body. The Gandhāra school made rep-resentations of these extravagances, but the old Indian school refrained for the simple reasons that the figure of the Buddha could not be repre-sented. Possibly that is the reason why the Southern tradition has shown more restraint in the use of fabulous fiction. On the other hand, the Northern tradition, in both its imagery and its canonical texts, knew no limits. Having used the "Twin Miracles" before, something new had to be invented for this occasion and it had to be done by the Buddha alone. This led to both the literary and the figured representa-tion of a phantasmagoric multiplication of Buddhas who, assuming the four consecrated poses—standing, walking, sitting, and lying down —filled the firmament and covered all surfaces. Indian imagination has never gone beyond this apocalyptic splendor; but with it the small core of historical reality seems to have vanished. Only unbelievers will find this sad.

The Second Cycle of Rājagṛha

It is easy to conceive that such prodigal miracles induced the later biographers to complete the series by having the Buddha ascend to the Heaven of the Thirty-three. There he could catch his breath while quietly converting his mother and her companions. But not having come to the end of his last earthly existence, he was not at the end of his tribulations. Back in Rājagṛha, he found that times had definitely changed. His old friend Bimbisāra was no more, having been not only dethroned by his son Ajātaśatru but allowed to starve to death in prison. Because of this act the son became the Master's enemy. Of the important zealots the only one left was the famous doctor, Jīvaka, whose many marvelous cures would make a long story.[9]

Little good did it do the Blessed One to confound the six heterodox scholars, two hundred leagues away, for it was now within the heart of his own Community that an unscrupulous rival fomented discord and sought to supplant him. The worst of it was that the villain found accomplices everywhere, in the monasteries, in the city, and at court. Such is humanity! Kindness, generosity, forgiveness, self-denial—even in India—will not be received with gratitude. The bitter irony is that love of your fellow man will bring forth enemies.

In history as well as in literature, there are few pathetic situations not brought about by treachery. In addition, no traitor has existed that novelists and dramatists do not love to blacken. Historians should be more objective, and we wonder what we should think of Devadatta, first cousin of Śākyamuni, who has often been called the Judas of Buddhism. When numerous pages of the Scriptures concerning him have been read, two distinct points of view emerge. One accuses him of all possible crimes because he has committed the worst by trying to create a schism or, as was said, "a rupture in the Order." That is the popular version. The other, more intellectually conceived, tries to show the plausible motives involved and the means he used in trying to achieve his criminal end. Both viewpoints condemn him utterly. Our own task is to try and weigh the pros and cons and to pick out in the bill of indictment the circumstances that to unprejudiced eyes could appear as extenuating circumstances.

Seen from this angle, Devadatta ceases to be the monster depicted. He becomes a man much like many others and often superior, but inflated with pride and ambition and gnawed at by the most common and despicable sin—envy. Whether he was among the first or the second group of young Śākyas who became monastic recruits, he asked for and obtained his ordination into the Order. It is recognized that he studied, that he attained high degrees of meditation, that he achieved supernatural powers, that he was well considered by the lay followers, and that he really only lacked two or three of the signs characteristic of the Buddha, of whom he was the equal by birth.

Feeling that the Master was getting old and that it was time for him to consider retirement, Devadatta offered to take his place as head of the Order.[10] His request was brushed aside without its being given the slightest consideration. As a matter of fact, since the Buddha had no idea of withdrawing in favor of his two Great Disciples, why should he relinquish his place and turn over his flock to a man in whose heart he read as in an open book not only the basest motives but envy as well? The rebuff made Devadatta furious and he changed tactics. Many monks in the Order were imbued with the old ascetic ideal and, impressed by the rigorous examples as well as disturbed by the taunts of rival sects, they criticized Śākyamuni's liberal concessions. These concerned five issues: residence, invitations to dinner, clothing, shelter, and food. Due to either his personal conviction or a pharisaical acceptation (as we are told), Devadatta became the leader of the rigid malcontents as well as their spokesman during one of the plenary meetings. In their name he requested of the Buddha that the old rules be applied in all their former severity. For the monks this meant leading a solitary life, eating only food received from begging, wearing robes made from mended rags, having no permanent shelter, and abstaining from eating meat or fish. A convinced liberal, the Buddha insisted that his disciples remain free to be their own judges as to these five restrictions. With the aid of an old and critical monk, Kokālika, who was also full of envy, Devadatta took advantage of the above refusal and vaunted his superior austerity before the lay faithful.[11] He even succeeded in drawing to himself five hundred new monks from Vaiśālī. However, we are told that the two Great Disciples, sent out posthaste by the Blessed One, soon brought these stray lambs back to the fold. This does not seem true to fact as told by the Chinese travelers, who recounted that they found at both ends of the Ganges religious groups, which, having remained loyal to Devadatta's principles, continued to venerate Buddhas of the past except Śākyamuni.

Thus the unforgivable presumption of the Buddha's cousin, as told by the ancient texts, seems confirmed by historical data, and legend's list of true or alleged crimes was based on this initial fact. First of all, Devadatta's hatred for his cousin became the heritage of a fabulous past, manifested through many previous lives.[12] In this particular existence it had already manifested itself in childhood and in youthful sports, becoming stronger with time. It would seem that it was Devadatta who incited Ajātaśatru to murder his father in the hope that, having become king, the former prince would in turn help him to dethrone the Buddha. So with impunity he premeditated three means of foul play. First he hired some killers to murder his cousin, but they could only fall at the Buddha's feet and become converted. Then he caused a huge rock to roll down upon his intended victim, but all that resulted were a few scratches on the Blessed One's foot. Finally, with royal approval, Devadatta attempted to have Śākyamuni trampled by a mad elephant.

When everything failed, the only recourse was to act himself and the enemy chose then a most execrable means. He joined the Blessed One in Śrāvastī and, under the guise of begging forgiveness, he threw himself at the Master's feet with the aim of scratching them with poisoned fingernails. This was too much for even the narrators' imagination, and with one accord they precipitated the would-be murderer into hell.

Subjugating the Mad Elephant

Though we cannot believe the theatrical solution to Devadatta's criminal attempts or many of his intrigues, it does not necessarily follow that we give the accused the benefit of the doubt, nor is it obligatory that he be the instigator of what became the spectacular miracle of the Rājagṛha pilgrimage. It might have been mere chance that brought the Buddha face to face with a mad elephant one day on the main street of the capital. The oldest texts agreed that Nālāgiri was mean and was known as a man-killer. The latter is a well-authenticated possibility. That Devadatta used his influence with the young king in persuading him to give orders that Nālāgiri be turned loose at the time of the Buddha's begging hour is not impossible. The later texts even suggested that at the traitor's instigation the keepers of the royal elephant made him drunk. Whether it was due to alcohol, to rut, or simply to innate evil, the huge pachyderm, "with trunk in the air, ears erect, and tail rigid," tore down the city street at a gallop. All fled before him, seeking shelter. Only the Buddha remained impassive, refusing to move.

Then came the miracle! The elephant, overcome by the radiance of kindness emanating from the Blessed One, suddenly became calm. Gentle and peaceful, he came and knelt before the Master, who lifted his right hand and patted the animal's forehead. What an admirable illustration, though not easily believed, of the authority of kindness over brute strength, which can only bring to mind Saint Francis' taming of the wolf of Gubbio. A sculptured medallion at Amarā-vatī represents this scene with great skill. Unfortunately, the devout tried to embellish the scene by exaggeration: they related that five lions sprang forth from the Master's extended hand and held the elephant at bay. Such was the tale as told to Hsuan Tsang and as it appears on Nepalese miniatures and in Chinese drawings, but it would be difficult to betray more completely the gesture and spirit of the Great Being. The ancient text itself ended with this futile statement:

> And the elephant Nālāgiri having returned to the stable stayed in his place and once more became the domesticated elephant Nālā-giri; and on this occasion the people sang this stanza:
>
> > People tame them with blows from sticks,
> >   gaffs and whips;
> > Without stick or weapon was
> >   the elephant tamed by the Great Sage.

The Tibetan version added a new touch to the tale by telling how the elephant, full of love for his new Master, followed him to the house where he was to dine. The Buddha, touched by this devotion, caused the walls to become transparent so that the elephant could still see him. The wicked king at once had a barrier built to hide the Blessed One from the poor elephant, who died of sorrow on the spot.[13] True, the author was anxious to hasten the worthy animal's rebirth in the Heaven of the Four Guardians of the World.

The Vaiśālī Cycle

ANOTHER fragment of the biography that is hard to place in the Master's career is going to lead him and us back across the Ganges to the free city of Vaiśālī. Here we find many traditional memories relating to the Blessed One. He had lived there during one of his previous existences; he had studied there with Arāda Kālāpa in his present life; and later, after becoming a Buddha, he was invited to come back and help put down a plague epidemic. Evil spirits, the microbes of those days, which were the cause of the plague were exorcised by his very presence and fled. At this time Gośringi had him invited to dinner by a talking parrot and at dessert presented him with the "Great Wood" in the northern suburb of the city.[14] It was in that very hermitage his aunt (also his stepmother), Mahāprajāpatī, came to beg of him to admit women into the Order. And it was also at Vaiśālī that the venerable Queen Mother was said to have attained saintliness and entered Nirvāna.

At this time Vaiśālī was a rich and prosperous city with a large population and it is said that there were 7777 palaces with terraces and the same number of costly houses and parks. Again, the lotus ponds numbered four sevens. One of its important inhabitants was the courtesan Ambapālī, who was known for her great beauty and charm.[15] She was among the first to receive the Buddha and his following at dinner, and after the meal was finished she turned her "Mango Grove" over to them. As was usual before leaving, the Blessed One made his little speech, designed to teach, encourage, stimulate, and gladden his hostess. From there he went on to the Great Wood, where he resided in Belvedere Hall whenever he was in Vaiśālī.

This is the place to which we shall lead the reader on a short archaeological excursion as of today. After crossing the Ganges at Patnā and going north-northeast through the rich plains of the Tirhut, we come to the village of Basārh, about twenty miles from the river's left bank. Nearby is a large, barren quadrilateral area surrounded by a wide ditch and known as "King Visāl's Castle," which was the emplacement of the royal palace of Vaiśālī. A two-mile journey further to the northwest will bring us to our goal.[16]

Of course we should be carrying with us our Hsuan Tsang as others carry their Pausanias. Sure enough, raising our eyes from our book, we find facing us the tall, monolithic column crowned with a lion, seen thirteen centuries ago by the Chinese traveler. And quite near, to the north, is the great *stūpa*, which he was told was also attributed to Aśoka.

To the south is the pond near which monkeys were said to have piously filled the Blessed One's bowl with honey. The Sanskrit canon tells us that Belvedere Hall, which was the Master's favorite lodging near Vaiśālī, was situated in the Great Wood "on the edge of the Monkey Pond." Nothing is left of the edifice and the trees are sparse, but the essential marks of the landscape are still before our eyes: the column, the tumulus, and the pond. We can be pretty certain of being on the site of the Vaiśālī miracle, thanks to our excellent Oriental guide.

So far so good, but a number of difficulties now arise. If, as is our habit, we turn to the texts to find more information concerning the monkey's gift, we find either omissions or contradictions. The Pāli canon entirely omitted the episode and our Sanskrit sources, though recognizing by place and name the Monkey Pond, made no mention of the incident for which it was named. Fa-hsien did no better, but Hsuan Tsang expanded the event by having the monkeys dig the pond, and insisted upon speaking of them in the plural. What is more disconcerting is that the same story was set here and there by various writers, and translators have persisted in calling the offering "honey." [17] It is quite out of the question that a monkey, no matter what his noble aim be, should steal honey from the fierce wild bees of India.

Fortunately, once more the figured monuments come to our rescue. First the representation of the Monkey's Offering on the north gate at Sānchī shows that the legend was popular before our era. Twelve centuries later the title on a Nepalese miniature locates it "at Vaiśālī in the Tirabhukti." Between these two we find several other sculptured versions of our story, and these images make it possible for us to give a completely coherent if not entirely believable version.

The imitative instinct of the monkey is well known and in India, where monkeys live freely and at large, they become not only friendly but often impudent. The sculptors have shown them sitting in the "yogī manner," imitating the Buddha's meditating attitude. The simian hero of the Vaiśālī Miracle goes further, and due to the artists we can follow his activities. He climbs the tall palm trees to fetch the *madhu,* the sweet syrup that comes from the incised tops of various palm trees but which is not honey. Our monkey knows full well what he is doing and, having brought this offering to the Buddha who graciously accepts it, he bows and politely withdraws. This is what is shown on the ancient bas-relief.

Such a simple act, however, could hardly satisfy our scribes, and various spectacular activities were described. Either, as in the Mathurā account, the monkey in wild joy flew from branch to branch and fell into the great ditch in which he perished, or later he voluntarily flung himself into a well. At Mathurā the miracle seems to have been that the content of the one begging bowl offered by the monkey, indefinitely extended with water, lost nothing of its flavor and was sufficient to quench the thirst of not only the Buddha but the whole Community as well. In Vaiśālī, where the monks' imagination was stirred by repetitions of monkeys in the images, it was only one step further to the adoption of the belief in the existence of many monkeys. Having achieved this, they decided to have this free labor corps dig the pond which immortalized its act of charity.

From the two last miracles—that of Rājagṛha and that of Vaiśāli—when stripped of their embellishments we have left two stories inconceivable anywhere but in India, where the belief in the transmigration of souls from childhood induces the recognition that "all species have individuals endowed with virtuous inclinations." [18]

CHAPTER XI

THE FOURTH GREAT PILGRIMAGE

WILL WE DARE PRETEND that reading the texts and studying the sculptured imagery have made it possible for us to restore a sufficiently convincing representation of the growing importance of the mission of salvation pursued by the "Teacher of men and gods"? Guided by the above witnesses, we have tried to understand his constant labor during this forty-five-year period, spent primarily in organizing and protecting his Order from the attacks of rival sects. Against a background of exhortation, teaching, and preaching, interrupted only by journeys on foot and by sedentary retreats during certain seasons spent here and there, we catch sight of a few striking episodes. These are often distorted or even contorted—bits of a legend that has never achieved integration into a genuine and coherent biography.

However, time passes and, according to the law of the impermanence of all things human, constantly preached by the Master, he aged and his decline was in sight. With the final separation approaching and the bitterness of impending loss upon the disciples, their attention became sharpened toward the incidents of the last days and these were deeply etched in their minds. Thus regret and sorrow did for the end of the Buddha's career what joy and enthusiasm had done for his early triumphs. It now becomes our task to follow him step by step until we reach the place and time of the last of the Four Great Miracles and the Fourth Great Pilgrimage—the Final Decease. In fact we have a relatively old and authentic detailed account of the Buddha's last year which at least is precise as to places as well as consecutive in recital.[1]

The Buddha, in spite of his advanced age, decided to pursue once more the same itinerary he had traveled when he first left home. This time the journey was to be made in reverse order. According to all indications, feeling that the end of his days was approaching, the

Blessed One wished to return to the land of his childhood and to see again from his favorite hermitage, Jētavana, the eternal snows of the Himālayan summits. His active youth, his life in the open, and his daily exercise of walking, coupled with his strong constitution, had until then kept him in fine health. At least we are told of only minor ailments, which the doctor Jīvaka had no difficulty in curing. A distance of ten or twelve miles a day was nothing to frighten his old age. However, he had banked too heavily on his strength, and death was to overcome him halfway on his journey.

It was in a little village in the neighborhood of Vaiśālī, where he was tarrying during the rainy season, that he was stricken with the first attack of the dysentery that finally killed him. Making a great effort of will, he overcame his illness and bravely started on his way again. At Pāvā, the sixth stopping place, an infringement of his diet due, to the well-intended but unwise persuasion of one of his zealots, caused a serious relapse. Still, he did not give up until the next stop at Kuśinagara, where he lay down never to rise again. Such, in brief, is the canvas upon which legend was to embroider many decorations.

Ajātaśatru's Visit

As the curtain rises upon the last act in our drama we find ourselves again one last time in the capital of the Magadha. The situation had changed since we were last there; the parricide king, no longer under Devadatta's evil influence, was feeling remorse for his crime and was beginning to fear retribution at the hands of his own son, Udāyibhadra. At this point there occurred an incident which has been celebrated in both literary and artistic form.

The most beautiful moonlight nights in India are those of early autumn when the skies have been freshly washed of all their dust by the rains and the light is far brighter than on many of our cloudy days during the same season. The story is that King Ajātaśatru, with his court, was enjoying one of those bright, moonlit evenings on his lofty terrace in late October or early November. Seeing the night so clear and feeling his conscience so troubled, the king sighed and wondered what saintly Brāhman or *samāna* could restore his peace of mind. After the six heterodox masters had been suggested and discarded, because of the king's lack of faith in them, his doctor Jīvaka told him that the Buddha was at this time in his Mango Grove with twelve hundred and fifty monks. "Your Majesty should go and visit him and peace will return to your heart." At once the king gave orders to have five hundred elephants made ready to take five hundred of his women while he mounted his own. The procession, lighted by torches, left by the southern gate of the new part of Rājagṛha and filed through the narrow pass, which is the access to the surrounding hills of the older city. Turning left, it proceeded to the Mango Grove as indicated by Jīvaka.

Suddenly the king, hearing nothing but silence, became afraid that he was being drawn into an ambush. How else could it be explained that, being so close to such a numerous assembly, they should hear no sound, not even that of a cough? Jīvaka reassured his majesty and pointed to lights in the distance illuminating the large circular hall that he had built for the Community's meetings. There they found the Buddha, seated near the central pillar and facing east, surrounded by his monks. After the usual salutations the monarch asked the Blessed One for permission to put to him a question that was most unusual under the circumstances. What were the benefits, substantial or slight, that could be found in asceticism? The Buddha amply satisfied the king's curiosity on this point and finally the story proceeded to its original beginning. After Ajātaśatru declared himself convinced and stated his desire to become a lay zealot, he made his confession:

> In my foolishness, in my blindness, in wickedness I have committed a sin, my Lord: for the love of sovereign power I have caused my father's death, this virtuous man and virtuous king. May the Blessed One, O Lord, accept the confession of my sin so that I shall not sin again.

The Buddha made reply:

> It is only too true, O great king, that you have sinned . . . , but as long as you recognize it as sin and that you make public penance according to the rule, we shall accept your confession. Such is, O great king, the blessing of the Noble Discipline, that whoever, recognizing his sin as a sin and makes public penance according to the rule, he will not sin again.

Upon hearing this the king left, apparently reassured. It must not be taken for granted, however, that according to Buddhist doctrine confession *ipso facto* brings about complete absolution. The monarch had not attained salvation. As the Buddha immediately pointed out to his monks, in spite of his evident contrition, his sin prevented "the vision of spotless truth to rise before him at this very place," according to the sacred formula.

From Rājagṛha to Vaiśālī

IT is necessary for us to be aware of the new turn of affairs between the Buddha and the son and murderer of his old friend Bimbisāra if we are to understand the beginning of the Book of the Great Decease (*Mahāparinibbāna Sutta*). Ajātaśatru, having come into power, conceived the desire of extending it over the neighboring states. Son of a Vidheha princess (Vaidehī), he claimed his right through her to bring the lands bordering the left bank of the Ganges, facing the Magadha, under his domination. His plan was to conquer the Vṛjjis after subduing the Licchavis of Vaiśālī despite or because of their riches and power. Before starting on this venture, Ajātaśatru wished to know what outcome the Blessed One would predict, for the words of Buddhas are invariably true. Consequently, he dispatched one of his ministers, the Brāhman Varshakāra, to Śākyamuni, who at this time was residing on the Vultures' Peak. As we know, the Master had long since shed all the bellicose prejudices of his class and had become an avowed pacifist. But he knew the world and recognized what made for strong and respected nations.

During the interview with Varshakāra he dealt with the minister's question by parrying with questions of his own which he put to his faithful Ānanda, who stood by fanning him. He asked his disciple what he himself knew better than anyone—namely, how the Vṛjjis behaved among themselves. In this ingenious manner he was able to define for his interlocutor the seven fundamental reasons for their prosperity: frequent public meetings, peaceful living, lawfulness, respect for the aged and for women, veneration of sanctuaries, and kindness to saints. As long as they practiced these virtues they would be invincible, and that was just what they were doing. As an astute politician, the minister concluded that the primary thing was to sow discord among the enemy before attacking, and so he took leave of the Buddha in the manner usual for statesmen, mentioning their great tasks to be accomplished.² The fact that we shall soon meet him again is our excuse for this interlude.

The passage we have just read deserves to be read and meditated upon in all countries, for it is only too true that the welfare of a country depends essentially upon concord among its citizens. It would, however, remain a strange opening for the account of the Buddha's last journey if it did not reveal the singular manner in which that book was composed. Not only was the preamble borrowed from another text, but it was entirely copied. And after the Master had enumerated the seven causes for the Vaiśālī inhabitants' prosperity, he enumerated the seven-times-five-plus-six conditions for the prosperity of his Order. And so the account continued, making more than half of the *Parinirvāna Sutra* nothing more than a mosaic of what could be called "plagiarisms from the Scriptures," loosely welded together by narrative passages.

Sometimes it is but a bare, stereotyped formula announcing the resumption of the successive journey: "Now when the Blessed One had stayed as long as was convenient at Rāgagaha he addressed the venerable Ānanda, and said: 'Come, Ānanda, let us go on to Ambalatthika.'"³ This was his first stop going north on that last trip. There the king had a summer house in a mango park, and it was in that spot that the Buddha stayed with his company of monks. He had already preached two well-known sermons there and he did not fail to preach another. The next stopping place was Nālanda, the village that was to become the great Buddhist university of medieval India and where the Archaeological Service has made such fruitful finds. It was also the birthplace of the great Disciple Śāriputra, and the scribe found nothing better than having him come back to earth and without hesitation take up *verbatim* the same conversation he had had once, before his death, with the Master.⁴ A third march at last brought the Buddha and his retinue to the bank of the Ganges and the village of Pātali (The Bignonia) where the lay faithful immediately organized a reception in his honor. At this point in the account there is a long section of interest taken from an old treatise on discipline.

Situated as has been noted by Fa-hsien just below the junction of several important rivers, the village of Pātali (to-day Patna) was from time immemorial the place for crossing the Middle Ganges. Its importance, both commercially and strategically, was evident. As a matter of fact, before too long it was to become the celebrated capital of the quasi-pan-Indian empire of the Mauryas under the name of Pāṭaliputra. It was therefore not surprising to find Ajātaśatru's two leading ministers, Sunīdha and Varshakāra, already there for the erection of a fortress to hold back the Licchavis, masters of the opposite shore, as well as to serve as base for the offensive they still contemplated. It can be easily admitted that under the circumstances the Buddha could predict the important future for this area and the dangers that threatened it: floods, fire, and internal discord.

As spring was well on there was no question of crossing the Ganges by stepping from sand bank to sand bank, for the great river, swollen by the melted Himālayan snows, was at its highest. Therefore, Śākyamuni had to go across on the ferry, and one of the usual topographic details remembered and later shown to pilgrims was the gate by which he left in order to reach the pier. Everything was about to take place in a most natural way—but that was just what a devoted zealot could not bear, and so the biographers took care of that. First of all, the Buddha's prediction about the future city referred not merely to its size; he made it precise that it would become a "metropolis," and this he based on the fact that his divine eye perceived a multitude of jinn haunting the area.[5] (Later this type of divination was condemned as a form of charlatanism unworthy of a religious prophet.) Finally as all were busy arranging for boats to ferry the Master and his monks across the river, he suddenly disappeared, as he had once before, this time from the right bank, and reappeared instantaneously on the left bank with his retinue of monks. Probability at this point is strained but edification is saved, and for many that is the essential.

The Rejection of Life at Vaiśālī

LET us not linger over two more stops and more repetitions, but go on to Vaiśālī. It goes without saying that we are not spared a second recital *in extenso* of visits and donations on the part of the courtesan Ambapālī and the noble Licchavis, but here at last is something new. The rainy season was approaching, and the Buddha advised his monks to spread themselves among the neighboring villages and to seek shelter with friends and acquaintances; he himself chose to remain in the village of Beluva. The following is the account given in the *Mahāparanib-bāna Sutta*:

Now when the Blessed One had thus entered upon the rainy season, there fell upon him a dire sickness, and sharp pains came upon him, even unto death. But the Blessed One, mindful and self-possessed, bore them without complaint.

Then this thought occurred to the Blessed One, "It would not be right for me to pass away from existence without addressing the disciples, without taking leave of the Order. Let me now, by a strong effort of the will, bend this sickness down again, and keep my hold on life till the allotted time be come."

And the Blessed One, by a strong effort of the will, bent that sickness down again, and kept his hold on life till the time he fixed upon should come. And the sickness abated upon him.

Now very soon after the Blessed One began to recover; when he had quite got rid of the sickness, he went out from the monastery, and sat down behind the monastery on a seat spread out there. And the venerable Ānanda went to the place where the Blessed One was, and saluted him, and took a seat respectfully on one side, and addressed the Blessed One, and said: "I have beheld, Lord, how the Blessed One was in health, and I have beheld how the Blessed One had to suffer. And though at the sight of the sickness of the Blessed One my body became weak as a creeper, and the horizon became dim to me, and my faculties were no longer clear, yet notwithstanding I took some little comfort from the thought that the Blessed One would not pass away from existence until at least he had left instructions as touching the Order."

"What, then, Ānanda? Does the Order expect that of me? I have preached the truth without making any distinction between exoteric and esoteric doctrine: for in respect of the truths, Ānanda, the Tathāgata has no such thing as the closed fist of a teacher, who keeps some things back. Surely, Ānanda, should there be any one who harbours the thought, 'It is I who will lead the brotherhood,' or, 'The order is dependent upon me,' it is he who should lay down instructions in any matter concerning the Order. Now the Tathā-gata, Ānanda, thinks not that it is he who should lead the brotherhood, or that the Order is dependent upon him. Why then should he leave instructions in any matter concerning the Order? I too, O Ānanda, am now grown old, and full of years, my journey is drawing to its close, I have reached my sum of days, I am turning eighty years of age; and just as a worn-out cart, Ānanda, can only with much additional care be made to move along, so, methinks, the body of the Tathāgata can only be kept going with much additional care. It is only, Ānanda, when the Tathāgata, ceasing to attend to any outward thing, or to experience any sensation, becomes plunged in that devout meditation of heart which is concerned with no material object—it is only then that the body of the Tathāgata is at ease.

"Therefore, O Ānanda, be ye lamps unto yourselves. Be ye a refuge to yourselves. Betake yourselves to no external refuge. Hold fast to the truth as a lamp." [6]

Thus the Buddha disclaimed ever having tried or desired to govern the Order. Perhaps on that point he himself was under an illusion, and we shall come back to it; but for the moment let us continue our reading, which has other surprises in store for us. Soon we shall find that our text is in complete discord with the whole doctrine. But when has a devout soul shunned a contradiction? The great theme of the Buddha's teaching, as we have seen over and over, was the impermanence of all things human, and yet here we find excuses being thought up for letting himself die! He had become for his faithful the "god superior to the gods," the unique Being, exceptional, autonomous, and above the laws of the universe. All this in spite of the fact that he had always proclaimed that all that is born must die and that he himself had promised Māra that once his task was accomplished he would enter Nirvāna never to return. But this was in the past and, just as he was supposed to have chosen all circumstances concerning his birth, it was thought he could do likewise for his death. He could and therefore should prolong his life indefinitely. Gifted with supernatural powers, why not work the same miracle which the Jews expected of the Messiah, and remain on earth for all time? How much more charitable it would be to continue to enlighten the world and thus keep the door to salvation wide open for all beings. Deliberately depriving us of his presence and assistance—us, the later unfortunate generations who have not had the inestimable privilege of being his contemporaries—would seem a cruel denial of all that could be expected from his infinite kindness. Such an admission of the Buddha's voluntary refusal to meet his obligations

as savior was inconceivable. Consequently, if this was not done on purpose, whose fault was it?

Here we quote again one of the accounts as given in the *Mahāpara-
nibbāna Sutta,* omitting some of the many repetitions:

> Now the Blessed One robed himself early in the morning, and
> taking his bowl in the robe, went into Vesāli for alms, and when he
> returned he sat down on the seat prepared for him, and after he had
> finished eating the rice he addressed the venerable Ānanda, and
> said: "Take up the mat, Ānanda; I will go to spend the day at the
> Kāpāla Ketiya."
>
> "So be it, Lord!" said the venerable Ānanda, in assent, to the
> Blessed One. And taking up the mat he followed step for step be-
> hind the Blessed One.
>
> So the Blessed One proceeded to the Kāpāla Ketiya, and when
> he had come there he sat down on the mat spread out for him, and
> the venerable Ānanda took his seat respectfully beside him. Then
> the Blessed One addressed the venerable Ānanda, and said: "How
> delightful a spot, Ānanda, is Vesāli, . . .
>
> "Ānanda! whosoever has thought out, developed, practised, accu-
> mulated, and ascended to the very heights of the four paths to Iddhi
> [psychic powers], and so mastered them as to be able to use them
> as a means of [mental] advancement, and as a basis for edification,
> he, should he desire it, could remain in the same birth for a kalpa,
> or for that portion of the kalpa which had yet to run. Now the
> Tathāgata has thought them out, and thoroughly practised and
> developed them [in all respects as just more fully described], and
> he could, therefore, should he desire it, live on yet for a kalpa, or for
> that portion of the kalpa which has yet to run."
>
> But even though a suggestion so evident and a hint so clear were
> thus given by the Blessed One, the venerable Ānanda was incapable
> of comprehending them; and he besought not the Blessed One, say-
> ing, "Vouchsafe, Lord, to remain during the kalpa! Live on through
> the kalpa, O Blessed One! for the good and the happiness of the
> great multitudes, out of pity for the world, for the good and the
> gain and the weal of gods and men!" So far was his heart possessed
> by the Evil One.
>
> A second and a third time did the Blessed One [say the same
> thing, and a second and a third time was Ānanda's heart thus
> hardened].

Now the Blessed One addressed the venerable Ānanda, and said: "You may leave me, Ānanda, awhile, and do whatever seemeth to thee fit."

"So be it, Lord!" said the venerable Ānanda, in assent, to the Blessed One, and rising from his seat he saluted the Blessed One, and passing him on the right, sat down at the foot of a certain tree not far off thence.

.   .   .   .

Now not long after the venerable Ānanda had been gone, Māra, the Evil One, approached the Blessed One, and stood beside him. And so standing there, he addressed the Blessed One in these words:

"Pass away now, Lord, from existence; let the Blessed One now die. Now is the time for the Blessed One to pass away—even according to the word which the Blessed One spoke when he said: 'I shall not die, O Evil One! until the brethren and sisters of the Order, and until the lay-disciples of either sex shall have become true hearers, wise and well-trained, ready and learned, versed in the Scriptures . . .'

"And now, Lord, the Brethren and Sisters of the Order and the lay disciples of either sex have become [all this], are able to do [all this]. Pass away now therefore, Lord, from existence; let the Blessed One now die!"

And when he had thus spoken, the Blessed One addressed Māra, the Evil One, and said: "O Evil One! make thyself happy, the final extinction of the Tathāgata shall take place before long. At the end of three months from this time the Tathāgata will die!"

Thus the Blessed One while at the Kāpāla Ketiya deliberately and consciously rejected the rest of his allotted sum of life. And on his so rejecting it there arose a mighty earthquake, awful and terrible, and the thunders of heaven burst forth. . . .

Now the following thought occurred to the venerable Ānanda: "Wonderful indeed and marvelous is it that this mighty earthquake should arise, awful and terrible, and that the thunders of heaven should burst forth! What may be the proximate, what the remote cause of the appearance of this earthquake?"

Then the venerable Ānanda went up to the place where the Blessed One was, and did obeisance to the Blessed One, and seated himself respectfully at one side and said: "Wonderful indeed and marvellous is it that this mighty earthquake should arise, awful and terrible, and that the thunders of heaven should burst forth! What may be the proximate, what the remote cause of the appearance of this earthquake?". . .

"Again, Ānanda, when a Tathāgata consciously and deliberately rejects the remainder of his life, then this earth quakes and trembles and is shaken violently. This is the seventh cause, proximate and remote, of the appearance of a mighty earthquake.

"Again, Ānanda, when a Tathāgata passes entirely away with that utter passing away in which nothing whatever is left behind, then this earth quakes and trembles and is shaken violently. This is the eighth cause, proximate and remote, of the appearance of a mighty earthquake. . . .

"Thus, Ānanda, the Tathāgata has now today at the Kāpāla Ketiya consciously and deliberately rejected the rest of his allotted term of life."

And when he had thus spoken the venerable Ānanda addressed the Blessed One, and said: "Vouchsafe, Lord, to remain during the kalpa! live on through the kalpa, O Blessed One! for the good and the happiness of the great multitudes, out of pity for the world, for the good and the gain and the weal of gods and men!"

"Enough now, Ānanda, beseech not the Tathāgata!" was the reply. "The time for making such request is past." . . .

[A second and third time Ānanda makes the same request in vain.]

"Hast thou faith, Ānanda?"

"Even so, Lord!"

"Then, O Ānanda, thine is the fault, thine is the offence—in that when a suggestion so evident and a hint so clear were thus given thee by the Tathāgata, thou wast yet incapable of comprehending them, and thou besoughtest not the Tathāgata, saying, 'Vouchsafe, Lord, to remain during the kalpa. Live on, O Blessed One! through the kalpa for the good and the happiness of the great multitudes, out of pity for the world, for the good and the gain and the weal of gods and men.' If thou shouldst then have so besought the Tathāgata, the Tathāgata might have rejected the appeal even to the second time, but the third time he would have granted it. Thine, therefore, O Ānanda, is the fault, thine is the offence!" [7]

Such is human injustice and variability. On one hand, the oldest account, gathered from those who had known Ānanda personally, tells us that he devoted twenty-five years of his life and constant attention to a demanding Master; now newcomers would make him responsible for the Blessed One's death. However, neither legend nor the Buddhist

Church on the whole would seem to bear Ānanda a grudge for what might have seemed unpardonable thoughtlessness. Evidently the expedient that was later thought of to account for the Master's *Parinirvāna* was only half believed. All this would seem to be quite unnecessary, since the Buddha himself declared that it was our fate to be condemned to separation from what we loved, and went right on recalling to Ānanda as a form of consolation the doom that cannot be escaped. Furthermore, he was to state it once more on his deathbed.[8]

The Last Meal, in Pāvā

THE reason we believe that the following episode was introduced later is that after it has taken place we are not much further along than we were before. However, the die was cast and the Buddha, barely recovered from his illness, left the pleasant and hospitable city of the Licchavis. Just beyond the city gates he turned to have a last look, saying: "It is the last time, O Ānanda, that the Predestined One looks upon Vaiśālī; he will never return." These simple words were cause for universal sadness, and to Ānanda's surprise large drops of rain fell from a cloudless sky. The Buddha then explained to his disciple that those were the tears shed by local heavenly divinities in sorrow for the imminent and final separation. Much later in time Hsuan Tsang was shown "fifty or sixty *li* northwest of the city" the spot to which the inhabitants in great numbers escorted the Predestined One. And in order to make the moaning crowd turn back it was necessary for him to use his magical powers and create a deep river between himself and the people.

The sixth journey brought the Buddha and his retinue to the small town of Pāvā without incident. This was the very place where his great rival Jina was to die a few years later. The pious group settled for the night in the mango orchard of Kunda, "the blacksmith's son," who, according to the custom of Indian castes, was himself a blacksmith. The latter at once invited the Buddha and his retinue to dinner the next day. Unfortunately the main dish decided upon for the feast was pork. This heavy food brought on a severe recurrence of the dysentery from which the Master had barely recovered. He bravely bore this new and no less painful attack but, with his strength already weakened, he was unable to overcome it. At least this is the account passed on by living witnesses, who still thought of the Buddha as of a man susceptible to human weaknesses. This meant that the Blessed One, the Predestined One, the Perfect One, died miserably in an obscure village from an attack of dysentery following a digestive upset caused by eating pork. What a comedown for the sublime Being who, a century or two later, would have been exempted by his devotees from any human failings! But also what a guarantee of authenticity to have a fact that would have been in the legend's interest to conceal or disguise!

As can be easily guessed, later generations did not hesitate to rebel against a testimony so devoid of any embellishment and which, as India became more and more strictly vegetarian, lent itself to adverse criticism. The text that we are following chapter by chapter revealed only two such manifestations. Nothing escaped the Blessed One's knowledge, as we all know, and since his kindness extended to all beings, we are told that, as soon as he was seated at the table, the Buddha begged the blacksmith to serve pork only to him and to give his monks the other foods. Also, at the end of the meal he advised his host of the day rapidly to bury the remainder of the meat, for the Master's all-seeing eye had discovered no one, man or god, who could digest such food after eating it—excepting the Predestined One, of course, naïvely added the scribe, forgetting that the Predestined One was the one who became ill.

The second attempt at embellishment, also a latecomer, arose from the same desire but was happier in its expression. The Buddha perceived that the pious blacksmith might be blamed for his death, and because he knew that his host's intentions were pure he was filled with pity and entrusted Ānanda with a consoling message for the poor man: "There are two offerings of food of equal merit and equal fruitfulness, more meritorious and profitable than any other: the one eaten by the Predestined One before supreme and perfect Enlightenment and the one eaten by the Predestined One before the Final Decease." Thus Kunda needed to have neither remorse for the past nor fears for the future.

Our source ends there and later texts only add small bits in the same direction. What they specially retained was a parallel between the last meal before *Sambodhi* and the last meal before the *Parinirvāna;* and having established the merits of both, these also had to become equally delicious. Further consideration made it impossible for such delicious food to be harmful, and thus Kunda could be completely exonerated. If the Buddha barely survived the invitation to dinner, it could only be due to his advanced age. Since there were at the time no absolute restrictions on the eating of meat and fish, there was no reason to modify an age-old tradition. This audacious feat was left to our epoch. After that the philologists became involved in a discussion of the exact meaning of the words used in the old texts, and from one translation to the other the meanings varied, going as far afield as possible and finally suggesting that what the Buddha had eaten was a mess of truffles—not more easily digested but far more distinguished.

The Last Stage of the Journey

IN spite of his great weakness the Buddha decided to resume his journey and bravely took to the road again. His lack of strength betrayed his courage and halfway between Pāvā and Kuśinagara he had to stop beneath a tree and call to Ānanda: "Well, Ānanda, fold my cloak in four; I am tired and wish to sit." At once he asked his faithful helper to bring him water to quench his fevered thirst. But this time, to our great surprise, Ānanda did not hasten to obey. He told the Master that a caravan of five hundred carts had just forded a little stream nearby, making the water churned and muddy; but, he added, a little farther on there was a clear, fresh river, Kakutthā, where the Blessed One could not only drink but bathe his tired limbs. But at that moment the Buddha was unable to move and insisted upon having drinking water. At the third request Ānanda finally gave in and went to the little stream to fill the begging bowl. To his surprise the water had become clear and bright again, which does not astonish us.

At this moment a Mallian nobleman, member of the ruling oligarchy of Kuśinagara, came by. We are told that he was the owner of the caravan which had just preceded him. He stopped to chat with the Buddha and they found that they had both studied with Āḷāra Kālāma.* The young Mallian, however, had remained faithful to his teacher's doctrine. In order to illustrate the amazing faculty of abstraction or withdrawal from the scene of which ascetics were capable, he told an anecdote concerning their former master. One day while Āḷāra Kālāma was seated in meditation on the side of a highway, five hundred carts went by without his being aware of them, and only the dust that covered him was proof of their having passed.

* (Pāli spelling. Previously referred to as Arāda Kālāpa.)

In answer to this the Buddha remarked that one of his own experiences was far more extraordinary. At the time he was staying near the village of Atumā in a barn. A tremendous thunderstorm came up, bringing with it torrential rains and violent thunder. Lightning struck very close by, killing two plowmen, who were brothers, and their four yoked oxen; but the Buddha's meditation was so profound that he neither saw nor heard anything. Now, was that not a feat superior to that of Āḷāra Kālāma?

Marveling at this exploit, the young Mallian immediately acknowledged its superiority and expressed his faith in the true Doctrine. He ordered one of his men to bring to the Buddha two pieces of cloth "the color of gold, shining and ready to wear." These were accepted, one for the Master and the other for Ānanda and the princely donor went on his way.

What is the meaning of this episode? Is it an old traditional recollection or is it rather an interpolation used to pave the way for the following episode? As soon as the Mallian had left, Ānanda clothed his Master in the two pieces of cloth and then there came a miracle. Outdone by the brilliance emanating from the Buddha's body, the splendid material suddenly lost its sheen. When the disciple called attention to this miracle, the Blessed One explained that on two occasions the Predestined One's complexion becomes prodigiously brilliant—on the eve of perfect Enlightenment and on the eve of the Final Decease. For those who wished to establish a connection between this scene and the Christian miracle of the Transfiguration on the mountain, there was need of much good will.

Then and there, without transition, the Buddha rose and started walking. He took a bath in the river Kakutthā and was momentarily revived, but this did not last long and again before crossing the next river, Hiraṇyavatī, he had to stop and rest. (In later accounts the number of these forced halts was increased to twenty-five, while our Stations of the Cross number only fourteen.) At the same time there was a familiar ring to a note brought in. Nothing could happen to the Predestined One to which he had not already given assent, and if, before his death, he was willing to exhibit such human misery and endure so much suffering, it was to give men one last warning of the suffering that awaits them and to teach them a supreme lesson in resignation. But it would be a vain search to seek in the ancient texts the emotional acknowledgments of the Savior's passion and urgent appeals for its imitation. The time was not yet ripe for that.

Arrival in Kuśinagara

THERE was still one more supreme effort to be made. "Let us go, Ānanda, to the other shore of the river Hiranyavatī, at Kuśinārā, to the *Śāla* Grove of the Mallas." No sooner had they reached it than the Buddha, worn with fatigue, said, "Come, Ānanda, spread for me a couch with its head to the north between the twin *Śāla* trees. I am weary, Ānanda, and would lie down. . . . And the Blessed One laid himself down on his right side, with one leg resting on the other and he was mindful and self-possessed." [9] And now he would rise no more.

This last description is to all of Asia what the images of the Crucifixion are to the Occident. The oldest Indian school for a long time could only represent this scene by a funeral tumulus, but the Greco-Buddhist school felt able to achieve a direct representation conforming absolutely to the letter of the texts. It is the only time that the Buddha is represented other than seated or standing. On a bed rather like the couches shown in the funeral banquets of our classical antiquity, the Buddha is lying on his right side, his head to the left of the spectator so that his face can be seen, and, as it has been written, the legs are somewhat stiffly stretched one upon the other. When Aśvaghoṣa wrote that "the Buddha had his right hand folded back under his head," it is easy to believe that he already had before him one of those representations. This particular detail, which is omitted from the old texts, appears constantly in the images.

Where has this painful journey brought us? The data on the direction taken and the distances covered would point to the present village of Kasia, located about thirty-seven miles east of Gorakhpur, at the intersection of two highways in the middle of fertile plains. Everything has led us to identify this with the original Kuśinagara (in Pāli, Kusinārā). Before the end of the last century the discovery, made near the ruins of an ancient *stūpa*, of a temple specially consecrated for sheltering a large stone image, six feet long, of the Buddha on his deathbed was a step in strengthening the hypothesis concerning the area. Twenty years later three archaeological diggings revealed further ruins going back to the time of the Kuśans and possibly of the Mauryas. There were also found seals of the "monastery of the Mahāparinirvāna." Though the final evidence had not yet been reached, enough was present to show that this had been the long-standing site of a well-frequented pilgrimage. Kasia did not wait to become that again. The devoted Burmese, not content to build a hostel for the modern pilgrims and to plant new *śālas,* raised enough funds to restore the great tumulus. Borings, made deep within the center of the mound during the reconstruction probings, brought forth a copper urn in the shape of a round jug, the opening of which was sealed with a copper plaque. This plaque bore an inscription stating that the urn had been deposited "in the sanctuary of the Parinirvāna." This time there could be no further doubt as to the authenticity of the site of the fourth Great Miracle, which the monument commemorated.

The Kasia finds have also revealed that this group of local Buddhist sanctuaries extended over a sacred area of about forty acres, closely rivaling the size of the Jētavana Park at Śrāvastī. But there is no question of Kuśinagara's having been a large city, and it would never have been deliberately chosen for the scene of the Ultimate Death. Ānanda actually reprimanded the Master about that very point:

> Let not the Blessed One die in this little wattle and daub town in the midst of the jungle . . . For, Lord, there are other great cities such as Kampā, Rājagṛha, Śrāvastī, etc. . . . Let the Blessed One die in one of them. There, there are many wealthy nobles and Brāhmans and rich heads of houses, believers in the Tathāgata, who will pay due honor to the remains of the Tathāgata.

The Buddha replied at once: "Say not so, Ānanda!" and he recalled that at a time when he was the greatest and most virtuous king of kings, Kuśinagara, under the name of Kusāvatī, was his capital and there was no fairer and mightier city.[10] If he wished to die in the place that witnessed his past splendors, who could blame him?

Ānanda's Role

WE left Śākyamuni stretched out on his deathbed, and truly his end was near but it was not immediately at hand. His life was to end during the third watch of the following night. It would be extremely difficult to follow the thread of the story through the incoherent incidents

and desultory talk that filled the remaining hours before death if
Ānanda, due to the complete immobilization of his Master, had not
taken matters into his own hands. He was the one who received the
Predestined One's last recommendations, he who took care of the
final errands and messages, he who watched over the last callers; and
all of this he did in spite of profound, though slightly selfish, grief. He
betrayed only one moment of weakness when, standing aside and leaning against a wall he wept, saying: "I am only a disciple with much to
learn, one who has yet to work out his own perfection. And the Master
is about to pass away from me—he who is so kind!" The Buddha was
not slow to note Ānanda's absence and called him in order to console
him affectionately:

> Enough, Ānanda! Do not let yourself be troubled; do not weep!
> Have I not already told you, on former occasions, that it is the very
> nature of all things most near and dear unto us that we must divide
> ourselves from them, leave them, sever ourselves from them? How
> then Ānanda can this be possible—whereas anything whatever born
> . . . contains within itself the inherent necessity of dissolution—
> how then can it be possible that such a being should not be dis-
> solved? No such condition can exist. For a long time, Ānanda, you
> have been very near to me by acts of love, kind and good, that never
> varies, and is beyond all measure. . . . You have done well,
> Ānanda! Be earnest in effort, and you too shall soon be free from
> the great evils . . .[11]

And after having thus comforted his disciple in private, he repeated
his praise in public, telling of Ānanda's qualities as an assistant, his
care in organizing the Predestined One's meetings to everyone's satisfaction, and his ability in handling visitors, be they monks, nuns,
zealots, or kings—or even members of the heterodox groups.

The Buddha gave further proof of his confidence in Ānanda by
sending him to Kuśinagara as his ambassador to the notables to tell
them of his approaching death. He was to ask them to hurry so they
would not reproach themselves later, saying, "In our village did the
death of our Tathāgata take place and we took no opportunity of visit-
ing the Tathāgata in his last hours." The call was only too well heard,
and all the Mallas—men, women, children—came forth and with evidence of great sorrow moved on to the *Sāla* Grove. Fortunately,
Ānanda was there to act as master of ceremonies to handle the difficult

problem of making so many presentations to the dying Buddha. Instead of taking the Mallas individually, he presented them as families with their "entourage" so that during the first watch of the night that task was finished.

But there was no rest for the disciples nor for the Master. Hardly had the Mallas left when a religious called Subhadra appeared, soliciting an interview with the Blessed One. He knew, said he, how rare in this world is the coming of a Buddha; and since he had heard that the Buddha was about to leave it, this was his only hope of finding a solution to the doubts that still plagued him. Three times Ānanda tried to lead him away, saying that the Blessed One had had enough and was weary; but the latter overheard the conversation from his bed and, as always, he welcomed a man with a sincerely troubled conscience. The interview ended, as one would expect, in a total condemnation of the doctrines of the six heretic masters and an exaltation of the Good Law. Subhadra was immediately convinced and converted and, as an exceptional favor, was ordained at once. The last disciple to be converted by the Buddha, he later became one of the saints. This gave rise to several legends concerning Subhadra, and we can recognize him on the figured representations of the *Parinirvāna* as the monk seated in meditation in front of the Buddha's deathbed.

Final Decease

DAYLIGHT was soon to come but the Buddha would not see it. He gave Ānanda a few more instructions and called his monks together. Did any of them have in their minds any doubts or perplexities concerning the Doctrine or the discipline? Let them hurry and state them before it was too late! After urging them for the third time and receiving silence in answer, the Blessed One said: "Behold now, brethren, I exhort you, saying, 'Decay is inherent in all composite things! Work out your salvation with diligence!'"[12] These were the Tathāgata's last words. Already the death struggle had begun, but a Buddha cannot die simply from physical exhaustion. As a finished adept of yogī he had to pass through a series of spiritual trances, which are meaningless to the uninitiated but which have been carefully catalogued by the initiates. From the peak of ecstasy he passed slowly through the series as a natural transition into the supreme and ineffable state of final Nirvāna.

Possibly the original version was simpler and Śākyamuni only had
to pass through the same four degrees of Meditation, that he discovered
at the dawn of his vocation under the immobile shade of the rose-apple
tree. Let us again turn to the text:

Then the Blessed One entered into the first stage of deep meditation. And rising out of the first stage he passed into the second.
And rising out of the second he passed into the third. And rising
out of the third stage he passed into the fourth. And rising out of
the fourth stage of deep meditation he entered into the state of mind
to which the infinity of space is alone present. And passing out of
the mere consciousness of the infinity of space he entered into the
state of mind to which the infinity of thought is alone present. And
passing out of the mere consciousness of the infinity of thought
he entered into a state of mind to which nothing at all was specially present. And passing out of the consciousness of no special
object he fell into a state between consciousness and unconsciousness. And passing out of the state between consciousness and unconsciousness he fell into a state in which the consciousness both of
sensations and of ideas had wholly passed away.
    Then the venerable Ānanda said to the venerable Anuruddha:
"O my lord, O Anuruddha, the Blessed One is dead!"
    "Nay! brother Ānanda, the Blessed One is not dead. He has en-
tered into that state in which both sensations and ideas have ceased
to be!"
    Then the Blessed One passing out of the state in which both
sensations and ideas have ceased to be, entered into the state between consciousness and unconsciousness. And passing out of the
state between consciousness and unconsciousness he entered into the
state of mind to which nothing at all is specially present. And
passing out of the consciousness of no special object he entered into
the state of mind to which the infinity of thought is alone present.
And passing out of the mere consciousness of the infinity of thought
he entered into the state of mind to which the infinity of space is
alone present. And passing out of the mere consciousness of the
infinity of space he entered into the fourth stage of deep meditation.
And passing out of the fourth stage he entered into the third. And
passing out of the third stage he entered into the second. And passing out of the second he entered into the first. And passing out of
the first stage of deep meditation he entered into the second. And
passing out of the second stage he entered into the third. And pass-

ing out of the third stage he entered into the fourth stage of deep meditation. And passing out of the last stage of deep meditation he immediately expired.[13]

The Funeral

IF we tried to reconstitute the funeral rites as prescribed by custom and local circumstances, we would have no doubt that the later accounts willfully altered the records in order to throw a pious veil over events that no longer fitted in with the new concepts. First of all, it is an accepted fact that the funerals of members of religious orders were left entirely in the hands of the lay faithful. Thus it would seem that at the news of the Buddha's death the zealots among the Mallas hastened with their families to the *Sāla* Grove.

Their first duty, according to ancient and universal custom, was to gather about the deathbed and lament. (It was then, that according to the old scribes the women had "sullied" the Blessed One's body with their tears.) Once grief had been duly manifested these people must proceed to washing of the body according to the rules, and that is why Ānanda might have been accused of having allowed the august nudity to be exhibited to the public eye. At the completion of all these preparations, the body was again robed in the monastic habit and laid on its stretcher, and voluntary pallbearers offered to carry it to the crematory area of the village. Upon the improvised funeral pyre, built according to the zealots' means, the mortal remains of Śākyamuni were laid and burned that very day, according to custom's and the climate's demands. Afterwards the helpers' only duty was to gather the relics from the ashes and purify themselves with a ritual bath and a change of clothes, for all dead bodies were considered impure and a source of contamination.

Thus, or in a similar fashion, must the Buddha's funeral have been carried out; otherwise, the innuendoes of blame later directed towards Ānanda would have no meaning. Later the biographers wished for grander ceremonies. According to our principal source, the gods were called on to intervene and the Buddha's body was paraded through the streets with garlands of "flowers from heaven, dance and song and music." The new tradition revealed itself in the statement that Ānanda had consulted the Master as to the kind of funeral rites that would be

appropriate. He is said to have answered that the body of the Predestined One should receive the same rites as those accorded a Universal Monarch—which meant a funeral with all the solemnity and
magnificence possible. Accordingly the notables knew what their duties
were and carried them out to the full, thereby delaying cremation a
whole week. It was, of course, no longer acceptable to have the dead
Buddha in his monastic robes, and we are given a graphic account of
the use of five hundred lay costumes, masses of cotton wool, and five
hundred twin pieces of new material in which to wrap the swathed
body, which was finally deposited in a metal container. This eventually
was taken to the pyre, now made of nothing but perfumed woods.
Even the lighting of the funeral pyre became a complex matter, for
though four Malla princes were ready with their torches, nothing could
happen until Mahākāśyapa, who was to become the high priest of the
Buddhist Church, appeared on the scene. Finally the pyre burst into
flame spontaneously and all that was left was to invent diverse means,
all the more extraordinary, to help put out the fire.

The Division of Relics

It is a well-known fact that in ancient civilizations death is not an end
for the individual, and the questions pertaining to funerals are too
important to his future life to be taken lightly. In the Buddha's case
such questions should not have existed, for "there was to be no rebirth
for him." Wise were the monks who refused to deplore the final liberation of the Presdestined One. But even so, after the lay faithful had
generously carried out their funeral duties, they had to be told how to
dispose of the Buddha's precious remains. We in the Occident are too
familiar with the cult of "saintly relics" to ask here for an explanation
of such matters. Buddhists recognized three kinds of remains: the or-
ganic remains found among the ashes; the various utensils used by the
Blessed One during his life, such as his begging bowl, basin, and broom;
and finally the objects or edifices commemorating the great events of
his career. It is written that the Buddha's body was entirely destroyed
by fire except for the bones of the skull and the teeth, and of the numerous shrouds only two, the inner and the outer, remained, by miracle,
quite intact. The Mallas, we are told, proud of the windfall that fate

had bestowed on them, carried off the relics in a procession to their assembly hall with song and dance.

The bas-reliefs show us the relics set on a throne, which is draped and overhung with stuff in the shape of a bell and over which is the royal parasol. Already warriors leaning on their lances are there as guardians. This is probably an indication that the Mallas had an inkling of what was to follow. When the news of the Buddha's death spread, the kings and chiefs of the various areas where the Buddha had sojourned sent requests for their share of the precious possessions. The notables sent word back that "the Buddha died on our territory; we shall not share his relics." Then the requests became summons and to make them more urgent the seven pretenders to shares came with their armies to lay siege to Kuśinagara. A lintel of Sānchī's southern gate represents this scene admirably. Fortunately a scandalous war over love for the apostle of peace was averted through the good offices of the wise Brāhman Drona. To him was turned over the task of dividing the relics in eight equal shares.

The distribution of the relics in their eight parts is shown on the old monuments, and the seven pretenders are also represented, carrying off their portions in small caskets ceremoniously set on the heads of their state elephants. Where are they going? To fulfill the demand attributed to the dying Buddha:

> And as they treat the remains of a king of kings, so, Vāsetthas, should they treat the remains of the Tathāgata. At the four crossroads a dāgaba should be erected to the Tathāgata. And whosoever shall there place garlands or perfumes or paint, or make salutation there, or become in its presence calm in heart—that shall long be to them for a profit and a joy.[14]

Thus we find at the end of the Master's life the association which was made at his birth—namely, that between the most powerful of monarchs and the most wise of the Enlightened. At the same time we come upon the origin of the cult of the *stūpa,* which, though it has never been in India the exclusive monopoly of Buddhists, has become and remained the characteristic monument of their faith throughout the Far East.

We have followed the Buddha to his innumerable graves and now our only task is to establish the date of his death. This has been the source of long and laborious discussions, on which we shall not spend much time. The Singhalese chronology, which seems most reliable, places the event in 543 B.C. The calculations of erudite Europeans bring it down to 477 B.C. On the other hand, we have faithfully followed the accepted tradition, which states that the Predestined One lived about fifty years after leaving home, thus making a total of about eighty years. This assertion is in no sense untrue, but it is also not confirmed by any facts. We do know that the Buddha owed it to himself and to his believers to live at least that long, for according to Indian ideas eighty years is the normal duration of a full human life, and it could not be admitted that the Buddha had died prematurely.

Now there arises the suspicion that the lack of agreement between the count of the Indians and that of the Indologists may simply come from the fact that in time the former might have mistaken the date of the death of their Master for that of his nativity. Not only is the number eighty too conventional to avoid being suspect, but again and again we have noted either in ancient or modern sources that the records of the last fifteen years of the Buddha's life remain practically blank. Then suddenly there are again active recitals of recollections at the approach of the *Parinirvāna*. The first explanation of this total lacuna is that those fifteen years were never lived and that in reality Śākyamuni died around the age of sixty-five, not eighty. Surely once again we claim no certainty and we would not dare insinuate that, because of the length of time involved, any error could be called insignificant. However, until we know more, we can be sure of not being too far wrong if we write after the name of our historical Buddha: *circa* 543–477 B.C.

23. The Final Decease.
Gandhāra school, 2nd–5th century A.D.

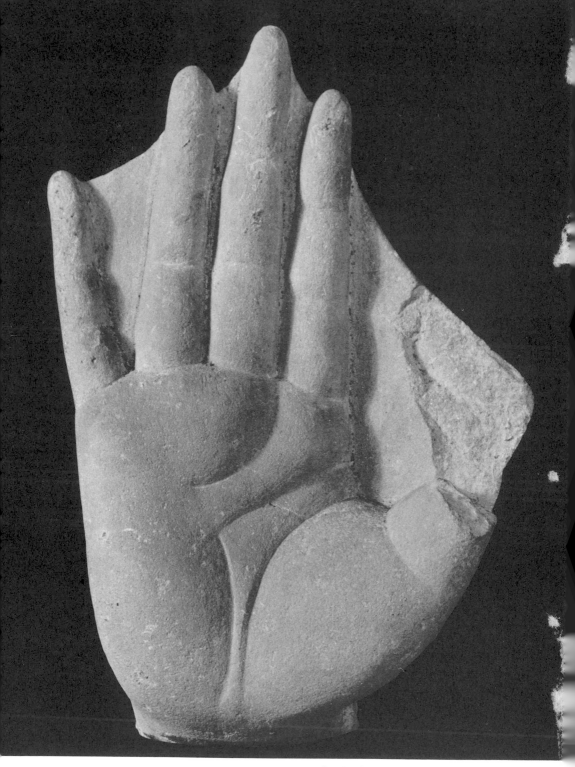

24. Hand of the Buddha. Sārnāth.

CHAPTER XII

CONCLUSIONS

WHEN WE BEGAN our study we warned the reader that according to Indian ideas the biography of this Great Being who was to become during his last existence the Buddha Śākyamuni could not have an actual or known beginning but that it had a certain ending. This we have just described. The Buddha died because he was only a man and all men are mortal. He died in the open air just as he had been born and where he had lived most of his life since the Great Renunciation. Death, which came at an advanced age, was caused by illness and, at the time, the Master was cared for by his disciples and surrounded by veneration. It was a quiet death, without violence or bloodshed, but it was a final death, without resurrection or after life. The Buddha could be admired and praised for his perfections; he could be loved for his kindness; but he could no longer be counted upon for any further assistance. As it was written in the original *Milindapañha,* the book designed to spread the doctrine among the Indo-Greeks, "he exists now only as his Law."

However, nearly twenty-five hundred years after his death his memory is still very much alive. Apparently as long as world suffering is to last—and it will last as long as the world—the memory of the great doctor of the soul whose life was spent in trying to find its cure will persist as a shining light on the horizon. "The Sage of the Śākyas" was, above all, the initiator of a religion that achieved world-wide renown, but he was also the founder of an important monastic order, and both are still flourishing. Besides this, he was, for his time, an understanding moralist as well as an independent and vigorous thinker. With this much certainty the memory of a great spirit—what the Indians call a *Mahātma* ("Magnanimous")—has been preserved for us, and we have no cause to stint our praise or restrain our criticism of him. He has the right to our complete respect.

The Religious

IT is hardly necessary to recall the actual facts that still confirm the Buddha's past greatness. Though no one who has visited Asia would want to be called upon to guarantee the absolute faith of five hundred million zealots assigned to Buddhism by geographical statistics, it is certainly true that it can claim as many true believers as Christianity, the other widespread religion of our time. And if the posthumous popularity of a historical personage can be measured by the number of figured representations of him, there is probably no one who can boast of more painted or sculptured portraits than the Buddha. These are actual facts on which it is useless to insist; but it may be necessary to impress on the Western reader's mind that all this has been achieved by a doctrine that disclaims the existence of a lasting soul to which immortality can be promised, or of a providential god who can answer the prayers of the faithful. To the Westerner, these would seem to be the essential elements of all religions.

It is only too true that in this world all is impermanence and suffering, and the only remedy found by the Buddha was not to be reborn. Upon this Buddhists are all agreed, be they monks or laymen. For both, the supreme goal or "sovereign good" is Nirvāna. This word, however, can be understood in various ways. The great majority of the faithful, without worrying over the scholars' theories concerning the disintegration of the soul after death, cling to the hope of joys in the heavens, promised to all the friends of virtue, graded according to their merits. For them Nirvāna is synonymous with Paradise—a haven or a refuge. Even those who remain within the Master's pure tradition, far from seeing in the cessation of all existence a distressing experience, hail this extinction as the happiest good fortune and the greatest of victories. It was with a shout of triumph and joy that, upon the simultaneous attainment of Enlightenment and Nirvāna, the Buddha at last broke the chains of destiny and forever liberated himself from his corporeal prison. Unquestionably, though Buddhism is at heart the most pessimistic of doctrines, it is permissible, without excessive paradox and with numerous precise citations, to speak of the "exuberant optimism" of its aherents.[1]

The attention of students of Buddhism should be called to the dual personality of its founder. For an infinite time he was the Bodhisattva, the being predestined to perfect Enlightenment, and as such during his numerous rebirths he was supposed to have performed a multitude of generous acts and exemplified all altruistic virtues to their maximum. As soon as he became, for a relatively brief but no less important time, the perfect Buddha, above all human vicissitudes, he turned practically all his attention to ensuring the salvation of the disciples who had put their trust in him. This he did with precepts, prohibitions, and protection. By remembering those two aspects of the Master, it is easier to understand the future development of his church.

On the one hand, the old Order of Central India clung particularly to the monachal and disciplinary character of his teaching, adopting the saintly but selfish ideal of the monk solely concerned with his escape from the sea of suffering and ruthlessly determined to overcome all obstacles, family or other, that stood in the way of his salvation. On the other hand, the northwestern sects, developing in another climate and accessible to Occidental influences, preferred to adhere to the example of the Prince of Charity, the hero forever ready to undergo all sacrifices. Thus they felt that they opened up a "Superior Way" to the one in which the ancients had become mired and which has continued to be known as the "Inferior Way."[2] So there arose the great schism that still divides the Buddhist Church into two camps. One has put the emphasis on compassion, universal good will, selfless devotion, and love of one's fellow man extended to all living beings to the point of forgetting oneself completely. The other advocates, above all, the withdrawal into the self, concentration of spirit, constant vigilance over acts and words and thoughts, solitary meditation, and the complete suppression of all emotion. In short, it could be said that the first imitates the Bodhisattva and the second the Buddha. It is more in the opposition of these two moral attitudes than in their different mythological creations and metaphysical speculations that the fundamental distinction between Mahāyāna and Hīnayāna is found.

This observation deserves to be further analyzed, for it helps us to understand the conflicts that have sometimes arisen among the members of the older Community as well as the differences in opinion that divide the more recent commentators on Buddhism. Both, due to their own intellectual and moral leanings, were drawn, and still are, to the two traditions that have remained dominant within the Church. In the Master's very entourage representatives of a generous humanity or of the most strict individualism could be found. Several of the disciples had been his childhood and youthful friends before accepting him as "Teacher of men and gods," and some accepted the doctrine only because of their affection for him. The love that Ānanda, for example, bore him already deserved the name of that passionate devotion, ready to spread over the world, which the Mahāyānists thought they had invented as *bhakti*. Opposed to this, some later converts, such as Mahā-kāśyapa, having come from the austere heterodox sects and imbued with all the ascetic prejudices, persisted in exemplifying the incarnation of the rigid, almost inhuman monk, indifferent to the suffering of mankind and remote from the world. Therein, probably, lay the basis for the fundamental disagreement between the two disciples, and this variance would have rapidly become a conflict if the sweet patience of one had not vanquished the uncompromising aggression of the other.

Still, the Chinese sculptors who carved gigantic images of Śākya-muni on the rocky cliffs of Long-men were basically right in representing him between those two disciples. The young, prepossessing monk on his right and the austere, thin, older man on his left admirably personify, physically as well as morally, the dual components which are completely merged in the pensive serenity of their Master, represented between them at a mature age. Despite their divergences, both ancient and later Buddhism have their origin in the personality of the Master, just as the Ganges and the Indus, though they flow into two different seas, gush forth from the same Himālayan mountain.

The above considerations may serve to make more precise Śākya-muni's historical role in the religious evolution of a large part of Asia. For one not born into his religion it is impossible to define exactly the nature of his spiritual influence and to gauge its depth. However, from the outside it is easy to determine its more apparent limitations. Three facts are immediately to be noted. First, it is incorrect to speak of the Indian "Savior," as we have done, for the term is only partially exact. To be a savior in the full sense of the word demands the sacrifice of one's person, followed by continued assistance due to an efficacious grace. A helping hand can then be held out to the suppliants in order to rescue them from their misery and guide them to him. Though the Buddha was known to carry out such gestures during his lifetime in order to bring about the salvation of more or less acceptable persons, if he saw fit, no help whatsoever could be hoped for after his *Parinirvāna* except that coming from his precepts and his past example. Each of his followers was given the task of bringing about his own salvation. For the present generations he has become the pioneer, the guide, who, before leaving this world, opened the way to salvation, for we must never forget that his system is, above all, a "path."

It is, therefore, all the more important to know where that path leads before entering upon it. The answer, which we already know, is perfectly clear: it is a way out of *samsāra,* the vortex of rebirths. The means of salvation was conceived only with this primary datum in mind, and therefore it follows that any value and meaning is dependent on this one concept. In fact, the Good Law can directly address itself only to those human beings who share a belief in transmigration of one kind or another, and who, wishing to be free of this pitiless cycle, are willing to face nothingness. The very nature of these ideas obviously restricts the field of activity of Buddhism, which becomes even narrower when the means of escape is made known. For the only one recommended as certain is entry into an order of begging monks. Such a necessity would hardly suit everyone's taste and its additional restriction —to propagate the Good Law—destroys for the doctrine the ecumenical character that its partisans would have it share with Christianity. The Christ of the Gospel could be called the "Man-God"; the Buddha of the old canonical scriptures was the "Monk-God."

The Thinker

ŚĀKYAMUNI'S philosophical system has received extravagant praise. But it has also been the subject of distortions and exaggerations. When, in accord with Sānkhya, the Buddha denied all divine intention and intervention in an uncreated universe, he seemed to be anticipating the most rigorous concepts of modern physics; when he professed a kind of phenomenalism, Hume comes to mind; and when he treated physiological and psychic data on the same plane, we are tempted to think of our psychobiologists. Such tempting *rapprochements* have little foundation, for we have proof that at the time of the Buddha's death physiology and psychology, physics and metaphysics, systematics and morality were far from being disentangled. We must not forget that this was still the time when the mind was situated not yet in the brain but in the heart.

These observations, though they may destroy certain illusions, may help us in suggesting a solution to the greatest difficulty in the interpretation of the Buddha's system—namely, the accord between his metaphysics and his ethics. As early as the First and the Second Sermon two distinct purposes were definitely set. While the conclusion drawn from the Four Truths asserted and sharpened a moralizing intention, that of the sermon on the illusion of the self brought troubling consequences for the moral law—so much so that more than one leader of a sect, contemporary with the Buddha, found in the transitory character of the soul an excuse to free himself from all responsibility.[3] And in fact, amid the constant integration and disintegration of the combinations of phenomena and the equally incessant appearances and disappearances of the phenomena themselves, the numerous occasions for suffering were evident. But what of the place for notions of right and wrong? If man is only a name and a shadow, is it not doubly so for virtue? Still, no one disputes the fact that the Predestined One taught with equal vigor the theory of the retribution for man's acts as well as that of the nullity of the agent. For the Buddha, the permanence of *karma* was as essential a dogma as the fleeting, unsubstantial character of beings and things. Innumerable are the passages in the scriptures which condemn with equal finality both the negation of the moral sanction and the affirmation of the reality of the individual against whom this sanction must be applied. The unbelievers have not waited until now to cry out against this lack of logic, nor the Buddhist theologians to try to reduce this contradiction. Various ways have been tried, but diluting the difficulty has not resolved it. The real question is to know when, why, and how the notion of quality, either good or bad, appeared in the mechanical unrolling of the series of phenomena to the point of modifying its value and altering its course. In other words, to the point of substituting for a vague causal link, which organizes them in sequences, a more and more strict determinism of the law, which classifies them according to their merits or demerits.

Because the Buddha never explained this point, modern exegetes have been called upon to invent an explanation for it. The first that comes to mind is that when Śākyamuni, as an adult, elaborated his philosophical system, he did not give up his childhood beliefs but simply annexed to them the doctrine of universal emptiness.[4] Having witnessed the same kind of thing occurring in our own day, when reputed thinkers hold two types of incompatible ideas, such as purely scientific concepts conforming to the demands of reason and religious beliefs, which simply remain objects of faith, we find the above a plausible hypothesis. However, while recognizing some truth in this theory, we prefer to suggest another, which we find historically more acceptable.

Ever since Descartes made the well-known distinction between "thinking" and "extension," philosophers have felt obliged to bridge the gap between these two antitheses. But the Buddha never felt the need of reconciling an antinomy of which he was not aware. Just as he never thought of reconstituting reality, broken down by pure reason, on the foundations of moral law, so he never thought he had to defend the sanction of our actions against the destructive effect of perceptual analysis. These difficult and perhaps insoluble problems were still well beyond the intellectual frontiers of his time. Amid the confused mixture of disparate principles, which methodical introspection was scarcely beginning to untangle, no fundamental distinction between the physical and the mental could be clearly discerned. It would, moreover, have seemed to be a complication more troublesome than useful. The romantic imagination of an Alfred de Musset could transform the mathematical law of universal gravitation into an erotic relationship among the planets. But what change does that bring in the spectacle of the heavenly sphere?

The same is true when we read in the texts that the five aggregates which form our apparent personality break up and are recomposed without cessation, and that while this is going on our acts "ripen" in these same aggregates. The two events are synchronous, and one does not prevent the other. Just as a tree, according to its species, naturally produces in the course of its growth fruits that are sweet, bitter, or tasteless, so every animate organism, after its kind, engenders while it grows a *karma* that is sweet, bitter, or neutral. What difference does it make to the phenomenal series of events that we are limited to observing their quasi-automatic history or that we anticipate their qualitative outcome? This is but a question of shifting one's point of view. Ethics and metaphysics are for the Buddha but two connected aspects of the single process of "becoming," or, if one prefer—since this process is known to us only insofar as it is grasped subjectively—of a single psychophysiological unit. If this seems to us to be even more obscure, we owe it to those students who, trying to think through the human complex after the Buddha, have clarified it a bit without, however, reaching the synthetic end of their analysis.

We are not lowering the stature of Śākyamuni by relocating him in his environment. It would be a betrayal of him to put him in ours. No impartial critic could avoid praising him for his objectivity and for the intellectual courage required to free himself from the mental routine of the great mass of mankind and to discover what seemed to so many of his contemporaries, as it still does to so many of ours, the most adequate solution to the painful problem of human fate. But vigor of thought is not synonymous with originality and breadth of mind. It seems more and more clear that the doctrine of Buddhism is in its main outlines only the faithful image of popular beliefs—we are far from calling them superstitions—and of philosophic doctrines that flourished in India in the sixth century B.C. Tradition itself agrees that its inspiration lay in the forms of Sāṅkhya and Yoga then current. From the former it took the mechanical conception of the universe; from the latter, its methods of psychotherapy. All things considered, the philosophic contribution of Śākyamuni can be reduced by way of the Four Noble Truths and what we may call the Fifth, the enumeration of the twelve events whose unchanging order beats out the rhythm of each individual life. Not only did he have no answer to the great questions about the beginning and the end of things; he never concealed his aversion to that type of teleological speculation.[5] In the most ancient texts the word which names it (*drishti,* literally "view") has always the pejorative meaning of "erroneous opinion." That his followers themselves felt the narrowness of his system and the limitations of his teaching, we have shown above by a twofold proof. For now they attempt to torture the formula of production in conditioned series or sequences into abstract generalizations and to give it a logical rigor, which it so obviously lacks. And also to save the dogma of their Master's omniscience, they have no other expedient than to pretend that he deliberately restricted the number and the range of his teachings. The liberties they take in interpreting his main thesis, like the embarrassed manner in which they excuse its limitations, bear eloquent testimony to their basic agreement with us that, much more than a philosopher, the Buddha was a moralist.

The Moralist

IN truth, Buddhism, as Emile Senart has judiciously said, is essentially a "moral discipline." It was as such that, as it came into being, it inspired the uplifting edicts of Emperor Aśoka, and it is as such that in our time it still exerts a profound influence that has won the respect of two hemispheres among both believers and unbelievers. Moreover, it is what the two main primitive outpourings of its enormous literature made clear in practically every line. While the symbol of the wheel of rebirths and the theory of universal nullity were constantly in the back of the Buddha's mind, it is true that in his discourses they rarely came to the fore, and then only when he was dealing with neophytes already trained to understand or having superior minds familiar with the handling of abstract ideas. The *Vinaya* and *Sūtra* treatises are, above all, collections of moral prescriptions and instructions. There is a great deal of truth in such statements as the following, which are attributed to the Master: "I only teach that there is suffering and the freedom from suffering"; or again, "I only teach the retribution of acts." A well-known quotation makes clear this general law: "Abstaining from all sin, practising the good, purifying thought, here is the teaching of Buddhas." [6] Because he knew how to restrict himself to the most urgent, if not the most fundamental, question, and by concentrating upon it the intensity of his thinking and teaching, Śākyamuni was able to found an Order that had the capacity to develop into a church of world renown centuries after his death.

Little does it matter to the historian if the Buddha's ethics be accused of lacking in originality. That was its guarantee of success. A moral code is not invented; living in social groups has already done that, and what remains to be done is to systematize it. The Predestined One's great merit was that he, particularly, saw clearly the conceptions and the aspirations of his environment and expounded them. Only where they have continued to exist has his exalted position endured. It is no less true that the reason for his being able to formulate them in such a seductive manner was that he shared them. The horror of *saṃsāra*, the recognition of the five cardinal sins, and so forth were common currency, and, as far as we can see, Śākyamuni's originality among leaders of non-Brāhmanic sects is found in his way of dealing with questions of method. In all things from the beginning to the end of his career he insisted upon following the middle way, precisely as in one's conduct there should be a just mean between hedonism and asceticism.

Secondly, it was with unrivaled spirit that he steadily refused to deduce from his frightening discovery of the unreality of the world any indifference concerning moral issues. He continued to place emphasis upon the unavoidable sanctions from acts, in spite of the unreality of the acting agent. Finally, he would have these acts themselves, be they of body, speech, or ideas, judged primarily upon their intention. For him and for his disciples, who were capable of understanding this, sin was not some slimy impurity, some kind of pus sticking to the soul that could be washed off by sacred baths or dried out by ascetic excess. Life's drama is entirely of the spirit, and man becomes not just what he has done but what he has wanted to do.

Buddhist ethics, then, is not so commonplace as some would hold it to be. What can truthfully be said is that no matter how great its service is to all men, it is fundamentally Indian, even in its contradictions. The latter seem numerous, as seen in many accounts. At times the Predestined One urged upon his flock the practice of good works, homely virtues, worship of divinities who would show gratitude; in short, all the practices considered worthy by devout people. In exchange he promised a paradise at the end of their lives. Inversely, he put them on their guard against the sins and causes of demerits that would not fail to plunge them after death into an unhappy rebirth or into a burning or freezing hell. Sometimes he insisted on the fact that gaining true knowledge (naturally, his doctrine) was the necessary and sufficient condition for salvation; while erroneous beliefs were the most certain cause of perdition. At other times he tended to have it understood that the secret of salvation was to be found in an ardent devotion to him and absolute faith in his law. In short, if we believe the words that are attributed to him, he would have recommended indifferently the three means of liberation that were so carefully segregated by later generations—namely, pious works, insight, and quietism. This would entail the same kind of confusion gained from contradictory principles such as we noted above in his psychobiology. Still, it would be easy to point out that the Buddha could not be held responsible for everything that has been written in his name and that these contradictions are more apparent than real. They can be attributed to adaptations of the Master's teachings to the moral levels of various audiences without his ever losing sight of the final goal set for humanity. The exegetes have, however, not been blind to this lack of unity, which has given rise to a variety of contradictory judgments concerning Buddhist ethics.

Finally, if we seek a comparison between the idea of charity in Buddhism and in Christianity, we find that they completely lack a common basis. In the latter the notion rests on the love of God and as a corollary on the love of one's fellow man in God. In Buddhism the concept of God in the Christian sense is totally absent, but this does not eliminate charity. In spite of the fact that each one is responsible for his own salvation and consequently must concentrate his effort on his own life, still we are reminded that "kindliness is the purification of the heart" and "doing good is the best way to love one's self." The older Buddhist doctrine, long before the later one, preached four responsibilities towards fellow beings, that is, all that lives. First there is "equanimity," which implies not simply a feeling of impartiality and disinterest but also complete calm towards the worst affronts. As a consequence, there is to be no resentment and no desire to return evil for evil. Then comes "compassion" towards all sufferings, which does not exclude trying to alleviate them as one can. The third responsibility is "joyous participation," which means sharing the happiness of others and thus doing away with the ignominious sin of envy. Finally, crowning all, is *maitri* or *metta* which is defined both in Sanskrit and Pāli as "the love that a mother or a father and mother bear towards an only son, even though it cost them their life." This clinches the matter, for that is not a neutral and passive feeling such as some have been prone to condemn. Each true Buddhist must be his own redeemer, atoning for his life by virtue. In accomplishing this he effectively works for universal happiness.

The Gentleman

LET us admit it. After we have gone the rounds of the texts of his early church and gazed upon the Buddha as a person, the rich complexity of his personality leaves us perplexed. We realize that this personality absorbed the contradictions, shed light on the obscure, gave meaning to the commonplaces of his moral or philosophical systems, and yet each time it is easier to state what he was not rather than what he was. It is difficult to accept Ernest Renan's opinion without restrictions when he says that "alone among the great founders of religions Śākyamuni was a metaphysician." It is true that he wished to have his doctrine a matter of reason and not of faith. We could go on at length into a series of pros and cons and conclude that, like the unknowable *ātman* of the ancient Upanishads, the Predestined One could be defined only in negative terms, and consequently admit that we could never know the basic make-up of his personality.

We shall not, however, declare ourselves defeated nor our study sterile. Too often along the way we have perceived the beating of a heart beneath the impassive bearing of a pretended god; too many typical anecdotes have been recounted, too many meaningful words have been recorded, credited to the Blessed One, not to leave an impression of his personality. And so the hope still exists of discovering the distinctive trait that will unite and vitalize the minute indications scattered among the texts and thus reveal his original character.

Perhaps it is not a mere illusion that the most constant characteristics of his personality were revealed to us in his youth. His noble birth, his training in sports and in intellectual matters, the life of luxury and pleasure that he led until he was almost thirty, determined the lordly quality that remained forever despite the monastic robe. His innate distinction always impressed his visitors, beginning with King Bimbisāra. At all times and everywhere, Śāriputra reputedly said, the Buddha was a model of urbanity and politeness. It was due to both his good education and his free intelligence that he scorned the foolish and indecent practices common to the religious sects of his time and that he would have nothing to do with their jealousies and intrigues. His constant concern with good manners and with physical as well as moral cleanliness in his Order can also be traced to his youth. The last sections of the Formulation of Confession are a genuine book of etiquette for the use of monks. Just as he condemned lust, theft, lies, and cheating, he forbade carelessness in dress, the licking of fingers when eating, speaking with a full mouth, and ogling the food in the bowl of one's neighbor. All behavior had to be, above all, "correct." And when he announced his determination, which would always remain with him, to adhere to the golden mean, can one not recognize there a manifestation of his innate and refined sense of decorum and fitness? With confidence we can keep in mind these first indications.

Thus encouraged, let us continue to watch closely for the statements and gestures of this strange monk. We quickly realize that he resembled only himself. Without doubt he was detached from society, but he did not systematically shun it, and even accepted dinner invitations. What is more, far from thinking only of his own salvation, he reognized his duties towards his fellow man and always welcomed anyone to his daily sermon. The number of consultations he held every day is beyond count, and, tireless, he went from town to village across the great Indian plain teaching the truths that he was the first to discover. His example was as convincing as his words. In the meantime he. acquired or won over more and more disciples, and he constantly watched the disciplinary status of his flock. Frequently he had to guide his monks back into the observance of decency and harmony and protect them from temptation. Surely this was no sinecure, and there were monks of a later vintage who complained that the slightest misdemeanor never escaped his vigilance.

When a rich landowner upbraided him for eating without producing, he was able to answer with a clear conscience that he, too, was engaged in continual labor. In fact, he died in harness. Even on his deathbed two of his last acts were to settle a question of protocol between monks and to put a black sheep in quarantine, so completely did he take to heart his task as a spiritual director. Only for short periods and at rare intervals did he allow himself the leisure and the pure joy of solitary meditation. His was far from a contemplative Order, but rather an active, militant one with instructions to be constantly on the alert. Far from allowing his monks to be idle, the Predestined One imposed on them the task of studying and preaching the Good Law for the edification and salvation of their fellow men. It would seem that he took to heart the justification of their enforced mendicity by their useful role in society. This is a most important point on which there is to be no doubt. Though the religious Gautama may have for some few years believed himself to be a hermit at heart, he soon awoke from this dream and he remained until the end of his life a busy man of action.

As we watched him rule this Order whose constitution, or rather lack of constitution, made it impossible to govern, we found that he succeeded only through his personal authority. His prestige impressed everyone and usually was sufficient to discourage failures in good conduct as well as to settle conflicts. Only once, as we saw, his conciliatory intervention failed, having been called in too late when things were out of hand. Offended in his dignity, he retired to solitude but did not have to wait long for the repentance of the sinners.

Without doubt he wished to be, and was, loved rather than feared, but his kindly attitude towards suffering humanity had nothing of bleating humanitarianism. His compassion was that of a surgeon towards his patient and it never diluted his severity in necessary interventions. Concerning means of salvation, he was inflexible and may have seemed implacable when he finally broke his old father's heart and shattered his dynastic hopes by insisting upon the enrollment in the Order of the King's younger son Nanda and grandson Rahūla. That was only because Śākyamuni's own confidence in his doctrine equaled his self-control.

Could he be accused of having the soul of a dictator? That would assume a deeper knowledge than he had of himself, for during his last illness he disclaimed ever having wished to rule his order. He did not "order," he "suggested," he told Ānanda. Whether this was so or not, from all evidence he was a leader, and he was legitimately called "the Leader who has no leader." Thus, to his innate and acquired distinction, his concern for good behavior, and his constant awareness of manners and fitness can be added an imperious leaning towards action and leadership. Before having been transfigured by the idolatry of his zealots into a monk-god, Śākyamuni owed it to himself to be during his life the noble-monk.

We may then conclude that the Buddha Śākyamuni was a gentleman to his fingertips, free from the slightest suggestion of charlatanism and fanaticism as well as endowed with a surpassing strength of mind and perfect serenity. He also was an austere moralist but without excess and considerate of others, an independent and judicious thinker as consistent an enemy of meaningless metaphysics as of vulgar superstitions. He became the founder of a religion completely imbued with a spirit of mercy throughout its secret despair, and was the first leader of men—at least in man's memory—to accuse the selfishness of desire of being the source of evil and hatred. The infallible cure Śākyamuni offered his fellowmen for their worst sufferings was mutual love. If only they had listened more closely!

NOTES

Chapter I: THE NATIVITY (1)

1. Hermann Oldenberg, *Buddha, sein Leben, seine Lehre, seine Gemeinde.*
2. Emile Senart, *Origines Bouddhiques,* XXV, 6.
3. See the extensive notes in the French edition of this work: A Foucher, *La Vie du Bouddha,* p. 345. (Translator.)
4. *The Questions of King Milinda,* trans. by T. W. Rhys Davids, XXV, 64.
5. Edward Conze, *Buddhism; Its Essence and Development,* p. 39. (Translator.)
6. *Ibid.,* p. 49. (Translator.) Cf. A. L. Basham, *The Wonder that was India,* p. 320. (Translator.)
7. *Śāntideva-Bodhicarya-avatara,* ed. and transcribed by L. de la Vallée-Poussin and trans. by L. Finot. Paris, 1920.
8. *Jātakas,* Nos. 499 and 547. See Bibliography for translation.
9. *Lalitavistara,* Chapter III, pp. 37–46.
10. *Mahāvastu,* ed. E. Senart, I, 227–280.
11. *Lalitavistara,* Chapter III, p. 36.
12. *Ibid.,* p. 44.
13. *Ibid.,* p. 56.
14. *Ibid.,* Chapter V, p. 73 and p. 88 n.
15. *Ibid.,* p. 74.
16. *Ibid.,* Chapter VI, pp. 94 and 112.
17. See Foucher, *op. cit.,* p. 356 n.
18. *Lalitavistara,* Chapter V, p. 76.
19. *Ibid.,* Chapter VI, p. 98.
20. *Ibid.,* p. 99.
21. *Ibid.,* p. 103.
22. *Ibid.,* p. 102.
23. *Ibid.,* p. 99.

24. A. Foucher, *On the Iconography of the Buddha's Nativity*, Archaeological Survey of India, No. 46, trans. by H. Hargreaves.
25. *Lalitavistara*, Chapter VII, p. 155 nn.
26. *Ibid.*, p. 123.

Chapter II: THE NATIVITY (II)

1. St. Jerome, *Contra Jovinianum*, Book I, sec. 42. (*Patrologia Latina*,
Vol. XXIII, 285.)
2. *Lalitavistara*, Chapter VIII, p. 126.
3. Matthew, 11:4–6.
4. *Lalitavistara*, Chapter VII, p. 124.
5. *Ibid.*
6. *Ibid.*
7. *Jataka Stories*, ed. E. B. Cowell, Book XXII, Vol. VI, 250.
8. W. W. Rockhill, *Life of the Buddha*, p. 16.
9. *Lalitavistara*, Chapter VII, p. 136.
10. *Ibid.*, Chapter VIII, p. 173.
11. *Ibid.*, p. 175.
12. *Ibid.*, Chapter VII, pp. 142 ff.

The thirty-two signs of a great personage:
1. coil of curly hair on his head; 2. hair blackish deep blue color and curl-
ing to the right side; 3. forehead large and even; 4. between eyebrows a
circle of hair of the color of snow or silver; 5. eyes black as a cow's; 6. teeth
40 in number; 7. closely set; 8. white; 9. voice like that of a Brahmana;
10. tongue full of moisture; 11. tongue large and slender; 12. lower jaw
like that of a lion; 13. neck well raised; 14. ends of shoulders raised like
the *saptachhada* flower (*Alastonia scholaris*); 15. radiance delicate, color of
gold; 16. and steady; 17. arms long and hanging; 18. upper part of body
like a lion's; 19. body as long as "his fathom"; 20. every hair on body detached, ascending upwards, and turned to right; 21. buttocks covered with
hair; 22. thighs well developed; 23. legs like a gazelle's; 24. fingers long;
25. hands and feet expansive; 26. also soft and fresh; 27. fingers and toes
webbed; 28. toes long; 29. on his soles a well-executed white wheel, "full
of light and radiance, and having 1000 spokes, a felly and a nave"; 30. feet
even and well set. NOTE. Only these thirty are given.

The eighty subsidiary signs of a great personage:
1. nails convex; 2. copper-colored; and 3. smooth; 4. fingers rounded; 5. and
well proportioned; 6. veins hidden; 7. so are ankles; 8. joints close; 9. feet
uniform, no irregularity; 10. feet and hands well spread; 11. markings on
hands smooth; 12. uniform on both hands; 13. deep; 14. uncrooked; 15. ar-

ranged in due order; 16. lips red; 17. speech not loud; 18. tongue soft, fresh, and copper-colored; 19. voice sweet and deep "like the bellowing of an elephant or the rolling of clouds"; 20. consonants fully sounded; 21. arms long; 22. skin pure; 23. body soft; 24. large; 25. unemaciated; 26. unrivaled; 27. well adjusted; 28. well proportioned; 29. knees large, swelling, and well developed; 30. body well rounded; 31. body well smoothed; 32. not crooked; 33. tapering; 34. navel deep; 35. not crooked; 36. and well fitted; 37. like a needle; 38. he is frisky as a bull calf; 39. brilliant without any shadow; 40. motion stately as that of an elephant; 41. like that of a lion; 42. or a bull; 43. or of a goose; 44. right stepped; 45. waist rounded; 46. not crooked; 47. belly like a bow; 48. body without perforations and faults, color of blue wood; 49. canines well rounded; 50. sharp; 51. and regular; 52. nose well pointed; 53. eye pure; 54. stainless; 55. laughing; 56. large; 57. broad; 58. like the petals of a blue lotus; 59. eyebrows joined; 60. beautiful; 61. well proportioned; 62. orderly; 63. black; 64. cheeks big; 65. not unequal; 66. faultless; 67. bridge of nose not sunk; 68. organs well apparent; 69. and perfect; 70. mouth and forehead in keeping; 71. head full; 72. hairs black; 73. born with hair; 74. hairs appropriate; 75. sweet smelling; 76. unrivaled; 77. untroublesome; 78. regular; 79. curly; 80. "whirled into the forms of Śrivatsa, Svastika, Nandyavarta, and Vardhamāna diagrams."

13. *Ibid.*, p. 138.
14. A. Foucher, *The Beginnings of Buddhist Art*, p. 271.
15. *Lalitavistara*, Chapter VII, p. 136.

Chapter III: CHILDHOOD AND YOUTH (1)

1. Cf. A. L. Basham, *The Wonder that was India*, p. 415. (Translator.)
2. *Lalitavistara*, Chapter VII, p. 138.
3. Cf. Basham, *op. cit.*, p. 256: "He was the son of a chief of the Śākyas, a small tribe of the Himālayan foothills." (Translator.)
4. *Lalitavistara*, Chapter VII, p. 138, gives him eight body-nurses to carry him, eight milk-nurses, eight nurses to keep him clean, and eight to play with him. (Translator.)
5. *Ibid.*
6. *Ibid.*, Chapter X.
7. *Divyāvadhāna*, ed. E. B. Cowell and R. A. Neil, Cambridge, England, 1886, p. 391.
8. See Basham, *op. cit.*, p. 398. (Translator.)
9. *Lalitavistara*, Chapter X, p. 204.
10. For the engagement and marriage, see *ibid.*, Chapter XII, pp. 198 ff.
11. *Ibid.*, p. 210.

12. See W. W. Rockhill, *Life of the Buddha*, p. 21. (Translator.)
13. *Mahāvastu*, ed. E. Senart, III, 150.
14. *Ibid.*, II, 115–117.

Chapter IV: CHILDHOOD AND YOUTH (II)

1. *Suttanipāta*, trans. by V. Fausboell (in *Sacred Books of the East*, Vol. X) III, i, 2.
2. *Lalitavistara*, Chapter XI.
3. *Ibid.*
4. *Suttanipāta*, III, i, 2 and 4.
5. *Lalitavistara*, Chapter XIV, p. 258.
6. Trans. by Ananda Coomaraswamy in his *Buddha and the Gospel of Buddhism*, p. 23. (Translator.)
7. *Lalitavistara*, Chapter XIV, pp. 280 ff.
8. *Buddhist Birth-Stories*, trans. by T. W. Rhys Davids., p. 62.
9. *Lalitavistara*, Chapter XIV, pp. 280 ff.
10. *Buddhacarita*, ed. E. H. Johnson, XXXII, 67, verse 53. (Translator.)

Chapter V: THE SEARCH FOR ENLIGHTENMENT

1. Marco Polo, *Travels*, trans. by Ronald Latham, pp. 255–257.
2. The Greek Orthodox Church preferred the date of August 26.
3. See S. Beal, *The Romantic Legend of Śākya Buddha*, p. 364.
4. *De Trinitate*, sec. viii, 4.
5. *Divyāvadhāna*, ed. E. B. Cowell and R. A. Neil, p. 547.
6. *Brihadāranyaka Upanishad*, trans. by Swami Nikhilananda, Book III, ii, 1.
7. See the beautiful volumes of Sir John Marshall, *Mohenjo-Daro and the Indus Civilization*.
8. The title of Chapter XVI in *Lalitavistara* is *"Bimbisāra-upāsankramana."* See also *Mahāvastu*, ed. E. Senart, II, 198, and *Suttanipāta*, ed. V. Fausboell, III, 1.
9. See H. C. Warren, *Buddhism in Translation*, p. 334.
10. *Lalitavistara*, Chapter XVII, *passim*.
11. On the much debated question, upon which we can but touch here, of the relation between Buddhism and Sāṅkhya, see Hermann Oldenberg, *Buddha, sein Leben, seine Lehre, seine Gemeinde*, p. 63; E. H. Johnston's preface to *Buddhacarita*, p. lvi; and E. H. Johnston, *Early Saṁkhya*. On the other hand, T. Shcherbatskoi has suggested the possibility of an influence of Buddhism on Sāṅkhya in his *Central Conception of Buddhism* (Calcutta ed.), p. 47. As a matter of fact, there

are several Sāṅkhyas, as there are also several Vedāntas; the classical
Sāṅkhya of Isvara-Krishna is only a Brāhmanized form, developed to
give the color of orthodoxy to a doctrine, the rational and quasi-sci-
entific content of which could not be overlooked by the teachings of the
schools.

12. See "Buddhisme et Yoga," *Revue de l'Histoire des Religions*, XLII
(1900), 345.
13. "Bellows" is the equivalent of *gargari*, but not its description.
14. For a description of the Buddha's body, see *Lalitavistara*, Chapter VII;
see also note 12, Chapter II, above.
15. For the bath, see *ibid.*, Chapter XVIII.

Chapter VI: ENLIGHTENMENT

1. See A. Foucher, *L'Art Gréco-Bouddhique du Gandhāra*, I, 383, and
figs. 194 to 198. See also Sir Alexander Cunningham, *Mahābodhi*, p. 34.
2. See *Buddhist Birth-Stories*, trans. by T. W. Rhys Davids, p. 188. (This
reference is given as a substitute for Foucher's, which is to Lermann's
translation into German of *Lalitavistara*, Halle, 1905. The English
translation, which has been used so far, stops short at the Great Departure.—Translator.)
3. The Four Noble Truths are: (1) birth is suffering, (2) old age is suffering, (3) disease is suffering, and (4) death is suffering. The Buddha's
sermon on them can be easily found in T. W. Rhys Davids, *Buddhism:
Its History and Literature*, p. 136. (Translator.)
4. The demand for comparisons runs throughout *The Questions of King
Milinda*, trans. by T. W. Rhys Davids. One of the best known is the
comparison between the soul and the oil in a lamp, to which reference
has already been made in the body of the text. But see also p. 63 and
pp. 71 ff. (Translator.)
5. Maurice Maeterlinck, *The Life of the Bee*, trans. by Alfred Sutro,
Chapter IV, sec. 62, p. 218.
6. Cf. *Rig Veda*, trans. by Ralph T. H. Griffith, Book III, Hymn 48;
Book IV, Hymn 18.
7. Foucher refers his readers to *Brihadāranyaka Upanishad*, I, iv. 10. But
see "Kutadanta Sutta" in *Dialogues of the Buddha*, trans. by T. W.
Rhys Davids, p. 173, where the Buddha preaches against sacrifices and
argues that the only proper sacrifice is self-discipline. Cf. *Dialogues of
the Buddha*, p. 96. (Translator.)
8. See W. M. McGovern, *Manual of Buddhist Philosophy*, I, 60.
9. *Mahāvagga*, trans. by T. W. Rhys Davids and H. Oldenberg, "First
Khandhaka," xxiv, sec. 5, p. 150.

10. *Suttanipāta*, III, ii, 30.
11. *Lalitavistara*, beginning of Chapter XVIII. E. Windisch, in his *Māra und Buddha*, translated two collections of these stereotyped temptations, *Māra Samyutta* (thirty-five tales) and *Bhikkhuni Samyutta* (ten tales) and tried to work out the chronological development of the legend of Māra (p. 213).
12. *Mahāvastu*, ed. E. Senart, p. 340. Cf. *Buddhist Birth-Stories*, p. 195.
13. *Buddhacarita*, ed. E. H. Johnston, XIV, 3, substitutes for the second of their traditional names Rati or Raga, Arati, and Trishnā, the name Prīti, or joy, which seems more appropriate. (Davids gives their names as Craving, Discontent, and Lust; see *Buddhist Birth-Stories*, p. 202.—Translator.)
14. *Divyāvadhāna*, ed. E. B. Cowell and R. A. Neil, p. 306.
15. Foucher gives no source for this quotation. (Translator.)
16. This simile comes from *Divyāvahāna*, p. 300, 17.
17. *Kathopanishad*, I, 6.
18. The formulas which follow in the text come from *Lalitavistara*, Chapter XX.
19. For a discussion of "The Wheel of Life," see Davids, *Buddhism, Its History and Literature*, p. 155.
20. *Bhagavad Gītā*, trans. by Swami Prabhavananda and Christopher Isherwood, p. 43. (Translator.)
21. The quotation is from *Lalitavistara*. See also *Mahāvastu*, II, 284.
22. For these sects, see McGovern, *op. cit.*, I, 172. For modern exegetes, see P. Oltramare, *La formule bouddhique des causes;* L. de la Vallée-Poussin, "Théorie des douze conditions," *Bouddhisme, études et matériaux;* P. Masson-Oursel, *Essai d'interprétation de la théorie bouddhique des douze conditions.* (In more recent English writings, see Edward Conze, *Buddhism; Its Essence and Development*, p. 43. Conze also gives a concise account of the Buddhist sects.—Translator.)

Chapter VII: THE FIRST SERMON

1. For a detailed study of the episodes between the Enlightenment and the First Sermon, see E. Tuneld, *Recherches sur la valeur des traditions bouddhiques pālie et non-pālie*, p. 54.
2. *Buddhacarita*, ed. E. H. Johnston, XIV, 94. Cf. Tuneld, *op. cit.*, p. 115.
3. *Lalitavistara*, p. 371.
4. *Mahāvastu*, ed. E. Senart, III, 281, puts this in the second, not in the third, week.
5. This accounts for the repetition of this incident in *Mahāparinibbāna Sutta* and *Divyāvadhāna*.

6. On self-ordination, see *Mahāvastu*, I, 2, 15. (Cf. *The Questions of King Milinda*, trans. by T. W. Rhys Davids, III, vi, 5, p. 118.—Translator.)

7. On Hsuan-Tsang, see T. Watters, *On Yuang Chwang's Travels in India*, I, 111. On the one hand, there may have been a play upon words, making the name of Bhallika stand for "Bactrian" (Bahlika); on the other, *trapuśa* is also the name of the tin which India imported from the coast opposite to that of the Bay of Bengal.

8. *Lalitavistara*, p. 405. Cf. *Mahāvastu*, III, 325; and S. Beal, *The Romantic Legend of Śakya Buddha*, p. 245.

9. McGovern, *Manual of Buddhist Philosophy*, 1890.

10. Cf. W. N. Brown, *The Indian and the Christian Miracles of Walking on the Water*.

11. See *Jātakas*, Book V, no. 359, trans. by H. T. Francis and R. A. Neil, III, 122. (Cf. W. W. Rockhill, *Life of the Buddha*, p. 138.—Translator.)

12. For a slightly different version of this incident, see *Mahāvagga*, ed. H. Oldenberg, I, vi, 10, p. 91. (Translator.)

13. *Lalitavistara*, p. 416; *Mahāvastu*, III, 331; *Mahāvagga*, I, vi, 17.

14. In the passage that follows in the text, it should be recalled that the names of the five *skanda* are *rūpa* (designating material bodies the differentia of which is impenetrability), *vedanā, sanjnā, samskāra vijnāna* (these four being mental *caitta* or *caitasika*). It is understood that only the *upādāna skandha* of the ordinary man are in question and, what is more, under the influence of the passions.

15. T. Stcherbatsky, in his *Central Conception of Buddhism and the Meaning of the word "Dharma,"* has shown this. The word *dharma* (*dhamma*), which may mean "norm," "statute," "custom," "law," "justice," "the right," "duty," "morality," "religion," and so on, here has the technical sense of "the ultimate ground of phenomena," for one has to stop at some point in decomposing aggregates into their elements. It should be noted in this connection that the old doctrine had no knowledge of atomic theory.

16. Oltramare, *Histoire des Idées Théosophiques dans l'Inde*, II, 166.

17. Trans. by Davids and Oldenberg in *Vinaya Texts*, I, 151 (*Sacred Books of the East*, Vol. XVII).

Chapter VIII: THE FIRST CONVERSIONS

1. *Lalitavistara*, p. 418, 1.19.

2. Other texts say "sixty years ago." See Tibetan version of *Buddhacarita*, trans. by E. H. Johnston, XVI, 15; *Mahāvastu*, I, 2, and III, 92; S. Beal, *The Romantic Legend of Śākhya Buddha*, p. 289. In any event,

the *Mahāvagga* says nothing of the sort and *Nidāna Kathā* (see *Buddhist Birth-Stories,* trans. by T. W. Rhys Davids, p. 88) brings in the miracle merely for the sake of Śuddhodhana's messengers.

3. This irreverent comment does not flow from my pen. It is already to be found in *The Questions of King Milinda,* ed. Trenckner, p. 74.

4. He is also called Nāradatta, Nārada, or Nālaka. See *Buddhacarita,* I, 81; *Mahāvastu,* III, 383; Beal, *op. cit.,* p. 279.

5. For this complicated story, see *Mahāvastu,* III, 382; Beal, *op. cit.,* p. 276. The legend is based on a transformation of the name Airāvata into *Ēlāpatra,* a cardamon leaf. Cf. J. Ph. Vogel, *Indian Serpent Lore,* pp. 10, 50, and 207.

6. Perhaps even "with dry feet." On this point see W. N. Brown, *The Indian and Christian Miracles of Walking on Water.*

7. *Mahāvagga,* I, xiv, 116.

8. *Ibid.,* I, xv–xxi; *Mahāvastu,* III, 424–432; Beal, *op. cit.,* p. 292; *Nidāna Kathā,* p. 82.

9. The Tibetan *Buddhacarita,* XVI, 54–57, makes much of this.

10. *Mahāvagga,* I, xxii, 13.

11. *Ibid.,* I, xxiii, 15, 18.

12. *Ibid.,* I, xxiii–xxiv.

13. *Mahāvastu,* III, 57. (Translated from the French of A. Foucher, pp. 224–227. Original spelling retained.—Translator.)

14. See the Tibetan *Buddhacarita,* XVIII; Beal, *op. cit.,* p. 316. The *Mahāvastu* dates the conversion of Mahākaśyapa before that of the two great disciples, III, 50.

15. See S. Beal, *Buddhist Records of the Western World,* Chapter 23, based on reports of Fa-hsien. Cf. T. Watters, *On Yuang Chwang's Travels in India,* II, 143, for the report of Hsuan Tsang.

16. *Mahāvagga,* I, xxiv, 5, trans. by Davids and Oldenberg, p. 150.

17. St. Luke, 18:29-30.

18. *Mahāvastu,* III, 92.

19. We follow the chronology of the *Mahāvastu* in counting seven years, much the most reasonable. The point which is unanimously granted is that Rāhula, the son of the Buddha, was six years old at the time of his father's return to Kapilavastu. Furthermore, the *Mahāvastu* has him born only "ten months" after the Great Departure, since it records him as entering his mother's womb on the very night of the *Abhiniṣkramana* (II, 159, line 3). The *Nidāna Kathā,* wanting the Bodhisattva to have learned of his son's birth before his flight, has to crowd together the events which took place immediately after the Enlightenment. After the first rainy season was over—a season passed, everyone

is agreed, in the Deer Park of Benares—the *Mahāvastu* counts three months for the miracles of Urubilvā and only two for the sojourn in Rājagrha. This brings us to the end of winter and permits us, by cutting out the second rainy season (spent in the Magadha) to refer to the spring the traditional stanzas on the journey. This journey occurred, according to the *Mahāvastu,* in the autumn, thus giving us an additional year. As for the Tibetan tradition, it recklessly piles up the difficulties, dating the return to Kapilavastu, not six years after the Great Departure, but six years after Sambodhi, making a total absence of twelve years. This forces us to conclude that Rāhula remained in his mother's womb for six years and came into the world only towards the end of the six years of austerity. It is odd to find this absurd legend interpolated without rhyme or reason in the *Mahāvastu* (III, 172) and even justified by an imagined "maturation" of an act committed in a previous birth. It will be noted that the Kapilavastu Cycle continues until at least the Master's thirty-sixth year and thus includes the sojourn at Benares and the better part of that of Magadha.

20. Kshemēndra, *Daśāvatāracarita, Kāvyamālā.* Translated from the French of Foucher. (Translator.)

Chapter IX: DUTIES OF A BUDDHA

1. E. W. Burlingame, *Buddhist Legends,* I, 2.
2. H. C. Warren, *Buddhism in Translation,* p. 91.
3. *Ibid.,* p. 95.
4. *Mahāvastu,* ed. E. Senart, pp. 418–420.
5. *Divyāvadhāna,* ed. E. B. Cowell and R. A. Neil, pp. 366 and 402.
6. *Ibid.,* p. 365.
7. *Mahāvibhanga,* ed. Sylvain Levi, p. 21.
8. *Divyāvadhāna,* pp. 44 and 184.
9. *Mahāvagga,* VI, 23, trans. by Davids and Oldenberg, pp. 84–86.
10. *Ibid.,* VI, 24, p. 87.
11. W. W. Rockhill, *Life of the Buddha,* p. 65.
12. Burlingame, *op. cit.,* XV, 12.
13. Bimbisāra was deposed and is said to have been murdered about 400 B.C. by his son Ajātsatru. See A. L. Basham, *The Wonder that was India,* p. 46. (Translator.)
14. *Mahāvagga,* I, v, vi, x, trans. by Davids and Olenberg, pp. 104–106.
15. *Mahāvastu,* III, 137.
16. *Suttanipāta,* ed. V. Fausboell, Book III, iv.
17. *Mahāvagga,* VIII, xxvi, 1–3.
18. *Ibid.,* VI, 40.

19. *Ibid.,* I, xxxi, 1, p. 174.
20. *Ibid.,* I, xlix, 1–2, p. 201.
21. *Cullavagga,* ed. H. Oldenberg, p. 416, n.1.
22. *Mahāparinibbāna Sutta,* trans. by T. W. Rhys Davids, Chapter V, sec. 23, p. 91.

Chapter X: FOUR SECONDARY PILGRIMAGES

1. *Mahāparinibbāna Sutta,* trans. by T. W. Rhys Davids, Chapter v, sec. 15–22, p. 90.
2. Mathurā is the Muttra of English maps, on the right bank of the Yamunā (Jamna) River, halfway between Agra and Delhi. The ruins of Sakēta are located in Aoudh, a few miles from Faizābād. Those of Kauśambī have been identified by Sir Alexander Cunningham with Kosām, on the left bank of the Yamunā, about thirty-three miles upstream from the junction of this river with the Ganges at Prayāga (Allahābād).
3. For this reason Maudgalyāyana is supposed to have gone to ask him in Heaven for the date of his advent, which would explain the crowds brought here on the date designated.
4. Hsuan Tsang's "Kapitha" appears to be only another name for Sankāśya. Fa-hsien alone puts the miracle in Kanyakubja (Kanauj). In any event, the capital of Aśoka's column, which has been found, has an elephant and not, as Hsuan Tsang says, a lion on it.
5. *Divyāvadhāna,* trans. by E. B. Cowell and R. A. Neil, p. 150, 11, 24–25.
6. See *Jātaka,* Book XII, no. 472, trans. by H. T. Francis and R. A. Neil, Vol. IV, pp. 117 ff. She fell into the Hell of Avisi, the lowest and most terrible of the eight hot hells. Cf. W. M. McGovern, *A Manual of Buddhist Philosophy,* p. 62.
7. For the Sanskrit tradition, see *Divyāvadhāna,* XII, p. 143; for the Pāli, *Jātaka,* Book XIII, no. 483. Translation cited, Vol. IV, pp. 169 ff.
8. For instance, see the sermon on the fruits of asceticism in *Dialogues of the Buddha,* trans. by T. W. Davids, I, 56.
9. *Mahāvastu,* ed. E. Senart, VIII.
10. There is every reason to believe that Devadatta was appreciably younger than the Buddha.
11. Another instance of such slanders is given in the *Suttanipāta,* III, 10.
12. See "Dēvadatta" in index of the *Jātakas,* translation cited.
13. See the *Cullavagga,* ed. H. Oldenberg, VII, iii, 12; W. W. Rockhill, *Life of the Buddha,* p. 93.
14. *Mahāvastu,* I, 251; McGovern, *op. cit.,* p. 244. The Great Wood (*Mahā-*

vana) was planted with *śāla* (*Shorea robusta*) trees, whence its other name, *Śālavana*.

15. *Mahāvastu,* VIII, 1 (cf. VI, 30). Amrapālī (meaning "who has a mango for a protector") probably owed her name to the fact that, in accordance with the custom of ladies of her profession, she had been married ceremoniously to a tree of that species.

16. Sir Alexander Cunningham, *Ancient Geography of India,* p. 443.

17. Cf. T. Watters, *On Yuang Chwang's Travels in India,* I, 309; II, 65. E. W. Burlingame fuses the same story with that of the elephant of Parileyyaka. See his *Buddhist Legends,* I, 5.

18. A. Foucher, *L'Art gréco-bouddhique du Gandhāra,* Vol. I, p. 605.

Chapter XI: THE FOURTH GREAT PILGRIMAGE

1. In *Mahāparinibbāna Sutta,* trans. by T. W. Rhys Davids.

2. *Ibid.,* Chapter 1, p. 1.

3. *Ibid.,* p. 12, secs. 13 and 15.

4. This conversation is also given in the *Sampasādaniya Sutta* of the *Dīgla Nikāya* and in the *Satipatthāna Vagga* of the *Samyutta.*

5. *Mahāparinibbāna Sutta,* XI, sec. 26, p. 18.

6. *Ibid.,* secs. 28–33, pp. 35–38.

7. *Ibid.,* Chapter 3, pp. 40 ff.

8. *Ibid.,* sec. 63, p. 58.

9. *Ibid.,* secs. 2 and 3, pp. 85 ff.

10. *Ibid.,* sec. 41, p. 99.

11. *Ibid.,* sec. 32, p. 95.

12. *Ibid.,* sec. 10, p. 144.

13. *Ibid.,* secs. 11–13, pp. 114 ff.

14. *Ibid.,* sec. 33, pp. 125 f.

BIBLIOGRAPHY

A. *Primary Sources*

Aśvaghosa. *Buddhacarita.* E. H. Johnston, ed. and trans. Publications of the University of the Punjab, Vol. XXXII. Tibetan version of the same, also translated by Johnston, in the *Acta Orientalia,* Vol. XV. Leyden, 1936.

Brihadāvanyaka Upanishad. In *The Unpanishads,* Swami Nikhilananda, trans. Vol. III. New York, 1949.

Cullavagga. H. Oldenberg, ed. In *The Vinayapitakem,* Vol. II. London, 1880. Trans. in *The Sacred Books of the East,* Vols. XVII and XX. Oxford, 1882–1885.

Dhāmmapada. E. B. Cowell and R. A. Neil, eds. Cambridge, England, 1886.

Dhāmmapada Commentary. In *Buddhist Legends,* trans. from the original Pāli text. 3 vols. Cambridge, Mass., 1921.

Dialogues of the Buddha. Trans. by T. W. Rhys Davids from the Pāli. In *The Sacred Books of the Buddhists,* Vols. II–III. London, 1899, 1910.

Divyāvadhāna. E. B. Cowell and R. A. Neil, eds. Cambridge, England, 1886.

Jātakatthavannana. V. Fausboell, ed. 7 vols. London, 1877–1897. Trans. under the direction of F. B. Cowell. 6 vols. Cambridge, England, 1895–1907. (Quotations in the text are from *Jataka Stories,* E. B. Cowell, ed. London, 1957.)

Kathopanishad. See E. Hume, *The Thirteen Original Upanishads.* Oxford, 1931. (Translator.)

Kshemendra. See A. B. Keith, *History of Sanskrit Literature,* Oxford, 1928. (Translator.)

Lalitavistara. S. Leimann, ed. Halle a. S., 1905. (Quotations in the text are from the translation of Rajendralala Mitra, Calcutta, 1881, as far as Chapter XV; thereafter from the French of A. Foucher.—Translator.)

Mahāparinibbāna Sutta. R. C. Childers, ed. *Journal of the Royal Asiatic Society,* N.S., Vols. VII and VIII, 1875–1876. Trans. by T. W. Rhys Davids in *The Sacred Books of the East.* Vol. XI. Oxford, 1881.

Mahāvagga. H. Oldenberg, ed. In *Vinayapitakem,* Vol. I. London, 1879. Trans. by T. W. Rhys Davids and Hermann Oldenberg, in *The Sacred Books of the East,* Vols. XIII and XVII. Oxford, 1881, 1882.

Mahāvastu. E. Senart, ed. 3 vols. Paris, 1882–1897.

Mahā Vibhanga. Sylvain Levi, ed. Paris, 1921.

Milinda Pañha (*The Questions of King Milinda*). Trans. by T. W. Rhys Davids. In *The Sacred Books of the East,* Vol. XXXV. Oxford, 1890.

Nidāna Kathā (Introduction to the *Jātaka*). Trans. by T. W. Rhys Davids under the title *Buddhist Birth-Stories.* London, 1880.

Rigveda. The Hymns of the Rigveda, trans. with a popular commentary by Ralph T. H. Griffith. 2d ed., 2 vols. Benares, 1896–1897.

Santideva Bodhicarya Avatara. Trans. by Cecil Bendall and W. H. D. Rouse. London, 1922.

Sūtralankāra. Trans. by E. Huber. Paris, 1908.

Suttanipāta. V. Fausboell, ed. Trans. by V. Fausboell in *The Sacred Books of the East,* Vol. X. Oxford, 1881.

B. *Secondary Sources and Modern Interpretations*

St. Augustine. *De Trinitate. Opera omnia,* Vol. VIII. Paris, 1841–1842.

Basham, A. L. *The Wonder that was India.* London, 1961. (Referred to by translator.)

Beal, S. *The Romantic Legend of Śakya Buddha.* London, 1875.

Bhagavad Gītā. Trans. by Swami Prabhavananda and Christopher Isherwood. London, 1947. (Referred to by translator.)

Brown, W. N. *The Indian and Christian Miracles of Walking on Water.* Chicago and London, 1928.

Burlingame, E. W. *Buddhist Legends.* Harvard Oriental Series. Cambridge, Mass., 1921.

Conze, Edward. *Buddhism; Its Essence and Development.* London, 1960. (Referred to by translator.)

Coomaraswamy, Ananda. *Buddha and the Gospel of Buddhism.* New York, 1916.

Cunningham, Sir Alexander. *Mahābodhi.* London, 1892.

Davids, T. W. Rhys. *Buddhism: Its History and Literature.* New York and London, 1896.

Foucher, A. *L'Art Gréco-Bouddhique du Gandhāra.* Vol. I. Paris, 1905.

———. *The Beginnings of Buddhist Art.* Paris, 1917.

———. *On the Iconography of the Buddha's Nativity.* Trans. by H. Hargreaves. Archaeological Survey of India, no. 46. Delhi, 1934.

St. Jerome. *Contra Jovinianum.* In Migne, *Patrologia Latina,* Vol. XXIII. Paris, 1883.

Johnston, E. H. *Early Sāṁkhya.* London, 1937.

McGovern, W. M. *A Manual of Buddhist Philosophy.* London and New York, 1923.

Maeterlinck, Maurice. *The Life of the Bee.* Trans. by Alfred Sutro. New York, 1923.

Marco Polo. *Travels.* Trans. by Ronald Latham. London, 1958. (Referred to by translator.)

Marshall, Sir John. *Mohenjo-Daro and the Indus Civilization.* 3 vols. London, 1931.

Masson-Oursel, P. *Essai d'interprétation de la théorie bouddhique des douze conditions.* Paris, n.d.

Oldenberg, Hermann. *Buddha, sein Leben, seine Lehre, seine Gemeinde,* 4th ed. Berlin, 1924.

Oltramare, P. *La formule bouddhique des douze causes.* Geneva, 1909.

———. *Histoire des Idées Théosophiques dans l'Inde.* Paris, 1923.

Rockhill, W. W. *Life of the Buddha.* London, 1884.

Senart, E. *Bouddhisme et Yoga.* Paris, 1900.

———. *Origines Bouddhiques.* Paris, 1907.

Shcherbatskoi, T. (elsewhere Stcherbatsky). *The Central Conception of Buddhism and the Meaning of the Word "Dharma."* London, 1928. (The translator has not been able to obtain these two volumes to compare them.)

Tuneld, E. *Recherches sur la valeur des traditions bouddhiques pālie et non-pālie.* Lund, 1915.

Vallée-Poussin, L. de la. "Théorie des douze conditions," in his *Bouddhisme, études et matériaux.* Ghent, 1913.

Warren, H. C. *Buddhism in Translation.* Vol. III. Harvard Oriental Studies. Cambridge, Mass., 1906.

Watters, T. *On Yuang Chwang's Travels in India.* London, 1904–1905.

Windisch, E. *Māra und Buddha.* Leipzig, 1895.

C. *Additional bibliography not given by A. Foucher*

Ashton, Leigh. *The Art of India and Pakistan.* New York, 1949.

Bareau, André. *Les Sectes Bouddiques du Petit Véhicule.* Saigon, 1955.

Bhattasali, Nalini Kanta. *Iconography of Buddhist and Brahmanical Sculptures in the Dacca Museum.* Dacca, 1929.

Cohn, William. *Buddha in der Kunst des Ostens*. Leipzig, 1925.

Conze, Edward. *Buddhism*. Oxford, 1954.

Coomaraswamy, Ananda. *Elements of Buddhist Iconography*. Cambridge, Mass., 1935.

Dasgupta, Shashi Bhusan. *An Introduction to Tantric Buddhism*. Calcutta, 1950.

Getty, Alice. *The Gods of Northern Buddhism*. Oxford, 1928.

Jennings, J. G. *The Vedantic Buddhism of the Buddha*. London, 1947.

Lamotte, Etienne. *Histoire du Bouddisme indien*. Louvain, 1958.

Lounsbery, G. Constant. *Buddhist Meditation in the Southern School*. London, 1950.

Masson, Joseph. *La religion populaire dans le Canon bouddique pali*. Louvain, 1942.

Mus, Paul. *Le Buddha paré*. Etudes Indiennes et Indochinoises. Paris, 1928.

Nyanaponika, Thera. *Guide Through the Abhidhamma-Pitaka*. Colombo, 1957.

Nyanatiloka. *Buddhist Dictionary*. Colombo, 1950.

Pratt, James Bissett. *The Pilgrimage of Buddhism*. New York, 1928.

Przyluski, Jean. *Le Concile de Rajagrha*. Paris, 1926.

Silva-Vigier, Anil de. *The Life of the Buddha*. London, 1955.

Zimmer, Heinrich. *Philosophies of India*. New York, 1951.

————. *The Art of Indian Asia*. New York, 1955.